MY BUSINESS IS CIRCUMFERENCE

Poets on Influence and Mastery

A. R. Ammons
L. S. Asekoff
Stephanie Brown
Hayden Carruth
Gillian Conoley
Amy Gerstler
Judith Hall
Hunt Hawkins
Jane Hirshfield
Claudia Keelan
Yusef Komunyakaa
Dana Levin
Lisa Lewis
Laurence Lieberman
Thomas Lux
Jane Mead
Jack Myers
Donald Revell
Len Roberts
Michael Ryan
Ira Sadoff
Hugh Seidman
Jennifer Snyder
Gerald Stern
Lucien Stryk
Karen Volkman
Theodore Weiss
Joe Wenderoth

Anonymous
John Ashbery
John Berryman
Elizabeth Bishop
William Blake
Bertolt Brecht
James M. Cain
Catullus
C. P. Cavafy
Geoffrey Chaucer
Hart Crane
Robert Creeley
E. E. Cummings
Emily Dickinson
Ralph Waldo Emerson
Robert Frost
Jack Gilbert
Louise Glück
Paul Goodman
Robert Hayden
George Herbert
Zbigniew Herbert
Gerard Manley Hopkins
Horace
Randall Jarrell
Ben Jonson
Roberto Juarroz
John Keats
Bill Knott
D. H. Lawrence
Philip Levine
Robert Lowell
Stéphane Mallarmé
W. S. Merwin
Charlotte Mew
Czeslaw Milosz
John Milton
Marianne Moore
Pablo Neruda
Frank O'Hara
Sharon Olds
Alexander Pope
Ezra Pound
Rainer Maria Rilke
Theodore Roethke
Jelaluddin Rumi
Sappho
Franz Schubert
William Shakespeare
Sei Shonagon
John Skelton
Jack Spicer
Wallace Stevens
Shinkichi Takahashi
Thomas Traherne
César Vallejo
Nathanael West
Walt Whitman
C. K. Williams
William Carlos Williams
James Wright
Thomas Wyatt

MY BUSINESS IS CIRCUMFERENCE

Poets on Influence and Mastery

Edited by STEPHEN BERG

PAUL DRY BOOKS
Philadelphia
2001

Paul Dry Books, Inc.
Philadelphia, Pennsylvania
www.pauldrybooks.com

Copyright © 2001 Paul Dry Books, Inc.
First Edition, 2001

Text type: Monotype Bembo and Trump Mediæval
Display type: Optima
Composed by Duke & Company
Designed by Adrianne Onderdonk Dudden

1 3 5 7 9 8 6 4 2
Printed in the United States of America

Library of Congress Cataloging-in-Publication Data
My business is circumference : poets on influence and mastery / edited by Stephen Berg.
    p. cm.
  Includes bibliographical references (p.) and index
  ISBN 0-9664913-9-4 (pbk. : alk. paper)
    1. American poetry—20th century. 2. Influence (Literary, artistic, etc.)
  3. Poetry—Authorship. I. Berg, Stephen

PS615 .M9 2001
808.1—dc21   2001028722

ISBN 0-9664913-9-4

Will you tell me my fault, frankly as to yourself, for I had rather wince, than die. Men do not call the surgeon, to commend—the Bone, but to set it, Sir, and fracture within, is more critical. And for this, Preceptor, I shall bring you—Obedience—the Blossom from my Garden, and every gratitude I know. Perhaps you smile at me. I could not stop for that—My Business is Circumference—An ignorance, not of Customs, but if caught with the Dawn—or the Sunset see me—Myself the only Kangaroo among the Beauty, Sir, if you please, it afflicts me, and I thought that instruction would take it away.

—Emily Dickinson to T. W. Higginson, July 1862

CONTENTS

PREFACE

When I first envisioned this book I hoped to learn what American poets had to say about the mysterious processes of influence and mastery. Here's a paragraph from the letter I sent to prospective contributors:

> The idea is that each contemporary American poet chooses 3–5 poems that have influenced his or her poetry, as well as a poem of his or her own. You would then write a short *essay* discussing the nature of the influence the poems have had on your work, and talk about the idea of mastery, what it is, and how you wrote your poem, what problems you faced—what the process was. I'm leaving the content of the essay as open as possible at this point. Please feel free to make any connections you like under the general categories of influence and mastery.

I am happy to say that twenty-eight of the finest contemporary poets in America accepted my proposal, and as you read *My Business is Circumference* you will see how each poet interpreted the invitation to muse on influence and mastery. In choosing the poems that have influenced them, in selecting their own poems, and in writing about influence and mastery, the contributors have created an intimate and helpful work. Poem by poem, essay by essay, the poets show the reader their distinctive involvement with writing and reading and how those nearly twin activities feed into one another.

This is a book for people who go to poetry because they believe it is a serious, almost miraculous activity, and who want to get as close as possible to the actual struggle of creating poetry, who want to know about a poet's relationship to language and experience. Many styles, many approaches to the craft of writing appear here. I hope that readers will feel as enriched as I do to be so happily contained by this eloquent circle of voices.

Scores of people have devoted a great deal of time and resources to bring this project to fruition. I want to thank each of the contributors, whose work and generosity have made the book all I had originally hoped it would be—and more. In addition to the contributors, several others worked hard to see the book to publication. Thanks go to Sarah Dry, Ilana Stanger, Martha K. Davis, and Elizabeth Scanlon for their involvement, and I am especially grateful to Rayna Kalas and William Schofield who oversaw the major job of editing and proofreading the selections.

Stephen Berg
Philadelphia 2001

THE POETRY DOES NOT MATTER
by STEPHEN BERG

For Jennie Q. Dietrich
(1943–2000)

Leaving one still with the intolerable wrestle
With words and meanings. The poetry does not matter.

. . . .

The only wisdom we can hope to acquire
is the wisdom of humility: humility is endless.

T. S. Eliot, *East Coker*

1 The first aim of poetry is to destroy the barriers of emotional distance that separate people. That can only be accomplished with a voice that includes the reader through its compassion, its acceptance, its understanding. A poem can be about anything and still include anyone. To the degree that a poem transcends the personality of the poet, it will be "about the reader."[1] Sincerity occurs when the speaker does not write in order to be perceived as one kind of person rather than another. Nothing is more destructive to community, to creativity, than the desire to be seen as a good person and the deceptions that are mobilized to make that happen.

> For as I detest the doorways of Death, I detest that man,
> who hides one thing in the depths of his heart, and speaks forth
>   another,[2]

utters Achilles.

But how is one to judge whether a poem accomplishes that sublime anonymity, intimacy, and honesty of consciousness that give the reader access to himself, that affect the reader through the language's act of love?

2   "A poet's words can pierce us. And that is of course causally connected with the use that they have in our life. And it is also connected with the way in which, conformably to this use, we let our thoughts roam up and down in the familiar surroundings of the words."[3] Wittgenstein's statement in *Zettel,* 155., can guide our thinking about influence and mastery, two terms which apply to both writer and reader. It's not only the writer's influences and his so-called mastery that we are seeking to understand. It's the fact that poetry enters us only when we sense that it will be useful to us; and once it does, only by letting "our thoughts roam up and down in the familiar surroundings of the words" may we discover what the poem really means to us.

3   I find it mysterious that certain lines, passages, phrases from poems have stayed with me. It isn't simply memory that makes this happen. I struggle to become more conscious, more open to others. I fail at this; my self-concern pulls me back into the protective self-deceptions that limit my ability to love, but the confusions of a self in relation to others rekindle the struggle. There are no rules for this process of destruction and resurrection, this coming to terms with who one is and who we are. So I believe that beyond the sheer beauty of the language itself, when it is forged well enough, one's need to use poetry to solve the problems rooted in simply being human makes memory embrace particular poems.

4   It is not Yeats's famous idea of speaking through a mask, it is the idea of speaking through fewer and fewer masks until truth and the reader are one. "The procedures of the great movement of art of the early twentieth century may serve to put us in mind of the violent meanings which are explicit in the Greek ancestry of the word 'authentic.' *Authenteo*: to have full power over: also, to commit a murder. *Authentes*: not only a master and a doer, but also a perpetrator, a murderer, even a self-murderer, a suicide."[4] Trilling's meditation on sincerity and authenticity leads us back to the point where word and deed somehow become a kind of enacted nakedness or piercing of the heart that binds us deeper to each other in the impossibility of ever fully comprehending our common fate. And yet there are poems that do function as permanent definitions of what we are trying to discover about ourselves so that we may enrich civilized feeling —that continue to work as a "momentary stay against confusion."[5] The compassionate intellect of Blake's startling poem addressed to a common housefly always touches me:

THE FLY
Little Fly,
Thy summer's play
My thoughtless hand
Has brush'd away.

Am not I
A fly like thee?
Or art not thou
A man like me?

For I dance,
And drink, & sing,
Till some blind hand
Shall brush my wing.

If thought is life
And strength & breath,
And the want
Of thought is death;

Then am I
A happy fly,
If I live
or if I die.

The humiliation of identification Blake undergoes in this poem dissolves personal identity and establishes the reader's relationship to God's power and the reader's power over creatures less powerful than himself. So great is the poem's morality that once you have read it, you can never again forget your own "flyness," your helplessness faced with that "some blind hand" which sooner or later shall brush your wing. That permanent humbling and consoling of the reader by the argument embedded in the lullaby rhythms of the poem—such a gentle, ironclad movement; a tone both impersonal and pitying—helps him to consider his own mortality differently. Blake's abrupt elevation of the term "thought" as an acceptable cause of death stops the reader. Mustn't Blake mean God's thought? The God above us, whatever the word God may mean; and the God a man is to the fly? It is consciousness as a moral state and thoughtlessness as immoral that screw down the logic of Blake's argument with himself, the fly, and the reader. All three become one: a single organism communing through the poem's spare, tender music. How often is one willing to talk to one's brother the fly, to offer one's apology in Franciscan humility? That gesture opens the poet to the rhetorical question, "Am not I/ A fly like thee?/ Or art not thou/ A man like me?" Why "or"? Perhaps because Blake is not convinced by his own argument at this point. In what way is a fly like a man? There must be something smaller than a fly. An ant, for example. A gnat. The fly becomes conscious in the poem, nature becomes conscious in the poem; poet, insect, and nature one conscious chain. "Thought" as defined by this poem fuses personal and cosmic awareness into an ecstatic, interdependent unity. The vast figure of a "blind hand," a purely physical, omnipotent instrument, a "thoughtless hand," is set against the idea of thought as responsible power, as conscious moral decision. Some version of universal love is being suggested here, and by the time this brief grave poem ends, Blake has become the very fly he killed at the beginning of the poem, the fly he spoke to, and he is now a "happy fly." But we will probably never unravel the meaning of those last two stanzas. The poet's passionate belief in his idea of life as thought and death as want of thought, both of which make him happy, will not quite yield to analytic reason. Nevertheless, it inspires faith, faith without an object of faith, blind faith, possibly, faith based not on reason but on Blake's gift of finally becoming—beyond personal identity—the fly whose joy breaks forth into the final pair of lines where life and death to him are the same. But not only the fly: Blake becomes the reader, God, and therefore fully himself. So few words to transfigure our view of death as personal threat and leave us less afraid! Twenty lines, all monosyllabic words but four; such resonant two-beat lines; so lean and large, an amulet of esoteric wisdom.   *yes.*

5   "[W]e don't want to be masters," Frost says, talking with Robert Penn Warren. "Somebody said to be a master writer, you don't have to wait for your moods. That'd be like Browning as he got older, you get to be a virtuoso and you aren't a poet anymore. He'd lost his moods somewhere. He'd got to be a master—we don't want to be masters."[6] Frost is referring to the influence of that vague inner state, a singular emotional direction that rises out of no clearly known source and gives each poem its inevitability, necessity, and sincerity. Mood's ultimate result is to allow the reader to trust the speaker, to listen, participate, and be moved. It is the speaker's tone of voice undefended by self-consciousness—by the desire to be loved by the reader. Beyond this union of speaker and reader is the intention to help both writer and reader "to live their lives," Wallace Stevens's definition of the purpose of poetry in *The Necessary Angel*.[7] It is not so much a moral purpose as a realization of the inarticulate vulnerability of our lives, of our need to be revealed so that we might see each other more clearly. Only then can we step out of ourselves for the sake of others. Mastery is really the gift of being able to give ourselves away, to "listen wholeheartedly," in Karen Horney's terms.[8] Then our responses to others will be what they can use. Jean-Paul Sartre called it "transparency" and believed it could eradicate the social illnesses of possessiveness and hatred of differences. The truly vital poems do this, in infinitely different ways. Let me refer once more to Frost. Though I can't find the citation in my notes, Frost said something like this: "In a poem you can kill all the babies you want to and it won't make me cry. And it isn't about bombs and things; nothing like that. It's always magnanimity—the heroism of magnanimity." And isn't magnanimity, in life and in art, having the strength to put oneself at the mercy of others' experience felt so completely that it becomes our own, at least for a moment, so that the other person knows he has been heard? We must feel with others as we feel ourselves.

6   On April 22, 1802, Wordsworth composed a stunningly direct haiku-like quatrain (which he did not publish) that inadvertently breaks through to a fresh intuition of one of his obsessions: how the passage of time can deaden intellectual perception. Its eerie voice embodies in the living speaker the fact of having been here, being dead, surrendering in the present to death as easily as a flower withers or a leaf falls:

> I have been here in the Moon-light,
> I have been here in the Day,
> I have been here in the Dark Night,
> And the stream was still roaring away.[9]

This is the speech of the dead—from a living voice—beyond past tense, even, where the stream no longer roars. It is a kind of epitaph in complete acceptance of one's own death, written by a living man. The tone is jubilant, I think. It says that the "I" lived "in" those times of day and night, was one with them, heard and followed the stream's syllables, and now is nowhere and everywhere. There is no argument to persuade. It is pure assertion, the ego in the world at peace, impartial attention, "A condition of complete simplicity/ (Costing not less than everything)."[10] Einstein recognized our need to solve this problem gnawing at our hearts and expressed his solution in a letter: "A human being is a part of the whole, called by us 'Universe,' a part limited in time and space. He experiences himself, his thoughts and feelings, as something separated from the rest—a kind of optical delusion of his consciousness. This delusion is a kind of prison for us, restricting us to our personal desires and to affection for a few persons nearest to us. Our task must be to free ourselves from this prison by widening our circle of compassion to embrace all living creatures and the whole of nature in its beauty. Nobody is able to achieve this completely, but the striving for such achievement is in itself a part of the liberation and the foundation for inner security."[11]

7   Listen to these words from the chapter "The Practice," a truly humane piece of literary criticism in William Carlos Williams's *Autobiography*. Williams is describing listening to his patients' complaints: "I lost myself in the very properties of their minds: for the moment at least I actually became them, whoever they should be, so that when I detached myself from them at the end of a half-hour of intense concentration over some illness which was affecting them, it was as though I were awakening from a sleep. For the moment I myself did not exist, nothing of myself affected me. As a consequence I came back to myself, as from any other sleep, rested. . . . We get the news and discount it, we are quite right in doing so. It is trivial. But the hunted news I get from some obscure patient's eyes is not trivial. . . . For under that language to which we have been listening all our lives a new, a more profound language, underlying all the dialectics offers itself. It is what they call poetry."[12]

8   God knows why what enters and influences us does so. As I walked with him out of his poetry workshop at Boston University, Robert Lowell said to me: "There are no rules!" That from a man who knew all the rules, and practiced them, rules learned from any poem he could devour, rules invented under the pressure of refusing to favor one technical approach above another. Years later when I was editing *Naked Poetry,* I asked each poet for an essay to accompany the poems. Lowell's remarks on the music of poetry arrived in a letter. It is one of the most instructive statements I know on this complicated topic—of how to make the music, in Stevens's words, "we need in our situation,"[13] that can help us to assess "emotions that form the substratum of our being."[14] I'll quote the letter completely:

Dear Stephen,

Oh dear, the many paths one might take, if there were time and energy! I really don't think I can stop what I am doing and knock off something worth printing about free verse.

My two rules in writing free verse are that I don't ever scan a line while I am composing it, and that the words must fall into lines. In the back of my head somewhere I am conscious that rhythm is usually made up of iambics, trochees, anapests and spondees. I think I feel the presence of these four feet when I write them, but the law and opportunity is that I am completely free. Complete freedom, though, is something I've used in very few poems. Usually even in more or less free verse I set down restrictions: stanzas with the same number of lines (most often quatrains), rhymes or off-rhymes sometimes at random, sometimes with a fixed place in the stanza, lines of more or less uniform length on the page, sometimes the lines are accentual and will scan, though this is a meter that allows great license, and the accenting of a syllable is often arbitrary. The joy and strength of unscanned verse is that it can be as natural as conversation or prose, or can follow the rhythm of the ear that knows no measure. Yet often a poem only becomes a poem and worth printing because it has struggled with fixed meters and rhymes. I can't understand how any poet, who has written both metered and unmetered poems, would be willing to settle for one and give up the other.

This is far short of what either you or I might desire, but it's the best I can do for the moment. I have never worked my intuitions into a theory. When I drop one style of writing, it's usually a surprise to me.

An afterthought—the glory of free verse is in those poems that would be thoroughly marred and would indeed be inconceivable in meter— first the translations of the Bible: Job, the Song of Solomon, the best psalms, David's Lament, great supreme poems, written when their translators merely intended prose and were forced by the structure of their originals to write poetry; then Whitman, whose *Song of Myself* is the only important long nineteenth century American poem, then Lawrence's bird and animal poems, Pound's *Cantos,* and most of William Carlos Williams. These works would have lost all their greatness and possibility in meter.

Yours as always, Cal

Here you can see a vigilant craftsman defining mastery as uncertainty and inclusiveness. He knows that poetry, in Eliot's words, is "a raid on the inarticulate"[15] and therefore demands an almost religious faith in music's power to satisfy the reader's longing to hear redemptive speech, the grace of a voice that can somehow give us a poetry to cope with the irremediables and to carry us beyond the failed limits of explanation. And there are poems that are barely poems, that are some kind of chaste, nearly speechless songs, weird woeful plaints, heartfelt, primitive, throaty laments, knotty, locked in a storyless self:

Erthe took of erthe, erthe wyth wogh:
Erthe other erthe to the erthe drough;
Erthe leyde erthe in erthen through:
Than hadde erthe of erthe erthe ynough.[16]

Let's call the music of poetry the theme beneath the conscious activity that makes sense of what we cannot understand by means of reasoned argument. Music helps us to surrender to life and accept it. It is like nature —undeniably present without explanation, a radiance of silent imagery.

9   "*My* business is to love. I found a bird, this morning, down-down-on a little bush at the foot of the garden, and wherefore sing, I said, since nobody *hears*?"[17] Dickinson's bird is deep inside us waiting to be heard. Yet sometimes nothing avails us. We hear nothing, not a note. We wait for the sound of a voice that will hear us. I said *hear* us. We feel we are heard by others' voices when we hear them as our own. This is a phenomenon of identity and anonymity, a simultaneous transference of one particular self to an anonymous voice. It is difficult to define it when it occurs or even to be aware of it when it does. We have a sense that we are known, relieved of a burden of isolation. It comes through the music. The tone. It occurs at the "frontiers of consciousness . . . where words fail but meaning still exists,"[18] according to Eliot. What are we straining to hear? What are we listening for? Frost once said, "The surest way to reach the heart is through the ear."

> As I me walked in one morning,
> I hard a birde both wepe and singe.
> This was the tenor of her talkinge,
> *Timor mortis conturbat me,*[19]

sang nobody-with-a-name-we-know in 1460 in the throes of feeling doomed by inescapable, pitiless death. He was trying to pray; he was trying to hear himself in the bird, man as a bird who both weeps out of grief and sings triumphantly; he knew that if he found the music he would be saved, if only for a moment. *Timor mortis conturbat me.* Church Latin for the congregation to chant. He is with us. He *is* us. Emily asks why the bird sings since nobody hears? Because it must sing, though it knows no audience, but in fact she heard it. Her love was her listening. A mastery in humility, an influence spontaneously bestowed upon her from deep among the leaves. The prayer of her listening, the answer of the bird.

MY BUSINESS IS CIRCUMFERENCE

Poets on Influence and Mastery

A. R. AMMONS

A. R. Ammons wrote: "I was born and raised on a farm outside Whiteville, North Carolina. After the Navy, I went to Wake Forest University, graduating with a B.S. in 1949. I was married that year to Phyllis Plumbo and we had a son in 1966. I taught at Cornell University until 1998, when I retired." Ammons's books of poetry include *Ommateum with Doxology* (Dorrance & Co., 1955), *Expressions of Sea Level* (Ohio State University Press, 1963), *Corsons Inlet* (Cornell University Press, 1965), *Diversifications* (Norton, 1975), and *Lake Effect Country* (Norton, 1983). In addition to his shorter verse, Ammons authored two book-length poems, *Tape for the Turn of the Year* (Cornell University Press, 1965) and *Sphere: The Form of a Motion* (Norton, 1974). His poetry has been collected in *Collected Poems* (1972), *Selected Poems* (1977), and *Selected Longer Poems* (1980), all published by Norton. A. R. Ammons died on February 25, 2001.

Hymn

I know if I find you I will have to leave the earth
and go on out
    over the sea marshes and the brant in bays
and over the hills of tall hickory
and over the crater lakes and canyons
and on up through the spheres of diminishing air
past the blackset noctilucent clouds

> where one wants to stop and look
> way past all the light diffusions and bombardments
> up farther than the loss of sight
>   into the unseasonal undifferentiated empty stark
>
> And I know if I find you I will have to stay with the earth
> inspecting with thin tools and ground eyes
> trusting the microvilli sporangia and simplest
>   coelenterates
> and praying for a nerve cell
> with all the soul of my chemical reactions
> and going right on down where the eye sees only traces
>
> You are everywhere partial and entire
> You are on the inside of everything and on the outside
>
> I walk down the path down the hill where the sweetgum
> has begun to ooze spring sap at the cut
> and I see how the bark cracks and winds like no other bark
> chasmal to my ant-soul running up and down
> and if I find you I must go out deep into your
>   far resolutions
> and if I find you I must stay here with the separate leaves

RALPH WALDO EMERSON
The Rhodora: On being asked, whence is the flower?

> In May, when sea-winds pierced our solitudes,
> I found the fresh Rhodora in the woods,
> Spreading its leafless blooms in a damp nook,
> To please the desert and the sluggish brook.
> The purple petals, fallen in the pool,
> Made the black water with their beauty gay;
> Here might the red-bird come his plumes to cool,
> And court the flower that cheapens his array.
> Rhodora! if the sages ask thee why
> This charm is wasted on the earth and sky,
> Tell them, dear, that if eyes were made for seeing,

Then Beauty is its own excuse for being:
Why thou wert there, O rival of the rose!
I never thought to ask, I never knew:
But, in my simple ignorance, suppose
The self-same Power that brought me there brought you.

WALT WHITMAN
Aboard at a Ship's Helm

Aboard at a ship's helm,
A young steersman steering with care.

Through fog on a sea-coast dolefully ringing,
An ocean-bell—O a warning bell, rock'd by the waves.

O you give good notice indeed, you bell by the sea-reefs ringing,
Ringing, ringing, to warn the ship from its wreck-place.

For as on the alert O steersman, you mind the loud admonition,
The bows turn, the freighted ship tacking speeds away under her
    gray sails,
The beautiful and noble ship with all her precious wealth speeds away
    gayly and safe.

But O the ship, the immortal ship! O ship aboard the ship!
Ship of the body, ship of the soul, voyaging, voyaging, voyaging.

WILLIAM CARLOS WILLIAMS
Poem

As the cat
climbed over
the top of

the jamcloset
first the right
forefoot

carefully
then the hind
stepped down

into the pit of
the empty
flowerpot

Hymns

I've been influenced by everything and everybody, especially by the only poetry I heard as a child, hymns. The mixture of song, form, and meaning became the basis of the flow for me, as well as the content I have engaged. A line such as "There's a land that is fairer than day" came much before Stevens's imagined land. And "Here I labor and toil as I look for a home, just a humble abode among men" describes my wrestling with myself and the highest challenge I have tried to meet. But those who speak of my poems most frequently mention Emerson, Whitman, Frost, Williams, and Stevens, along with occasional mention of everybody. I feel like a kiosk. Anything can stick to me. My own poems keep sounding about the same through time, but they do change, so I think the best triad of sequence would be something like Frost and Emerson, say from my *Ommateum,* something like Whitman—my *Hymn*—and, say, a Stevens stanza, like my *The Spiral Rag.* I will choose *Hymn* as the closest figure for my early work —from Emerson, *The Rhodora,* from Whitman, *Aboard at a Ship's Helm,* and from Williams, *Poem* (about the jamcloset).

L. S. ASEKOFF

L. S. Asekoff, director of the M.F.A. Poetry Program and faculty associate of The Wolfe Institute for the Humanities, was the Donald I. Fine Professor of Creative Writing at Brooklyn College for 1998–99. His two books of poetry are *Dreams of a Work* (Orchises Press, 1994) and *North Star* (Orchises Press, 1997).

iii.29.86

Lifted from black plumage of ashes
my words come back to me

   MEXICO
 nobody goes on, with a wo

   nship between la
    of went
the

    mirrors

ally, but polishe

     & 18d ever see

Strange to myself as I am these days
who damned by the light of my own match
set these paper boats upon a lake of fire.
"The mystery of mastery," I say . . .

The Mysteries of Mastery

Language is thy mistress.
& thy master? Silence.
Hôtel du Tour

Black Swan

Cast loose in the middle of his life, shipwrecked by love, he knew his long apprenticeship was over. In his crazy solitude, he sat alone waiting for the voices. Slowly, they came to him, one by one, & then all in a rush. Taking dictation, writing furiously, he could barely keep up with them—twenty-five poems in twenty-five days—until it seemed to him anything he thought or said could, *would,* be a poem, even a throwaway list, a note to the postman. Soon, exhausted, overwhelmed by the continuous presence of those clamoring voices, he cursed what had once been a blessing, prayed for silence.

Outside the window he could see against late winter sky a flock of blackbirds unscroll the wild improvisatory music, jangling silvery half- & quarter-notes of their liquid flight, shrill cries. He struck an Ohio blue-tip against stone, threw the lit match into the fireplace where the green wood hissed its smoky, resinous whisper, lascivious, sibilant, licking piles of crumpled paper that as they rose burst into flame—each letter blackly luminous on the white fire of the page.

In his diary he wrote that night: "Today I burned 'The Black Swan.'"

First Transcendental Etude

Opening *The Book of Borrowed Breath,* he reads: *"Attention is the natural prayer of the soul."* & what, he muses, is poetry if not an act of supreme attention? Then what is the difference between poetry & prayer? Not who speaks, I would say, but who listens. He puts the book aside & looks up at me. Dear boy, every dog cocks his ear for the whistle of his master. Whose whistle do you hear? Whose dog are you? (& when life has you by the throat, who do you pray to?)

The Never-Ending Sentence

He is compiling a personal dictionary of the language according to historical principles, cataloguing each word as to the occasion & frequency of its appearance. His goal is to chart all the words he has ever encountered *in the exact sequence in which they came to him.* It begins with the source, trickles of sound, liminal phonemes, musical trills bubbling up into speech, moves on through a babble of syllables, lullabies, full-blown baby talk to, as the shallow brook deepens, first-words, strings of words, entire phrases, until moving more swiftly now, gathering into itself tributaries of the widening worlds of reading & writing, it picks up momentum & becomes a freshet, a spring stream, a broad, majestic river flowing grandly on & on past language's sleepy port towns, alluvial harbors, distant towering polyglot cities to this very moment of . . . *a way alone a last a loved* . . . for never, he says, will we reach the mouth, & the sea. He is not unaware of the perils of such an ambitious, if eccentric, adventure, each word existing not only in itself but altered as it were by the climate of its occasion, the swirling currents of usage & time, & if this were not daunting enough, the whole enterprise is further threatened by a telling objection—its virtual impossibility, i.e., that, like a full-scale map of the world, it needs to be as large as the world it maps, using language to depict *ad seriatum* an ongoing experience of language, his dictionary is doomed to be unable to contain the ever-expanding linguistic universe it continues to add to, "the never-ending sentence of our lives."

Second Transcendental Etude

"You think, after all, you must be weaving a piece of cloth,
because you are sitting at a loom, even if it is empty,
and going through the motions of weaving."

"Not one word is original to me," he laughs, "therefore, I am my own master."

White Rose

He is convinced that the liar's paradox, like Zeno's speeding arrow or a zen koan, shows us the glories of the imagination as well as the limits of logic & language. How paltry a tool is reason when blindly mapped on a mere two-, three-, four-dimensional surface. To see the world "whole" —in its *quintessence,* as the old theologians used to say—one must take into account, he tells us, its dynamic, self-revising, ever-flowing nature—its indeterminate determinacy, unbounded boundedness, cursive recursiveness. From infinitesimal to infinite, he insists, the world is less fractured than fractal. & while he agrees with Pascal & the quantum mechanics that God may play dice with the universe, he has faith that beyond the laws of probability chance is to time what fate is to eternity. The world is a manifold, unfolding at every instant, if we but see it. A many-petaled luminous white rose! The poet's paradise & our only heaven! & counter to it—what? The blank shadow of its non-existence? The black rose? No, he retorts, we must give up such easy windows, step through the binary mirror, abolish the laws of identity & contradiction! We must cultivate an imageless imagining. This is our task. The zero sum game, the wager worthy of challenging the most daring minds. He calls it "the masterless mastery of the master," or "the holding-on of letting-go."

Third Transcendental Etude

& here, he points to the page, are the lessons for the day:

"You are the task. No pupil far and wide."
"There is a goal, but no way; what we call a way is hesitation."
"The animal wrests the whip from its master and whips itself in order to become master, not knowing that this is only a fantasy produced by a new knot in the master's whiplash."

& this is a little song I translated to amuse myself. It is called *Viento Azul:*

There is a horse & there is a man.
There is a whip & there is a whisper.
& there is a man mounting a horse.

The horse is a blue wind.
Who can ride him?

Fourth Transcendental Etude

He says we write *from* & we write *toward*. We write out of the eclipsing shadow & we write into the haloed light that blinds us. How often, he laments, have I woken from a dream of a dream holding in my hand no white rose? O, faceless one, universal author of the ongoing poem of the world, your pale shadow blankens the blackest wall! Thus, he concludes, the son sires the father. *"Each of us creates his own precursors."*

Seer/Over-Seer

It was after our quarrel, she confesses. In my dream, I said, *My love is a paper boat set on a lake of fire,* & you said, *Damned by the light of my own match, I stared into the dark refrigerator. Choose,* you said. *All the unasked questions are answered in time.* I reached into the black box & pulled out the shining letters *I* & *M*. I could feel the subtle vibrations flowing to me—influenza, starlight, intelligence from afar. Like a current, they rippled through the pure medium I had become. Then there was a jolt, like the shock of an electric eel. It stopped me in my tracks. I felt the whip (& the whisper), the laying on of hands, the firm controlling touch. I was no longer transparent to myself, but opaque, not fluid, but solid, & restrained. Surrendering, I bowed to kiss your gleaming buckle. Yet even as my lips touched cold metal I could hear myself think, *Idolatry—the servant's revenge on the master.*

Oracle

Thirty-six years ago, he reminisces, I stood all night between cars on a crowded train from Athens to Paris sharing my cigarettes with a sallow Greek who claimed to have relatives in Astoria, Queens. When I told him I wanted to be a writer, he stared for a moment into the starless dark & said, in halting English, "Just when you think you will never write again, that is when you will begin to be a writer." What is strange is not what he said, though strange it was, but that out of all the things said to me over the years I chose to remember it. So, following where we go, we write the story of our lives.

Fifth Transcendental Etude

& here, he confides, is what brought me to the last line—the severities & silences, the (false) etymologies of my (true) taskmaster who parsed my soul &, whether comparing a semi-colon in a sentence of Henry James to the woodcuts of Hokusai or the "aesthetic shock" of a Sufi inscription over the lintel of a prayer hall in Isfahan to "drifting water lilies longing to open," taught me how to balance a wheel & the true beauty of thought.

"Do you think that she was writing about you?

No, not at all. It would be vanity to think so. The writer she describes is a master of illusion.

And you are the master of non-illusions?

You mean to be kind, but mastery itself is the illusion. You haven't touched that machine. Does it start itself?

Yes, it's voice-activated.

You should avoid attributive nouns. Don't use voice as an adverb, it's a noun. Do you mean that if I remain mute the machine will stop? That it won't record my silence?

It will for several seconds. It has a time-lag device.

Then I am afraid that your interview will misrepresent me if it elides my silences. Aside from silences, my speech consists chiefly of quotations, what Horatio Greenough complained of: 'Extraneous and irrelevant forms invade that silence which is alone worthy of man when there is nothing to be said.' Perhaps the machine will record the ruffle of pages as I look up quotations.

I would say that voice-activated *is a compressed prepositional phrase, by voice-activated tape recorder. The* by *is silent.*

If you are writing a thesis on my work, I hope that you write better than you speak. Did you know that the fifteenth-century mystery plays were mastery plays, performed by masters of a guild, men whose craft was a mystery? They must have felt that their work was authorized and added something. If you are going to know my books, you need to know what I know. That is why I have agreed to this interview.

I'm sorry that you resent this.

I haven't said that I resent anything. Don't interpret me to myself: wait until you get home and listen to the tape. You seem to think that you have something to say about my writing that my writing doesn't say, and I am eager to discover what it could be. Perhaps you will use your skills as a Master of Arts in Literature to teach me what I have been trying to learn about myself by writing. I have quoted Polanyi's words to explain my writing: 'It is a systematic course in teaching myself to hold my own beliefs.'"

Ticket to Continuum

Writing is a continuum, he says. Words come from everywhere & nowhere, snatches of music in the air, a shout in the street, the murmurous sea of language. Everything vibrates with tiny filaments of meaning & sound: hammer of pulse, anvil of breath, vast unheard cycles of neutron, lepton, solar wind, star, the swarming electrons of the table we write on, paper, inkwell, flowing pen. & all are borrowed like our breath, bestowed & owed, given out & taken back, again & again. We live in a world we did not make. Yet here we are at the farthest reach of time casting our brief wild spark into the abyss. What keeps us company as we go along? Beneath all breath & speaking springs that great subterranean river, wordless song, darkly flowing toward silence & the sea.

Sixth Transcendental Etude

He says drowsily, Sometimes the book is a boat, drifting, drifting in the wake of its wake, as *"A sail ! A veil awave upon the waves."* Lotused on the rug, he reads: *"In the sounding of* mantra, *one lets the eternity of soundlessness, which is the enchanted origin and being of language, silently and musically resound. In the gesture of* mudra, *one effaces the ego by erasing its writing: this act of devotion lets the luminous writing of light, as well as the dark writing of shadow, gracefully alight on the white-surfaced paper. In this manner, one realizes the visible emptiness of light, which is also the invisible space from whence language comes forth."* Perhaps that is why, (he touches his finger to my lips), the poet came to remind us, *"Language is Delphi."*

Seventh Transcendental Etude

The rabbis tell us, *"the white fire is the written Torah, the black fire the oral Torah."* & one of them even suggests that *"the white spaces in the scroll of the Torah consist of letters we cannot see. Only when the Messiah comes will God reveal to us the white invisible letters of the Torah."*

Hence, the poet writes, *"Then where is the truth but in the burning space between one letter and the next."*

Gate

It began alone in a room with others. Thirteen years ago. Jewish leap year, a year of thirteen moons. He thinks back to those brief luminous winter days & long starry ice-age nights of excitation & exhaustion & renewal, of joy & despair & joy again, when writing seemed like copying only, tracing shadows, listening to voices, taking dictation. He had written himself to the center of what he had to say, & found there nothing but a hollowness, a hole, & a great forgetting, a farewell that was in its way a greater welcoming, the selfless self some call the soul. In his gnomic script, he wrote: *Civilization: the conversation of ghosts. Existence: a circle whose circumference is everywhere.*

Thirteen years later, sitting in this room of perfumed paper-whites & raked ashes, reading these words rescued from the transient foxfires of time —love letters, elegies, failed & finished poems—the burning (of writing) saved by the writing (of burning)—even now, they shine back at him, illuminating the dark—signals, semaphors, shattered light—each wounding shard a tiny illusory mirrorworld—vertiginous, dazzling, dizzyingly self-reflective. *The gloss is a glass,* he says. *Aleph a gate.*

So, passing back through the shadow of ourselves, we bow to the angel of morning.

Ox-Herding Pictures

He shows me the xerox of a xerox of a xerox. (Is it faintly graying, this blank page?) "Once we valued the faded original," he says, "then the fresh copy. Now we must be true to our originless origins. Coinless coins. Echo without word." Pausing now to face the surface. "Whiteness is witness,

my friend. What you see is what you get! & because there is no differ-
ence," he smiles, "we can choose."

Eighth Transcendental Etude

"Empty-handed I go, and behold the spade is in my hands;
I walk on foot, and yet on the back of an ox I am riding;
When I pass over the bridge,
Lo, the water floweth not, but the bridge doth flow."

In the Scriptorium

He sits alone in a room with others faithfully copying what lies before
him. In perfect stillness, he can hear the bell ringing before it has rung, in
his mind's eye follow the migratory network of flocks of returning swal-
lows before they take flight. Above him the clerestory ceiling weakly reflects
cloudy undulations of a late winter sun. Shadow fish swim through a
shadow net. Just this morning, he woke to the words, *Stars pale to meaning,*
& one by one they vanished—snowflakes—melting like memories in a
lake of light. Turning his gaze from faded original to the bright surface of
this page glistening with lines of ink, he wonders if the net *is* its minute
reticulations or the empty spaces between them. Then he picks up his pen
& begins to write: *He sits alone in a room with others . . .*

iii.29.99

Italicized passages from *The Book of Borrowed Breath:*

First Transcendental Etude:	Malebranche
Second Transcendental Etude:	Wittgenstein, *Philosophical Investigations*
Third Transcendental Etude:	Kafka, "Reflections on Sin, Suffering, Hope, and the True Way"
Fourth Transcendental Etude:	slight paraphrase of Borges, "Kafka and his Precursors"
Fifth Transcendental Etude:	William S. Wilson, "Metier," in *Why I Don't Write Like Franz Kafka* (Ecco Press, 1977)
Sixth Transcendental Etude:	James Joyce, *Finnegans Wake*

David Michael Levin, "The phenom-
enon and noumenon of language: the
twin paths of *mantra* (perfect speak-
ing) and *mudra* (perfect writing)," "In
the Wake of the *Wake*," (*Triquarterly*
38, Winter, 1977)
Novalis

Seventh Transcendental Etude: paraphrase of Gershom Scholem,
On the Kabbalah and its Symbolism
(Schocken Books, 1969)
Edmond Jabes, *From the Book to
the Book: An Edmond Jabes Reader*
(Wesleyan University Press, 1991)

Eighth Transcendental Etude: Lao-Tzu, *The Way*

STEPHANIE BROWN

Stephanie Brown was born in Pasadena, California, in 1961 and grew up in Newport Beach. She attended Boston University and the University of Iowa Writers' Workshop. She holds a Master of Library Science from the University of California at Berkeley. Brown's first book of poetry was *Allegory of the Supermarket* (University of Georgia Press, 1998). Her work was included in the 1993, 1995, and 1997 editions of *Best American Poetry* and has also been anthologized in *The Body Electric* (W. W. Norton, 2000) and *American Poetry: Next Generation* (Carnegie Mellon University Press, 2000). Brown is married and has two sons. She lives in San Clemente.

No Longer a Girl

The city was a gray city.
I was dreaming of nothing then.
I had no hopes of love anymore.
My back was breaking.
My heart was cracked.
Though it wasn't broken by another person.
I liked to shout, but there was no one to listen.
I was no longer a girl: no one looked and they once did.
It was dark but there were no storms to create verdant forests.

Drizzle, steady, on the train which ran down the freeway, then went
    underground.
I remember those guys nodding out, that kid playing with himself
All the way home from the airport. In the cute house I rented
There was this stain on the planked floor which trailed
directly from the bathroom to the around-the-corner bedroom door.
Someone had walked that path, dripping wet, for years.
I wasn't doing it, I swear.
It's hard to believe, but there was a crematorium on the corner.
Really. And there was a graveyard where my street dead-ended.
I found the graves of the Civil War soldiers, marked by cannons.
There were ponds, bent trees, and leaves floating in the waters.
And if you walked to the top of the hill
You could see Merritt Lake downtown.
You could see the Pacific beyond.
You could see light shimmer on the water but everything
Inside of me held still.
Not afraid of the feel of the dead,
Not afraid of the living sitting in cafés or walking the dog:
On Sundays I'd walk down to the street near my house
Where there were stores and things to do, even a movie theater,
Because I thought: "I'll take a walk and that will be fun"
But everything was sad, even the joy I once felt opening the big
Sunday newspaper was gone.
After a while I left that city, when I was done.

NATHANAEL WEST
Excerpt from *The Day of the Locust*

Around quitting time, Tod Hackett heard a great din on the road outside
his office. The groan of leather mingled with the jangle of iron and over
all beat the tattoo of a thousand hooves. He hurried to the window.

An army of cavalry and foot was passing. It moved like a mob; its
lines broken, as though fleeing from some terrible defeat. The dolmans
of the hussars, the heavy shakos of the guards, Hanoverian light horse,
with their flat leather caps and flowing red plumes, were all jumbled to-
gether in bobbing disorder. Behind the cavalry came the infantry, a wild
sea of waving sabertaches, sloped muskets, crossed shoulder belts and

swinging cartridge boxes. Tod recognized the scarlet infantry of England with their white shoulder pads, the black infantry of the Duke of Brunswick, the French grenadiers with their enormous white gaiters, the Scotch with bare knees under plaid skirts.

While he watched, a little fat man, wearing a cork sun-helmet, polo shirt and knickers, darted around the corner of the building in pursuit of the army.

"Stage Nine—you bastards—Stage Nine!" he screamed through a small megaphone.

The cavalry put spur to their horses and the infantry broke into a dogtrot. The little man in the cork hat ran after them, shaking his fist and cursing.

Tod watched until they had disappeared behind half a Mississippi steamboat, then put away his pencils and drawing board, and left the office. On the sidewalk outside the studio he stood for a moment trying to decide whether to walk home or take a streetcar. He had been in Hollywood less than three months and still found it a very exciting place, but he was lazy and didn't like to walk. He decided to take the streetcar as far as Vine Street and walk the rest of the way.

. . . When the Hollywood job had come along, he had grabbed it despite the arguments of his friends who were certain that he was selling out and would never paint again.

He reached the end of Vine Street and began the climb into Pinyon Canyon. Night had started to fall.

The edges of the trees burned with a pale violet light and their centers gradually turned from deep purple to black. The same violet piping, like a Neon tube, outlined the tops of the ugly, humpbacked hills and they were almost beautiful.

But not even the soft wash of dusk could help the houses. Only dynamite would be of any use against the Mexican ranch houses, Samoan huts, Mediterranean villas, Egyptian and Japanese temples, Swiss chalets, Tudor cottages, and every possible combination of these styles that lined the slopes of the canyon.

When he noticed that they were all of plaster, lath and paper, he was charitable and blamed their shape on the materials used. Steel, stone and brick curb a builder's fancy a little, forcing him to distribute his stresses and weights and to keep his corners plumb, but plaster and paper know no law, not even that of gravity.

On the corner of La Huerta Road was a miniature Rhine castle with tarpaper turrets pierced for archers. Next to it was a little highly colored shack with domes and minarets out of the *Arabian Nights*. Again he was charitable. Both houses were comic, but he didn't laugh. Their desire to startle was so eager and guileless.

It is hard to laugh at the need for beauty and romance, no matter how tasteless, even horrible, the results of that need are. But it is easy to sigh. Few things are sadder than the truly monstrous.

JAMES M. CAIN
Excerpt from *The Postman Always Rings Twice*

We didn't say anything. She knew what to do. She climbed back, and I climbed front. I looked at the wrench under the dash light. It had a few drops of blood on it. I uncorked a bottle of wine, and poured it on there till the blood was gone. I poured so the wine went over him. Then I wiped the wrench on a dry part of his clothes, and passed it back to her. She put it under the seat. I poured more wine over where I had wiped the wrench, cracked the bottle against the door, and laid it on top of him. Then I started the car. The wine bottle gave a gurgle, where a little of it was running out the crack.

I went a little way, and then shifted up to second. I couldn't tip it down that 500-foot drop, where we were. We had to get down to it afterward, and besides, if it plunged that far, how would we be alive? I drove slow, in second, up to a place where the ravine came to a point, and it was only a 50-foot drop. When I got there, I drove over the edge, put my foot on the brake, and fed with the hand throttle. As soon as the right front wheel went off, I stepped hard on the brake. It stalled. That was how I wanted it. The car had to be in gear, with the ignition on, but that dead motor would hold it for the rest of what we had to do.

We got out. We stepped on the road, not the shoulder, so there wouldn't be footprints. She handed me a rock, and a piece of 2 x 4 I had back there. I put the rock under the rear axle. It fitted, because I had picked one that would fit. I slipped the 2 x 4 over the rock and under the axle. I heaved down on it. The car tipped, but it hung there. I heaved again. It tipped a little more. I began to sweat. Here we were, with a dead man in the car, and suppose we couldn't tip it over?

I heaved again, but this time she was beside me. We both heaved. We heaved again. And then all of a sudden, there we were, sprawled down on the road, and the car was rolling over and over, down the gully, and banging so loud you could hear it a mile.

It stopped. The lights were still on, but it wasn't on fire. . . .

I ran back, picked her up, and slid down the ravine with her. . . .

I set her down. The car was hanging there, on two wheels, about halfway down the ravine. He was still in there, but now he was down on the floor. The wine bottle was wedged between him and the seat, and while we were looking it gave a gurgle. . . .

I began to fool with her blouse, to bust the buttons, so she would looked banged up. She was looking at me, and her eyes didn't look blue, they looked black. I could feel her breath coming fast. Then it stopped, and she leaned real close to me.

"Rip me! Rip me!"

I ripped her. I shoved my hand in her blouse and jerked. She was wide open, from her throat to her belly.

My Southern California: West, Cain

As a child, I didn't really like to read all that much, but I liked books (I even made a card catalogue of all my books in junior high). I have an early memory of sitting in my room with Robert Louis Stevenson's *A Child's Garden of Verses,* reciting *My Shadow* again and again. I loved the simple rhymes. They were easy to memorize. I could hold them in my mind and remember them if I wanted to, or I could turn to the book and enjoy both the words and Tasha Tudor's illustrations. In third grade, I read, memorized, and mused dramatically over *The Eagle* by Tennyson because I had read it in my English textbook. I wrote out the stanzas again and again because I loved how they looked. That one short poem lasted me a whole year. My mother had an old edition of Tennyson which I looked at, turned the pages of, and basically mooned over. I loved the idea: poet, poems, and big leather-bound books.

I found books of poetry at the mall bookstore, and I took special pleasure from my purchase of E. E. Cummings and Gary Snyder. On one trip to the mall (high on amphetamines) I went to the bookstore while my sister shopped. There was something new: *The American Poetry Anthology* edited by Daniel Halpern. That anthology became my companion during my junior and senior years in high school. I read and reread every poem in that book. I read them out loud in my room, wrote them out on lined notebook paper. I was particularly drawn to *Herbert White* by Frank Bidart and *Legs* by Kathleen Fraser. Those poems felt young and contemporary. They felt like something I wanted to do. Reading widely, even compulsively, as I have done in the twenty years since then, I've gone through serious one-sided love affairs with poets such as Yeats, Frost, Bishop, Lowell, and Merrill, to name a few, and there were many others on whom I had crushes. I was a shameless imitator of Kenneth Koch and Frank O'Hara for a while; I love their work.

Perversely, perhaps, I don't want to write an essay about those influences. Instead, I want to explore the influence of two novelists, Nathanael West and James M. Cain. Their depiction of Southern California and their use of language shaped my poetry and influenced my work for many years.

I

I remember as a child seeing the New Directions single-volume paper-back edition of Nathanael West's *Miss Lonelyhearts* and *The Day of the Locust* in my sister's box of books that she brought home from her first year at Berkeley. The black-and-white photo of the faces on the cover fascinated me, like the ads for baby dolls "100 for $1.00!" on the back cover of comic books: creepy, but I also wanted them. I used to open the box just to look at the cover. In my senior year of high school, I took the book out of the box that had sat there for ten years and read it during a week-long trip to the Colorado River with my boyfriend and friends. I read during the day while sitting on a beach chair at the river's edge, drinking a beer. I was not sure I even understood what was going on. Still, I was drawn to both novels and especially to *The Day of the Locust* because of its funny, gar-goyle-ish, and thoroughly believable depictions of Californians. The people who "had come to California to die,"[1] who had found themselves restless in Los Angeles and environs—I recognized them; I knew their descen-dants. Fools, idiots, whores, entertainers, cowboys, schemers, con artists, artists—they populated the world I knew, not the "California Dream" version of Southern California. West's characters, even as early as the 1930s, had been betrayed by the dream.

> All their lives they had slaved at some kind of dull, heavy labor, behind desks and counters, in the fields and at tedious machines of all sorts, sav-ing their pennies and dreaming of the leisure that would be theirs when they had enough. Finally that day came. They could draw a weekly in-come of ten or fifteen dollars. Where else would they go but California, the land of sunshine and oranges?
>
> Once there, they discover that sunshine isn't enough. They get tired of oranges, even of avocado pears and passion fruit. Nothing happens. They don't know what to do with their time. They haven't the mental equipment for leisure, the money nor the physical equipment for plea-

sure. . . . They watch the waves come in at Venice. There wasn't any ocean where most of them came from, but after you've seen one wave, you've seen them all. The same is true of the airplanes at Glendale. If only a plane would crash once in a while so that they could watch the passengers being consumed in a 'holocaust of flame,' as the newspapers put it. But the planes never crash.[2]

The California writers who came after West, such as Joan Didion and Bret Easton Ellis, depicted that same restless boredom. And I knew what it felt like.

California was rarely revealed to us in the literature we read in high school. We might read Steinbeck or something like Twain's "The Celebrated Jumping Frog of Calaveras County," but nothing about the world we knew. It was as if we were colonists in a remote part of the world, reading about the fatherland. West knew that California was not a thing like New England, New York, or the South, the places where, it seemed, all American stories were grown. He rightly saw that in order to capture the off-kilter world of Southern California, one needed to turn for models to artists of satire and the grotesque rather than to those of Yankee realism. His character Tod, an artist and set designer who comes from Yale to Hollywood to work for the movies, envisions throughout the novel a painting he calls "The Burning of Los Angeles," an apocalyptic vision of fire, destruction, and terror. Tod knew that

[T]he fat lady in the yachting cap was going shopping, not boating; the man in the Norfolk jacket and Tyrolean hat was returning, not from a mountain, but an insurance office; and the girl in slacks and sneaks with a bandanna around her head had just left a switchboard, not a tennis court. Scattered among these masqueraders were people of a different type. Their clothing was somber and badly cut, bought from mail-order houses. While the others moved rapidly, darting into stores and cocktail bars, they loitered on the corners or stood with their backs to the shop windows and stared at everyone who passed. When their stare was returned, their eyes filled with hatred. At this time Tod knew very little about them except that they had come to California to die.

He was determined to learn much more. They were the people he felt he must paint. He would never again do a fat red barn, old stone wall or sturdy Nantucket fisherman. From the moment he had seen them, he

had known that, despite his race, training and heritage, neither Winslow
Homer nor Thomas Ryder could be his masters and he turned to Goya
and Daumier.[3]

I, too, have always been drawn to artists of satire and caricature: Goya,
Daumier, Hogarth, Grosz. Serious humor. West was the first writer I'd
found, at seventeen, who tried to do that with words. I was drawn to the
1930s as well. I loved everything about them: the American and European
painters, the architecture, the clothes, Jean Harlow and the black-and-
white movies, the hard-drinking newspapermen in suits and hats, the *feel*
of it. Perhaps it was from listening to stories of my mother and father grow-
ing up in Los Angeles in the 1930s and from the sepia-toned photos from
that era of my grandparents at Capistrano Beach.

When I was growing up, it seemed that everyone showed symptoms
of pathological grandiosity. The people I knew expected to be rock stars
and models. Our world didn't overlap much with Hollywood, but the
people I knew bragged about selling cocaine to movie stars. Even those
who were part of the soil of California reinvented themselves through self-
improvement regimes, New Age religion, and restricted diets. I knew raw-
food vegans and Breatharians; followers of est, Lifespring, Transcendental
Meditation; students of Zen, Alistair Crowley, Sai Baba, Paramahansa Yoga-
nanda, and Kathryn Kuhlman; Fundamentalist-Christian commune-dwellers,
Hare Krishnas, and pagans; tax resisters and survivalists. I recognized the
gatherings that Tod attends in search of faces to draw:

> He visited the "Church of Christ, Physical" where holiness was attained
> through the constant use of chestweights and spring grips; the "Church
> Invisible" where fortunes were told and the dead made to find lost ob-
> jects; the "Tabernacle of the Third Coming" where a woman in male
> clothing preached the "Crusade Against Salt"; and the "Temple Moderne"
> under whose glass and chromium rood "Brain-Breathing, the Secret of
> the Aztecs" was taught.
>
> As he watched these people writhe on the hard seats of their churches,
> he thought of how well Alessandro Magnasco would dramatize the contrast
> between their drained-out, feeble bodies and their wild, disordered minds.
> He would not satirize them as Hogarth or Daumier might, nor would he
> pity them. He would paint them with respect, appreciating its awful, an-
> archic power and aware that they had it in them to destroy civilization.[4]

I recognized as well the grandiosity displayed by the character Faye Greener in her conversation with Homer Simpson. She reminded me of many people I had met along the way, of listening to someone's emphatic voice high on cocaine:

> "My father isn't really a peddler," she said, abruptly. "He's an actor. I'm an actress. My mother was also an actress, a dancer. The theatre is in our blood."
> "I haven't seen many shows. I . . ."
> He broke off because he saw that she wasn't interested.
> "I'm going to be a star some day," she announced as though daring him to contradict her.
> "I'm sure you . . ."
> "It's my life. It's the only thing in the whole world that I want."
> "It's good to know what you want. I used to be a bookkeeper in a hotel, but . . ."
> "If I'm not, I'll commit suicide."
> She stood up and put her hands to her hair, opened her eyes wide and frowned.[5]

That scene still makes me laugh. I love the bleak, nasty, and on-target comedy of Nathanael West. His Los Angeles—with its silly-crass mixture of architectural periods and styles, its cinematic blending of past, present, and future, its mingling of high and low—was the world I lived in, too. I knew people—like the movie producer Claude Estee in the book—who were rich, thought themselves witty, and collected rare cars, art, and yachts. I knew people who drove cast-off Cadillacs and lived in sheds and garages, like the cockfighters who live at Homer Simpson's house. I knew the appeal of the lurid, as a cockfight appeals to Tod and Claude; I knew the ease with which Faye Greener flirts and finds herself drunk and in bed with someone. Among my acquaintances were a mother and daughter who had had sex with the single guys who lived across the street from them, one pair in one room, one in the other. I knew boys who grew up playing golf with their doctor fathers but lived, after their parents' divorce, in rental apartments with mothers who struggled to survive and finally gave up, releasing their sons into the wild.

II

> Cain writes a scene in *The Postman Always Rings Twice* where Frank rips
> Cora's blouse and says, as if she'd been in a car wreck, "You got that climb-
> ing out. You caught it in the door handle." Then he punches her in the
> eye and says, "And this you don't know how you got." I thought if I could
> write a line like that I could be happy for the rest of my life, at least for
> the rest of the day.
>
> —Stephen King, in a *New Yorker* Profile[6]

I remember lying on the couch reading the book I'd picked out at the
bookstore, attracted by its cover and its title, which I recognized as a movie.
I was twenty. Outside the sliding glass doors, boats slipped and glided
through the calm bay water. It was a beautiful spring day. My boyfriend
had gone out on our ski boat with two of our friends. This was my par-
ents' boat. Where were they? I don't remember, but I remember being
alone in the house while I read this book cover to cover without stopping.
"No one has ever put down one of James M. Cain's books"—it said some-
thing like this on the back cover of *The Postman Always Rings Twice*.

It was considered strange, among my friends, to want to spend a day
inside reading, especially a beautiful day. We liked to drink, go out in the
ocean in fast boats, go to concerts and punk rock clubs and parties and
brunch, and drink and cheat on our boyfriends and girlfriends. My boyfriend
and his friends were part of the outer fringe of surfer culture, not of peace-
loving green types, but of violent, drunken, petty criminal types. I was
prone to violence myself. I liked the excitement and the wild emotions.
I would goad the guys into fistfights by playing one off the other. I re-
member throwing a clog that barely missed my boyfriend's head; a couple
of times, he bashed my head into a sidewalk during fights I started. Once,
when we were drunk and driving in a hard rain, I slapped him so hard I
cut his eye with the diamond in a ring that I was wearing, and he pulled
on the emergency brake and ran from the car.

On the flip side of the drinking, the fighting, the sex, and the adrena-
line were the afternoons spent watching TV while rolling joints and sitting
in a vague haze and the three- or four-a.m. mornings watching old TV
shows while coming down from cocaine, my jaw going back and forth,
my head nodding as I listened to someone go on and on about his future

plans and starry ambitions. The guys surfed and did their thing, while the girls evolved from companion to caretaker, though sometimes the situation was reversed, depending on who had the bigger drug problem. Predictably, couples lived together for a while, changed partners, moved on and moved in with the next one. I suspected that marrying one of these guys might turn me into a harridan supporting a perpetually childish ne'er-do-well. I was watching myself turn into a "shrew" and a "bitch" where once I had been "fun," but I still wanted to marry my boyfriend. Some couples, of course, were different: the young businessmen who owned the surf store, and their wives, seemed successful and able to live both within and without the low surf culture. They seemed to possess a beatific, blissful sense of the world; they were cool; I wanted to have a life like that: *cool.*

What was the appeal of *The Postman Always Rings Twice*? Like West's novels, Cain's took place in the 1930s; they were set in L.A.—characters lived in Pasadena, where I had been born; they vacationed at Lake Arrowhead, where my family did; they drove to Malibu and Laguna, to downtown and to Glendale. It was like the sepia-toned photos of my grandparents come to life. As in *The Day of the Locust,* the characters lived in the grip of obsessions, were self-destructive even when they had luck on their side. Like me—I was like that. The story of my great-aunt who died from alcoholism, her little bungalow filled with gin bottles—that could be me. The high school friend of a friend in a dive bar trying to pick me up by bragging about his time in San Quentin, where he had been sent for manslaughter—I could be his victim. I was about to cross a threshold. I longed to try heroin, but I saw a friend go to jail for it, steal from friends and parents, disappear, and something in me held back just a little bit. I actually felt terror while reading the book; I could understand being a loser, being consigned to doom. I knew how it appealed to me. But more than anything else, I liked how Cain wrote: I liked the short, clipped phrases. I liked his sympathy for the characters. I was moved by his novels. I wanted to tell a story the way Cain did. I wanted to grasp my reader and compel him to keep reading.

In *Postman,* Cain also described a raw sexuality that I hadn't found written about anywhere else. It showed how our fantasies often fuse sex and violence. When Frank first sees Cora, he thinks:

> Then I saw her. She had been out back, in the kitchen, but she came in to gather up my dishes. Except for the shape, she really wasn't any raving

beauty, but she had a sulky look to her, and her lips stuck out in a way that made me want to mash them in for her.[7]

When he finally kisses her:

> I took her in my arms and mashed my mouth up against hers. . . . "Bite me! Bite me!"
> I bit her. I sunk my teeth into her lips so deep I could feel the blood spurt into my mouth. It was running down her neck when I carried her upstairs.[8]

Today when I read that, it seems kind of silly. But when I first began to write poetry and short stories with serious intent, I wrote a lot about sex. I published some erotic poems in *Yellow Silk*. The appeal of all that has worn off. I haven't been able to write an erotic poem in years. But it was probably the first subject I explored in any depth. When I wrote about sex, I wrote about sex in a deadpan, violent, and sometimes smirking hard-boiled style. Cain's books struck an erotic note that I understood, as did West's evocation of Faye Greener in *The Day of the Locust,* a destructive seductress who incites men to violence.

III

While writing the poem *No Longer a Girl,* I was consciously trying to imitate both Cain and West. I wanted to echo the cadence of Cain's hard-boiled writing as I began: "The city was a gray city./ I was dreaming of nothing then./ I had no hopes of love anymore./ My back was breaking./ My heart was cracked." I wanted to introduce a tough, or at least numb, persona, like the narrators of crime novels with their "here's what I see; no comment" descriptive style: "I remember those guys nodding out, that kid playing with himself/ All the way home from the airport." And there was the strange, sad (and also bizarre) fact that I lived near both a crematorium and a graveyard—it's a landscape I think West would have appreciated. My main homage to West, though, is the insertion of comedy at odd moments: "Someone had walked that path, dripping wet, for years./ *I wasn't doing it, I swear.*" I was hoping to make the reader feel unsettled, as West does by his mixture of dark humor and detached visual accuracy.

In *Miss Lonelyhearts* he describes a cuckolded, grotesque man in this way: "As he hobbled along, he made many waste motions, like those of a partially destroyed insect."[9] When I first read that line, I could not help laughing because it is so mean and funny, yet I also felt the pathos of his hopeless existence. I admire the way West does this; by being detached in his observations, by using humor, he avoids bathos and sentimentality.

I chose *No Longer a Girl* not only because I can so easily trace the influence of these two writers but also because, while writing it, I experienced for one of the first times a sense of mastery. I wrote this poem as I always did: I let anything come out, got it down, and revised within the bounds of what was on the page. I was not very good at seeing out of the frame I'd composed for myself. I hadn't really learned to be subtle, to layer a poem with meanings, to bring in paradox or ambiguity. Those techniques were something I strove for, but if I managed to achieve them, it was mostly by accident. I wrote this poem during one of those periods of great creative activity, when the poems come every day and you almost can't keep up with them. I would come home every evening after work and write and revise. I did not have a feeling of writer's block or frustration, and I did not hurry my revisions. After I wrote the first draft of this poem, I felt something essential was missing. Instead of working on the mood of the person in the poem, I saw that it needed more concrete description of the landscape. So I started to think about the actual neighborhood where I had lived, the neighborhood I was trying to describe. A crematorium was at one end of my street and the graveyard entrance was at the other end. The streets that fanned out from the graveyard entrance were home to florists, headstone makers, mortuaries. In the first draft I had not written anything about the graveyard/mortuary/crematorium area. It was like a blow to the head: how could I have overlooked that!?

I saw that I had been living in a literal landscape of death. Here was a rich—indeed, *obvious*—metaphor that I could use. But because it had been a real experience, I hoped that my descriptions of the actual place would transcend the metaphor's obvious quality. Then I made an intuitive leap: I had, for some reason, chosen to live in a funereal setting. I thought of the myth of Persephone, abducted by Hades to the underworld (death) but eventually able to leave for six months of each year. I decided that I would write the poem as if I were a contemporary Persephone describing her life in, and her return from, Hades' kingdom.

I revised with that in mind and shaped the poem to tell that story. I consciously added the Persephone myth into the poem: in lines like "Drizzle, steady, on the train which ran down the freeway, then went underground"; in the detail of the planked wood floor that tries to evoke the idea of "walking the plank"; in the descriptions of being "no longer a girl," neither seen nor heard, but living in a gray city among other spirits, like Civil War soldiers or the people on the subway. I also tried to bury the myth within the story and not call attention to it. That took a new kind of confidence to keep from laying all my cards on the table, to be subtle. Emboldened by my confidence, I added some unconventional line breaks which I felt helped to propel the emotion in the poem: "You could see light shimmer on the water but everything/ Inside of me held still" and "But everything was sad, even the joy I once felt opening the big/ Sunday newspaper was gone" instead of breaking after "water" in the first instance and "felt" in the second. To be able to revise in such an intentional way was a breakthrough for me.

I still read *No Longer a Girl* with pleasure. It is a favorite of mine. I'm happy with the way it turned out, and I happily remember the satisfaction I had while writing it. I remember very well the time in which I wrote it because it was a period of change for me. Around the time I finished this poem I happened to read again the quotation from 1 Corinthians: "When I was a child, I spake as a child. . . . but when I became a man, I put away childish things."[10] That phrase became my motto for a while, something I turned over in my mind again and again. I myself was "no longer a girl." When I looked carefully at the world around me I saw that I had moved on from these two artists who had influenced my youth, and the poem was like a fond farewell.

HAYDEN CARRUTH

Hayden Carruth was born in 1921 and for many years lived in northern Vermont. He lives now in upstate New York and has retired from teaching in the Graduate Creative Writing Program at Syracuse University. He has published 41 books, chiefly poetry, but also including a novel, four books of criticism, and two anthologies. His most recent books are *Reluctantly* (Copper Canyon Press, 1998) and *Beside the Shadblow Tree* (Copper Canyon Press, 1999). He has been editor of *Poetry;* poetry editor of *Harper's;* and, for more than 25 years, an advisory editor of the *Hudson Review.* He has received fellowships from the Bollingen Foundation, the Guggenheim Foundation, the National Endowment for the Arts, the New York Arts Foundation, and others. He has been presented with the Lenore Marshall Award, the Vermont Governor's Medal, the Sarah Josepha Hale Award, the Brandeis University Award, the Carl Sandberg Award, the Whiting Award, the Ruth Lilly Prize, the National Book Critics' Circle Award for poetry, and many others. In 1988, he was appointed a Senior Fellow by the National Endowment for the Arts.

WILLIAM SHAKESPEARE
Excerpt from *Cymbeline*

Song

> Fear no more the heat o' the sun
> Nor the furious winter's rages;
> Thou thy worldly task hast done,

Home art gone, and ta'en thy wages.
Golden lads and girls all must,
As chimney-sweepers, come to dust.

Fear no more the frown o' the great;
Thou art past the tyrant's stroke.
Care no more to clothe and eat;
To thee the reed is as the oak.
The sceptre, learning, physic, must
All follow this and come to dust.

Fear no more the lightning flash—
Nor th'all-dreaded thunder-stone;
Fear not slander, censure rash;
Thou hast finish'd joy and moan.
All lovers young, all lovers must
Consign to thee and come to dust.

No exorciser harm thee!
Nor no witchcraft charm thee!
Ghost unlaid forbear thee!
Nothing ill come near thee!
Quiet consummation have;
And renowned be thy grave!

BEN JONSON
Epitaph on Elizabeth, L. H.

Would'st thou heare, what man can say
In a little? Reader, stay.
Under-neath this stone doth lye
As much beautie, as could dye:
Which in life did harbour give
To more vertue, then doth live.
If, at all, shee had a fault,
Leave it buryed in this vault.
One name was Elizabeth,
Th'other let it sleepe with death:
Fitter, where it dyed, to tell,
Then that it liv'd at all. Farewell.

ALEXANDER POPE
Excerpt from *Epistle to Dr. Arbuthnot*

Shut, shut the door, good John! fatigu'd I said,
Tye up the knocker, say I'm sick, I'm dead.
The Dog-star rages! nay 'tis past a doubt,
All Bedlam, or Parnassus, is let out:
Fire in each eye, and papers in each hand,
They rave, recite, and madden round the land.

What walls can guard me, or what shades can hide?
They pierce my thickets, thro' my Grot they glide,
By land, by water, they renew the charge,
They stop the chariot, and they board the barge.
No place is sacred, not the Church is free,
Ev'n Sunday shines no Sabbath-day to me:
Then from the Mint walks forth the Man of rhyme,
Happy! to catch me, just at Dinner-time.

Is there a Parson, much be-mus'd in beer,
A maudlin Poetess, a rhyming Peer,
A Clerk, foredoom'd his father's soul to cross,
Who pens a Stanza, when he should *engross*?
Is there, who, lock'd from ink and paper, scrawls
With desp'rate charcoal round his darken'd walls?
All fly to Twit'nam, and in humble strain
Apply to me, to keep them mad or vain.
Arthur, whose giddy son neglects the Laws,
Imputes to me and my damn'd works the cause:
Poor Cornus sees his frantic wife elope,
And curses Wit, and Poetry, and Pope.

EMILY DICKINSON
422

More Life—went out—when He went
Than Ordinary Breath—
Lit with a finer Phosphor—
Requiring in the Quench—

A Power of Renowned Cold,
The Climate of the Grave

A Temperature just adequate
So Anthracite, to live—

For some—an Ampler Zero—
A Frost more needle keen
Is necessary, to reduce
The Ethiop within.

Others—extinguish easier—
A Gnat's minutest Fan
Sufficient to obliterate
A Tract of Citizen—

Whose Peat lift—amply vivid—
Ignores the solemn News
That Popocatapel exists—
Or Etna's Scarlets, Choose—

ROBERT FROST
Brown's Descent, or The Willy-Nilly Slide

Brown lived at such a lofty farm
    That everyone for miles could see
His lantern when he did his chores
    In winter after half-past three.

And many must have seen him make
    His wild descent from there one night,
'Cross lots, 'cross walls, 'cross everything,
    Describing rings of lantern light.

Between the house and barn the gale
    Got him by something he had on
And blew him out on the icy crust
    That cased the world, and he was gone!

Walls were all buried, trees were few:
    He saw no stay unless he stove
A hole in somewhere with his heel.
    But though repeatedly he strove

And stamped and said things to himself,
    And sometimes something seemed to yield,

He gained no foothold, but pursued
    His journey down from field to field.

Sometimes he came with arms outspread
    Like wings, revolving in the scene
Upon his longer axis, and
    With no small dignity of mien.

Faster or slower as he chanced,
    Sitting or standing as he chose,
According as he feared to risk
    His neck, or thought to spare his clothes,

He never let the lantern drop.
    And some exclaimed who saw afar
The figures he described with it,
    'I wonder what those signals are

'Brown makes at such an hour of night!
    He's celebrating something strange.
I wonder if he's sold his farm,
    Or been made Master of the Grange.'

He reeled, he lurched, he bobbed, he checked;
    He fell and made the lantern rattle
(But saved the light from going out.)
    So halfway down he fought the battle,

Incredulous of his own bad luck.
    And then becoming reconciled
To everything, he gave it up
    And came down like a coasting child.

'Well—I—be—' that was all he said,
    As standing in the river road,
He looked back up the slippery slope
    (Two miles it was) to his abode.

Sometimes as an authority
    On motor-cars, I'm asked if I
Should say our stock was petered out,
    And this is my sincere reply:

Yankees are what they always were.
    Don't think Brown ever gave up hope

Of getting home again because
    He couldn't climb that slippery slope;

Or even thought of standing there
    Until the January thaw
Should take the polish off the crust.
    He bowed with grace to natural law,

And then went round it on his feet,
    After the manner of our stock;
Not much concerned for those to whom,
    At that particular time o'clock,

It must have looked as if the course
    He steered was really straight away
From that which he was headed for—
    Not much concerned for them, I say;

No more so than became a man—
    And politician at odd seasons.
I've kept Brown standing in the cold
    While I invested him with reasons;

But now he snapped his eyes three times;
    Then shook his lantern, saying, 'Ile's
'Bout out!' and took the long way home
    By road, a matter of several miles.

Influences

Influences. I suppose it's okay to be interested in them. Lots of people are. But it's always seemed rather weird and futile to me. Napoleon was influenced by Plutarch, Tamerlane, and Savonarola. So what? He'd have debauched Europe just the same if he'd never heard of any of them.

In my writing, I've been influenced by at least ten thousand poems written by at least one thousand poets. That's a fact—fat with factitude. My estimate is *very* conservative. After all, I began reading in 1924, and before then poems were recited to me. Now it's 2000.

Everyone is influenced, even if minimally, by everything read, everything heard, seen, encountered in any way, no? That's what the psychoneurotechnologists say. A poem by a third-grader from Abilene can enlarge one's sensibilities and set them ticking. It happens more often than the Big-Ass Poets are generally willing to admit.

I was asked to choose, for this assignment, five poems that have influenced me. I've done it, but I could just as well have chosen a hundred other sets of five.

Consider the opening couplet of Ben Jonson's lovely little epitaph:

Would'st thou heare, what man can say
In a little? Reader, stay.

This is a prosodic, musical wonder—yet it is simple enough. The first line consists of seven monosyllables of equal resonance. The reasonably experienced reader will recognize cataleptic dactylic tetrameter right away and will read the line with variation of pitch but practically no variation of stress or volume. It's a very strong beginning for a lyric poem. But then immediately comes the second line, with its run-over first phrase: "In a little." The two syllables—"a" and "tle"—are so low in stress that they are hardly more than murmurs, and "In" is not much stronger. The hard "lit," the only real stress, is still a low one. This combined with the rhyme of "a" and "tle," plus the nice assonance of the short "i"s and the mellifluent softness of the "n" and "l"—such a contrast to the strong first line—makes, to my ear, a triumph of musical verbalism. There follows a complete and abrupt stop, almost a standstill, before the language resumes with the very brief sentence, "Reader, stay."

I cannot say these beautiful lines aloud with anything like the delicacy of rhythm, tone, and texture I hear in my head. I doubt that any reader, even the most professional elocutionist, can do it. I could play these lines on my clarinet, and Bill Basie could have played them on his piano—he often did things with just such intrepid restraint. But the fact that I cannot enunciate the full loveliness of this poem with my actual voice does not diminish its importance for me. This is what *writing* is, so much more than speaking. And printing takes it one step further. Only a few years after I began to read, I also began to set type. The printed page is for me a treasure that can never be replaced by so-called video imagery.

As for the enigma in Jonson's epitaph, often I've wondered what part it plays in the poem's effectiveness. Some part, I'm sure. Who was Elizabeth? More to the point, how old was she? What was her fault? Why was the place of her death more defaming than the fact of her death? What did Jonson mean when he implied—no, stated—that the death of her name was more important than the death of her person? As far as I know, the scholars have discovered the answers to none of these questions, and we are left to our own delicious surmises.

Little is such a nice word, isn't it?—what we call "awfully nice" in our strange way of speaking. Is it beautiful? No. Unusually significant? No. Mellifluous, grand, noble? None of these things. It's just awfully nice. It makes me think of the old lullaby I love so much, which begins:

> Lollai lollai litil child
> Whi wepistow so sore?

Somewhere in Britain's rainy past was a man, or, more likely, a woman, who felt about language exactly as I do. Does this let me feel less lonely? No, but at least we are lonely together.

Once when I had a little boy I recited rhymes for him, as any parent does.

> Higgeldy piggeldy my black hen,
> She lays eggs for gentlemen.
> Gentlemen come every day
> To see what my black hen doth lay.

Then one night he said to me, "Papa, what does hendothlay mean?" It's a hell of a good question. Come to think of it, what *does* hendothlay mean? It's an awfully nice word. It has just the quality of smooth toughness I like best. But is it a word?

What is a word? I am thinking and writing in words at this moment and within the taut unstable limits of my sanity I cannot accept the idea that they are all meaningless. Higgeldy piggeldy, indeed.

Nevertheless, somewhere in this great improbable universe exists a race of "aliens" that has hit upon a way to communicate, fully and elaborately, without language, without abstraction. Think of that.

Each of the five poems I've reproduced at the beginning of this piece is flawed. Ben Jonson, for instance, should have written: "Would'st thou heare, what *words* can say?" This makes better sound and better sense. Similarly, toward the end of Frost's narrative, which I like greatly for its accuracy of language, its acute observation, and its good humor, qualities that any resident of northern New England can verify and appreciate, the poet should have put a damper on his didacticism; his fear that his poem could not elucidate its own meaning is too blatant—a common fault with Robert Frost. But then, I've never read a poem I couldn't improve. And this, believe me, is the most important way in which influences work among capable artists.

I've been asked to include one of my own among the poems quoted here.

What To Do

Tell your mind and its
    agony
to the white bloom
    of the blue plum tree,

a responding beauty
    irreducible
of the one earth and ground,
    for real.

Once a year
    in April
in this region
    you may tell
    for a little while.

A small, inconsequential piece, yet it pleases me greatly. I feel lucky, genuinely and gratefully, to have written it. Maybe I didn't write it. Two Bens have been immensely influential in my life, Ben Jonson and Ben Webster. Probably one of them wrote it.

GILLIAN CONOLEY

Gillian Conoley was born in Austin, Texas, in 1955. She studied journalism as an under-graduate at Southern Methodist University and went on to earn her M.F.A. in creative writing from the University of Massachusetts, Amherst. She has published four books of poetry with Carnegie Mellon University Press: *Some Gangster Pain* (1987), *Tall Stranger* (1991), *Beckon* (1996), and *Lovers in the Used World* (2001). *Tall Stranger* was a nomi-nee for the National Book Critics Circle Award. Conoley was winner of the Pushcart Prize in 1996, and her work was included in *Best American Poetry* in 1997. She was awarded the Jerome K. Shestack Poetry Prize for 1999 from the *American Poetry Review*. She is married to the novelist Domenic Stansberry. They live in the San Francisco Bay area with their daughter, Gillis.

Training Films of the Real

I.

Late shank of the evening: ligustrum pollen   on yellow walnut leaves,
two small girls   playing,   in sun,   young retinas   virtually empty

as: while pumping gas one sees   immaterial ones randomize rest
    stops,
as: in life,

black is,   blue is,   as in life   green becomes.
A red slashes

a red divides   white scallions   along a scaly riverbank.

A few new sprouts of cress   a crazed environmentalist
    shouting   *get off.*

As in life, I had meant the yellow
gaze of an ecstatic   over the unstainable industrial carpeting.

In the weedy old Victorian   sheltering the beakers, scales   of the
    meth lab,
oh yes   it's karmic   to print money.

Woman in creamy white slip   lacy bodice   a can of Colt .45
one finger fastening   the small rusty buckle of a strap.

May the baby wake.   Restoring respect   to the teamsters.
    Tremelo in the pipes
as cold and heat   trade places.

For the sound of a lute   out on water   she applies light makeup
    and sings,   *Don't Explain.*

II.

Teenagers xerox
genitalia.   Well that's a big if
what could they   *mean* by that

expanding moment
leaves falling
entire afternoon

                    spent looking

at the inscrutable,

days,   days

each blind
poet

                          with magnifying glass over OED

                                                akin

to Dostoyevsky's
never,

no sound of the gun   to come ringing through   the ears,

nevermore,

nevermore,

                    Green

bottle of pills   scattering across   a tile floor

POW in a recliner   tuning his ear   to the choir of his camp

as winter   and spring   depart.

III.

For better feng shui
I'd eat a low stack of silver dollars.

The key to it all   dangling on the tool shed wall
within   a soda's reach.

The aliens   haruspicating overnight   my heart   spleen which has   nothing to explain   to the chest cavity.

Nor to the forest's blondest wood.

If you have to   smooth grammar   to get clear,
—most imperial   royal model

bits of jade at her   clavicle—   may we
twin   the nouns,

may we twin   the whole experience
while   better demons   butter   the downtown.

The wind tithes.
The wind
                  tithes   and punctures   trying a piece of scenery.

People slow   to see the lights   across the pond.

May the time   come.   Loved,
unmocked conduit   stretching a whole figure   over the sun dial.

Mail the jail cell   house   one's valuables   in the dell.

STÉPHANE MALLARMÉ
Saint
Translated from the French by Henry Weinfield

At the window frame concealing
The viol old and destitute
Whose gilded sandalwood, now peeling,
Once shone with mandolin or flute,

Is the Saint, pale, unfolding
The old, worn missal, a divine
Magnificat in rivers flowing
Once at vespers and compline:

At the glass of this monstrance, vessel
Touched by a harp that took its shape
From the evening flight of an Angel
For the delicate fingertip

Which, without the old, worn missal
Or sandalwood, she balances
On the plumage instrumental,
Musician of silences.

EMILY DICKINSON
1090

I am afraid to own a Body—
I am afraid to own a Soul—
Profound—precarious Property—
Possession, not optional—

Double Estate—entailed at pleasure
Upon an unsuspecting Heir—

Duke in a moment of Deathlessness
And God, for a Frontier.

280

I felt a Funeral, in my Brain,
And Mourners to and fro
Kept treading—treading—till it seemed
That Sense was breaking through—

And when they all were seated,
A Service, like a Drum—
Kept beating—beating—till I thought
My Mind was going numb—

And then I heard them lift a Box
And creak across my Soul
With those same Boots of Lead, again,
Then Space—began to toll,

As all the Heavens were a Bell,
And Being, but an Ear,

And I, and Silence, some strange Race
Wrecked, solitary, here—

And then a Plank in Reason, broke,
And I dropped down, and down—
And hit a World, at every plunge,
And Finished knowing—then—

JACK SPICER
Phonemics

No love deserves the death it has. An archipelago
Rocks cropping out of ocean. Seabirds shit on it. Live out their lives
    on it.
What was once a mountain.
Or was it once a mountain? Did Lemuria, Atlantis, Mu ever exist
    except in the minds of old men fevered by the distances and the
    rocks they saw?
Was it true? Can the ocean of time claim to own us now adrift
Over that land. In that land. If memory serves
There (that rock out there)
Is more to it.

Wake up one warm morning. See the sea in the distance.
Die Ferne, water
Because mainly it is not land. A hot day too
The shreds of fog have already vaporized
Have gone back where they came from. There may be a whale in this
    ocean.
Empty fragments, like the shards of pots found in some Mesopotamian
    expedition. Found but not put together. The unstable
Universe has distance but not much else.
No one's weather or room to breathe in.

On the tele-phone (distant sound) you sounded no distant than if you
    were talking to me in San Francisco on the telephone or in a bar
    or in a room. Long
Distance calls. They break sound
Into electrical impulses and put it back again. Like the long telesexual
    route to the brain or the even longer teleerotic route to the heart.
    The numbers dialed badly, the connection faint.
Your voice
        consisted of sounds that I had

To route to phonemes, then to bound and free morphemes, then to
    syntactic structures. Telekinesis
Would not have been possible even if we were sitting at the same table.
    Long
Distance calls your father, your mother, your friend, your lover.
    The lips
Are never quite as far away as when you kiss.
An electric system.
"Gk. ηλεκτρον, amber, also shining metal; allied to ηλεκτωρ,
    gleaming."

Malice aforethought. Every sound
You can make with music.
Tough lips.
This is no nightingale. No-
Body's waxen image burned. Only
Believe me. Linguistics is divided like Graves' mythology of
    mythology, a triple goddess—morphology, phonology, and syntax.
Tough lips that cannot quite make the sounds of love
The language
Has so misshaped them.
Malicious afterthought. None of you bastards
Knows how Charlie Parker dies. And dances now in some brief
    kingdom (Oz) two phonemes
That were never paired before in the language.

Aleph did not come before Beth. The Semitic languages kept as strict
    a separation between consonant and vowel as between men and
    women. Vowels somehow got between to produce children. J V H
Was male. The Mycenaean bookkeepers
Mixed them up (one to every 4.5)
    (A=1, E=5, I=9, O=15, U=21)
Alpha being chosen as the queen of the alphabet because she meant
    "not."
Punched
        IBM cards follow this custom.
What I have chosen to follow is what schoolteachers call a blend, but
    which is not, since the sounds are very little changed by each other
Two consonants (floating in the sea of some truth together)
Immediately preceded and/or followed by a vowel.

The emotional disturbance echoes down the canyons of the heart.
Echoes there—sounds cut off—merely phonemes. A ground-rules
    double. You recognize them by pattern. Try.

Hello shouted down a canyon becomes huhluh. You, and the canyons
    of the heart,
Recognize feebly what you shouted. The vowels
Are indistinguishable. The consonants
A pattern for imagination. Phonemes,
In the true sense, that are dead before their burial. Constructs
Of the imagination
Of the real canyon and the heart's
Construct.

My Masters

> A poet is a time mechanic not an embalmer.
> —Jack Spicer

> For the Master has gone to draw tears from the Styx.
> —Stéphane Mallarmé

> I've got a cough as big as a thimble—but I don't care for that—
> I've got a Tomahawk in my side but that don't hurt me much. (If you)
> Her master stabs her more—
> —Emily Dickinson, *Letters*

One needs many masters. Requires many masters, for, as Donald Bar-
thelme noted, one keeps slaying them off. If one master replaces another
at different times in one's life, it is even better to have more than one simul-
taneously. This lends the work further complication, further multiplicity,
and protects it from being derivative. Most importantly, company keeps
the masters in conversation with one another, and quite alive.

A remaking of the real is at stake. A remaking of the real within a
method of language. God absent. What is present in the absence? What
lingering trails of God? What surfaces in the empty space from which Fou-
cault asks, "Who, or what, is speaking?" Void, not as a place of engulfing
despair, as an end, but *as a place of departure*. This "Nothing" was the pre-
cise point from which Emily Dickinson, Jack Spicer, and Stéphane Mal-
larmé wrote: they are our poets at the very gates of existence.

"Who, or what, is speaking?" This is still our big and basic question.
I do not wish to get too theoretical, because that would be against the
basic spirit of Dickinson, Spicer, and even Mallarmé, but a few passages

from Foucault will better serve as foundation than my paraphrasing of them. Here is Foucault on Nietzsche, on the death of God, and on the death of the human being:

> Nietzsche rediscovered the point at which man and God belong to one another, at which the death of the second is synonymous with the disappearance of the first, and at which the promise of the superman signifies first and foremost the imminence of the death of man. . . . It is no longer possible to think in our day other than in the void left by man's disappearance. For this void does not create a deficiency; it does not constitute a lacuna that must be filled. It is nothing more, and nothing less, than the unfolding of a space in which it is once more possible to think.[1]

And here is Foucault once again on syntax:

> Where, at the end of the eighteenth century, it was a matter of fixing the frontiers of knowledge, it will now be one of seeking to destroy syntax, to shatter tyrannical modes of speech. . . . God is perhaps not so much a region beyond knowledge as something prior to the sentences we speak, and if Western man is inseparable from him, it is not because of some invisible propensity to go beyond the frontiers of experience, but because his language ceaselessly foments him in the shadow of his laws.[2]

Dickinson:

> As all the Heavens were a Bell,
> And Being, but an Ear,
> And I, and Silence, some strange Race
> Wrecked, solitary, here—
>
> And then a Plank in Reason, broke,
> And I dropped down, and down—
> And hit a World, at every plunge,
> And Finished knowing—then—[3]

Mallarmé:

> I allowed the discourse forbidden to that scion of arctic sites to gush forth tacitly: 'Be so kind' (that was the meaning), and rather than lack charity,

explain to me the virtue of this atmosphere of splendor, of dust and voices, in which you have taught me to move.[4]

Spicer:

> Let us tie the strings on this bit of reality.
> Graphemes. Once wax now plastic, showing the ends. Like a red light.
> One feels or sees limits.
> They are warning graphemes but also meaning graphemes because
>   without the marked ends of the shoelace or the traffic signal one
>   would not know how to tie a shoe or cross a street—which is
>   like making a sentence.
> Crossing a street against the light or tying a shoe with a granny knot
>   is all right. Freedom, in fact, providing one sees or feels the
>   warning graphemes. Let them snarl at you then and you snarl
>   back at them. You'll be dead sooner
> But so will they. They
> Disappear when you die.[5]

Jack Spicer is a great master of the serial poem. According to Spicer, "you have to go into a serial poem not knowing what the hell you're doing. You have to be tricked into it, it has to be some path that you've never seen on a map before. . . ."[6] Spicer, who saw God as "a big white baseball," brought a particularly American quality to the void he languaged. He sought "a composition of the real," emptying himself so that he could receive a language other than his own; he called this dictation. He liked to think of poets as radios. I like to think that it is his spirit who hangs over my lines: "For better feng shui/ I'd eat a low stack of silver dollars."

The spirit of Mallarmé can perhaps best be glimpsed in the presence of a language that evokes rather than describes (his old dictum), and also in the use of white space in the poem (feng shui?) to indicate space as a pictoral element, or the chasm itself, as in his great masterpiece, *A Throw of the Dice*.

Dickinson's influence, if I am lucky, can be traced in the poem's desire to push through the floors of knowledge, bottoming out what can be known. "May the time come. Loved,/ unmocked conduit stretching a whole figure over the sun dial."

It makes me horribly uncomfortable to even place my own lines anywhere near the names and work of my masters. What hubris. For one must always pale before them. It is a frightening thing to think too long of one's masters, for one can never do them justice. One must always remain humble before them, in fear. They never arrive directly. They point ultimately to the place of no master, where their masters took them, where one must write, all alone.

AMY GERSTLER

Amy Gerstler was born in San Diego, California, in 1956. She attended Pitzer College, where she studied psychology. Her books of poetry include *Nerve Storm* (Viking Penguin, 1993), *Crown of Weeds* (Viking Penguin, 1997), *Bitter Angel* (Carnegie Mellon University Press, 1997), and *Medicine* (Viking Penguin, 2000). She has published numerous other books and chapbooks of both poetry and fiction, including *Past Lives,* a book made in collaboration with visual artist Alexis Smith (Santa Monica Museum of Art, 1989). Gerstler is married and lives in Los Angeles.

Nearby

When the spiritual axe fell, did you wake up inside *The White Orchard,*
that snowy Van Gogh we both admired? Are you lost in his chilly
idyllic painting, under skies filled with white dots he smeared in
with his thumbs? How dare you. How dare you die. Now you
express an absolute restfulness. A sober way of existing, unlike mine.
A shot of tequila gleams on the table by my side. Its vinegar-ish
drip gilds my innards—that's my report from the salt mine
of the senses tonight. You're supposed to be a ghost now, living on
in shipwrecked tatters like a shredded sailboat sail; sans dirty linen,
gritty winds, and the bane of shaving every day, which you hated.
Once you began to lose your mind, you wisely refused to shave

or be shaved. You put up surprisingly big fights, and I found
myself glad to see you so vehemently defying your keepers,
including me, as I chased you around with a red and white striped
can of shaving cream. Not that you could run much by then. So.
You've had a fortnight's silence. An autumnal lull. Sat out a break
between quarters in the cosmic basketball game. Come back
as a crawfish, a leek, a handful of gravel hens ingest to use as teeth,
a fake preacher who can't control his wolfish streak. I don't care
what you wear. But come back soon. Not seeking revenge
or relief, to which you're mightily entitled, but to meet your new
darkhaired niece and answer a few routine questions.

SIR THOMAS WYATT
They Flee from Me

They flee from me that sometime did me seek
With naked foot stalking in my chamber.
I have seen them gentle, tame and meek
That now are wild and do not remember
That sometime they put themself in danger
To take bread at my hand; and now they range
Busily seeking with a continual change.

Thanked be fortune it hath been otherwise
Twenty times better, but once in special,
In thin array after a pleasant guise,
When her loose gown from her shoulders did fall
And she me caught in her arms long and small.
Therewith all sweetly did me kiss
And softly said, "Dear heart, how like you this?"

It was no dream: I lay broad waking.
But all is turned through my gentleness
Into a strange fashion of forsaking:
And I have leave to go of her goodness
And she also to use new-fangledness.
But since that I so kindly am served
I would fain know what she hath deserved.

WILLIAM SHAKESPEARE
Prologue to *Romeo and Juliet*

Two households, both alike in dignity,
In fair Verona, where we lay our scene,
From ancient grudge break to new mutiny,
Where civil blood makes civil hands unclean.
From forth the fatal loins of these two foes
A pair of star-cross'd lovers take their life;
Whose misadventured piteous overthrows
Do with their death bury their parents' strife.
The fearful passage of their death-mark'd love,
And the continuance of their parents' rage,
Which, but their children's end, nought could remove,
Is now the two hours' traffic of our stage;
    The which if you with patient ears attend,
    What here shall miss, our toil shall strive to mend.

WALT WHITMAN
You felons on trial in courts

You felons on trial in courts,
You convicts in prison-cells, you sentenced assassins chain'd and
    handcuff'd with iron,
Who am I too that I am not on trial or in prison?
Me ruthless and devilish as any, that my wrists are not chain'd with
    iron, or my ankles with iron?

You prostitutes flaunting over the trottoirs or obscene in your rooms,
Who am I that I should call you more obscene than myself?
O culpable! I acknowledge—I expose!
(O admirers, praise me not—compliment me not—you make me
    wince,
I see what you do not—I know what you do not.)

Inside these breast-bones I lie smutch'd and choked,
Beneath this face that appears so impassive hell's tides continually run,
Lusts and wickedness are acceptable to me,
I walk with delinquents with passionate love,
I feel I am of them—I belong to those convicts and prostitutes myself,
And henceforth I will not deny them—for how can I deny myself?

SEI SHONAGON
Excerpt from *The Pillow Book*
Translated from the Japanese by Ivan Morris

29. Elegant Things

A white coat worn over a violet waistcoat.
Duck eggs.
Shaved ice mixed with liana syrup and put in a new silver bowl.
A rosary of rock crystal.
Wisteria blossoms. Plum blossoms covered with snow.
A pretty child eating strawberries.

47. Rare Things

A son-in law who is praised by his adoptive father; a young bride who
    is loved by her mother-in-law.
A silver tweezer that is good at plucking out the hair.
A servant who does not speak badly about his master.
A person who is in no way eccentric or imperfect, who is superior in
    both mind and body, and who remains flawless all his life.
People who live together and still manage to behave with reserve
    towards each other. However much these people may try to hide
    their weaknesses, they usually fail.
To avoid getting ink stains on the notebook into which one is copying
    stories, poems, or the like. If it is a very fine notebook, one takes
    the greatest care not to make a blot; yet somehow one never seems
    to succeed.
When people, whether they be men or women or priests, have
    promised each other eternal friendship, it is rare for them to stay
    on good terms until the end . . .

101. Squalid Things

The back of a piece of embroidery.
The inside of a cat's ear.
A swarm of mice, who still have no fur, when they come wriggling out
    of their nest.
The seams of a fur robe that has not yet been lined.
Darkness in a place that does not give the impression of being very
    clean.
A rather unattractive woman who looks after a large brood of children.
A woman who falls ill and remains unwell for a long time. In the mind
    of her lover, who is not particularly devoted to her, she must
    appear rather squalid.

A Servant of My Work

The grand word "mastery" doesn't rumble into my thinking very often. I feel wary of the term. I have to admit, it makes me nervous. For me—perhaps, in part, because I am female—"mastery" elicits images of dominators and the dominated; monolithic judgments; a supplicating address to a man of a higher caste; rock-hard certainties which I feel I must mistrust on principle; a mustachioed arrogance that seems a far cry from the way I try to look at the world. Where there are masters there are bound to be servants. While I sometimes like to think of myself as the servant of my work (a painter I like goes around saying he is the slave of his paintings), when I think about my complicated, fraught relationship to writing, something like the Buddhist phrase "beginner's mind" conveys the respect, curiosity, devotion (and maybe even awe, if that doesn't sound too corny) that I want to bring to writing better than the word "mastery" does.

One of the first poetry anthologies I dipped into as I was growing up, which still sits on my shelf, swiped from my generous parents, was a daunting, fat, black clothbound book whose spine proclaimed, in letters stamped in gold: MASTER POEMS OF THE ENGLISH LANGUAGE. It's a somber-looking tome, resembling an old, overweight hymnal. It seemed to be the kind of book a child might need special permission to read. The first poem in the book is Sir Thomas Wyatt's astonishing *They Flee from Me*. I felt back then, as I still do now, that I could never completely pin down, tire of, or shake off this poem. There are so many terrific, heartfelt, deceptively simple lines and images in that brief lament. I wish I could remember to tell myself "Thanked be fortune it hath been otherwise" when something bad happens. I've always wanted to whisper "Dear heart, how like you this?" before kissing someone. Or maybe afterward. So perhaps what is best meant by "mastery" here is that when poems really stun you, tickle your soul, perplex and inflect you, they can never be "mastered." They master you. That's fine with me. That's a way I don't mind being mastered. I crave it.

"Influence," on the other hand, a word with "fluid" in its sounds, is something that frequently occupies my mind. I pray for good influences to inspire and to seep into my work, as the parched pray for rain. My house is crammed with books, read and unread, that I hope will exert their salutary persuasions on me. To fill me up. Influence, from all kinds of sources, is something I hope I am always open to and can make judicious use of.

The poem of mine I chose to submit here is an address to a ghost by a living person. After I had written a few drafts of it and was looking for more things to put in, I came across a note I'd made about a painting by Van Gogh called *The White Orchard*. I'd seen a reproduction of the painting in a coffee-table book that was actually on my brother-in-law's coffee table. So I put the painting in at the beginning, as something the speaker toys with: a sort of whited-out version of a possible heaven to which the dead loved one has retreated. Because the poem is an entreaty for the dead loved one to return, it invokes pungent earthly tastes and smells to serve as lures or reminders: salt, tequila, vinegar, leeks. There are flat off-rhymes in the poem that sound right, to my ear, for the minor-key notes of bereavement, jangly and protesting. Since we have been asked to mention something about problems we may have had in composing our poems, I'll say that difficulties I wrestled with in writing *Nearby* included managing the emotions of intimacy and distance in the poem; balancing, in the speaker's tone, love and anger, clarity and restraint; and trying to smooth out the lines so they might read haltingly but not so awkwardly that the reader would stumble out of the poem altogether. At first I tried to find a form that would suggest sobbing by alternating long and short lines, but in the end I settled on these longish lines, giving the poem a boxy shape, which might look a little like a headstone, if you really stretch it.

The editor of this anthology asked that, when choosing poems that had meant a lot to us, the participating writers try to pick works in the public domain; the publishers understandably didn't wish to spend years and their inheritances obtaining permissions. This constraint spared me the agony of trying to decide between work by authors of more recent vintage, a list including but not limited to: Philip Larkin, Jane Kenyon, Alice Notley, Sylvia Plath, Charles Simic, Ai, Elizabeth Bishop, James Tate, Tom Clark, Wislawa Szymborska, Sharon Olds, Tim Dlugos, Bert Meyers. As it is, I merely agonized over selecting older favorites.

My choices for poems that are dear to me, and that I therefore hope have affected my writing, begin with the aforementioned Wyatt poem. In the version reproduced here, the original early modern spellings have been modernized. I also chose the Prologue to *Romeo and Juliet*. I'm afraid my sensibility is rather romantic. I have this speech memorized and repeat it in my head when I need to calm down or focus or cheer up. *Romeo and Juliet* is full of so much gorgeous poetry you can get high by whispering it. Among many other things in this speech, I love the idea that the whole plot of the play is condensed into a sonnet. The sound of this prologue, its sense, and its rhymes always give me the shivers. It's so tiny and dramatic. The end of the Prologue acknowledges that what's about to unfold is a play (as opposed to something we are supposed to pretend is reality) and that the actors will "toil" to bring it to life in the presence of the audience. The note, in that self-effacing final couplet—that if the Prologue whizzed by too fast, the company will try to "mend" that error through their performance—creates an instant intimacy between performers and audience, or writer and reader, as well as a pleasurable sense of informed expectation.

Like so many of his legion admirers, I love Whitman for his compassionate hedonism, his full-to-bursting heart, his celebration of the humane and the carnal, his willingness to implicate himself and, in doing so, exonerate all his fellow men. Lines like "The curious sympathy one feels when feeling with the hand the naked meat of the body" deserve to be read forever.

Sei Shonagon's *Pillow Book* was written by a lady-in-waiting to the Japanese Empress in the eleventh century. The only translation of the book into English I have ever seen is by Ivan Morris, and it is divided into titled sections, some of which are lists like the ones I have selected. Other sections are more like diary entries. While her work is usually regarded as prose, I include it here because I think that, by contemporary measures, sections from this work could also be regarded as prose poems, and I am very interested in work that straddles the line between poetry and prose. The snippy, witty, discerning, smart, self-possessed—and at times self-indulgent —tone of her voice always enlivens me: her tone is so crisp and acidic that it seems as though she is still alive, taking someone to task for a clumsy action or expressing her preference for one color of silk over another. Her eagle eye for tiny details and her tendency to aestheticize everything is amusing, human, enviable.

JUDITH HALL

Judith Hall lives in Los Angeles, California. Her first book of poems, *To Put The Mouth To* (William Morrow, 1992) was a National Poetry Series selection. She is also the author of *Anatomy, Errata* (Ohio State University Press, 1998). Hall has received grants from the Ingram Merrill Foundation and the National Endowment for the Arts. She serves as poetry editor for the *Antioch Review* and teaches at the California Institute of Technology.

Complaint of the Poet to Her Empty Purse

> Logic is the money of the mind.
> —Karl Marx

Marx as my witness, I tried. Work the line, I thought; turn out
Over 29,000 lines per annum. (Not bad. A bard for a bull market.)
Nearly a middle-class wage, if markets hold at a $1.00/line:
Eighty a day, say 5 great sonnets and a battle cry Monday; Tues.;
Years conceived in *ellipses,* dedicated to them . . . keep production up.

More, hurry. " ? , ." *Steal,* or perish. Monopolize.
Or? Collapse? From entrepreneurial "negative capability"?
Not to mention a positive incapability for alternatives? Or
Else *what,* I whispered, erasing the last line (whispering, as if for
You: Is money, as a long-remembered music, a moot rescue fantasy?).

My purse is empty, my purse-lipped pudendum, emptied.
O must I patronize myself—divested in toto—to eat?
No one pops out (pater-accomplice, *pis aller*) eager to fund,
Eager to fill—"Deliver me," I begged one long rough night, "from
Yielding to"—*what,* I scratched out, faster, "'*or elles moot I die*'!"

"Yielding to me?" Hermes laughed. "Sing me your annual yield! Or—
Expect me to come in as income, gross income?" Winged shoes tickled
Slowly, until I laughed. "Of all Chaucer," he added, "'*or else must I die*'?"

    Envoy

"Must? My dear, nihilism is the poor man's ultimatum." He turned in,
  Occupied, ignoring "Money is the poor woman's sovereignty."
"Narcissism is—" "*Money,*" I thought (this, the logic), "insures
  Each unlikely song beyond accounting—" "Aw, you economize awe,
Yes, with human sacrifice." So I wrote, "*Awfully happy* in winged shoes."

GEOFFREY CHAUCER
The Complaint of Chaucer to His Purse

To yow, my purse, and to noon other wight
Complayne I, for ye be my lady dere!
I am so sory, now that ye been lyght;
For certes, but ye make me hevy chere,
Me were as leef be layd upon my bere;
For which unto your mercy thus I crye:
Beth hevy ageyn, or elles moot I dye!

Now voucheth sauf this day, or yt be nyght,
That I of yow this blissful soun may here,
Or see your colour lyk the sonne bryght,
That of yelownesse hadde never pere.
Ye be my lyf, ye be myn hertes stere,
Quene of comfort and of good companye:
Beth hevy ageyn, or elles moot I dye!

Now purse, that ben to me my lyves lyght
And saveour, as doun in this world here,
Out of this toune helpe me thurgh your myght,
Syn that ye wole nat ben my tresorere;
For I am shave as nye as any frere.
But yet I pray unto your curtesye:
Beth hevy agen, or elles moot I dye!

    Lenvoy de Chaucer

O conqueror of Brutes Albyon,
Which that by lyne and free eleccion
Been verray king, this song to yow I send;
And ye, that mowen alle oure harmes amende,
Have mind upon my supplicacion!

WILLIAM SHAKESPEARE
Sonnet 29

When, in disgrace with fortune and men's eyes,
I all alone beweep my outcast state,
And trouble deaf heaven with my bootless cries,
And look upon myself, and curse my fate,
Wishing me like to one more rich in hope,
Featured like him, like him with friends possessed,
Desiring this man's art and that man's scope,
With what I most enjoy contented least;
Yet in these thoughts myself almost despising,
Haply I think on thee, and then my state,
Like to the lark at break of day arising
From sullen earth, sings hymns at heaven's gate;
    For thy sweet love remembered such wealth brings
    That then I scorn to change my state with kings.

EZRA POUND
The Lake Isle

O God, O Venus, O Mercury, patron of thieves,
Give me in due time, I beseech you, a little tobacco-shop,
With the little bright boxes
        piled up neatly upon the shelves
And the loose fragrant cavendish
        and the shag,
And the bright Virginia
        loose under the bright glass cases,
And a pair of scales not too greasy,
And the whores dropping in for a word or two in passing,
For a flip word, and to tidy their hair a bit.

O God, O Venus, O Mercury, patron of thieves,
Lend me a little tobacco-shop,
        or install me in any profession
Save this damn'd profession of writing,
        where one needs one's brains all the time.

ANONYMOUS
Hard Times Cotton Mill Girls

I've worked in a cotton mill all of my life
And I ain't got nothing but a Barlow knife,
It's hard times cotton mill girls,
It's hard times everywhere.

        Chorus:

It's hard times cotton mill girls,
It's hard times cotton mill girls,
It's hard times cotton mill girls,
It's hard times everywhere.

In nineteen and fifteen we heard it said,
Go to the country and get ahead.
It's hard times cotton mill girls,
It's hard times everywhere.

Us girls work twelve hours a day
For fourteen cents of measly pay.
It's hard times cotton mill girls,
It's hard times everywhere.

When I die don't bury me at all,
Just pickle my bones in alcohol,
Hang me up on the spinning room wall,
It's hard times everywhere.

ANONYMOUS
Berber Song
Translated from the Kabyle by W. S. Merwin

She has fallen in the dance,
None of you knows her name.
A silver amulet
Moves between her breasts.

She has hurled herself into the dance.
Rings chime on her ankles.
Silver bracelets.

For her I sold
An apple orchard.

She has fallen in the dance.
Her hair has come loose.

For her I sold
My field of olive trees.

She has hurled herself into the dance.
Her collar of pearls glittered.

For her I sold
My orchard of fig trees.

She has hurled herself into the dance.
A smile flowered on her.

For her I sold
All my orange trees.

Notes in Medias Res

Mastery is stasis. And if a poet seeks security more than invention, then the illusion of mastery might be possible through repetition. If I repeat myself, very well, I may appear a master, but only as the echo of a narcissist. With each new poem, and each substantial draft, mastery overturns. How much of what I learned writing the last poem affects the unfinished heap over there on the desk? Not much. Not enough.

Then study the unexpected slant rhymes midline, the "throb" that D. H. Lawrence mentions. Study Sappho's apostrophes—the Davenport Sappho—and the suspended complications of Horace's sentences. Study Shakespeare's late plays, where the lines roughen; and study the early ones, all of them—why not? Study the vowels that open longer and remain open, then peak like a shift in Wallace Stevens from clarinet to swan. Study seven languages, a few ancient, one hieroglyphic. Am I a poet yet? A master? If permeable? If protean? Gertrude Stein: "To try is to cry, but I did try to write. . . ."[1]

Watch how the line ends, and learn where the light shifts away from alleged subjects, where a burnt-sienna vagueness intervenes. Virginia Woolf to Elizabeth Bowen:

> As usual, the rightness seemed to me unconscious; something that you didn't notice yourself, & the wrongness when it got cold, & you added with bright but rather steely ink something too exact, too definite for the context. But this is only my old grumble, that we are afraid of the human heart (& with reason); & until we can write with all our faculties in action (even the big toe) but under the water, submerged, then we must be clever, like the rest of the modern sticklebacks.[2]

Read Woolf again and Bowen. Read Dante, Cervantes, Blake. Tu Fu again, as in the old days, with a giant lemonade. Study the reversal in a phrase; Ashbery, Berryman, Celan. Memorize the King James Song of Songs, then Ovid's gospels, Catullus's affairs. How much of this assists the poem through all its various permutations? Reading is a luxury that writing requires. One text recommends another. Yeats recommends Spenser, Rossetti, Auden, or Pessoa or Beckett, Plath, O'Hara, Merrill, Homer, Whitman, Wilde.

T. S. Eliot: "For last year's words belong to last year's language/ And next year's words await another voice."[3] Then this silence and doubt between poems. "Faulkner said that once you're satisfied with everything you've done, you might as well break the pencil and cut your throat. I mean, the whole damn thing is over with. So you never really finish. Not if you are a writer. And it never gets any easier."[4] So said Ernest J. Gaines. Read Gaines. Read Faulkner.

Each poem has its own constellation of influences. My *Complaint of the Poet to Her Empty Purse* is an obvious homage to Geoffrey Chaucer's *The Complaint of Chaucer to His Purse.* His ballade sparkles and charms, so much so that critics have argued for six hundred years whether he needed money at the end of his life. He complains of his purse as of a disinterested lover. He parodies the troubadour and the traditional begging poem. Chaucer did not write earnest "rhymed bills," as his patron-dependent contemporaries did, when the winter wood ran low. I intended to transpose Chaucer's complaint into a market economy, into the peculiar American style of advanced capitalism. "The economy, stupid," I laughed, thinking of American ambivalence about leisure, production, and reward. What I intend to write rarely resembles what evolves. When the poem becomes specific out of its possibilities, some of the dream is lost; a smaller vividness replaces it. Mastery, the idea of it, seems far away from the actual complications of writing, and its bliss. Mastery is no more than a hope in retrospect, a dream of hieratic control.

HUNT HAWKINS

Hunt Hawkins was born in the District of Columbia in 1943. He attended Williams College as an undergraduate and received his Ph.D. in English literature from Stanford University in 1976. He is the author of *The Domestic Life* (University of Pittsburgh Press, 1994). He is currently at work on two books: another poetry manuscript and a book on Joseph Conrad and the Congo. He is chair of the department of English at Florida State University. He lives in Tallahassee with his wife, Elaine Smith, and their two children, Sam and Molly.

At the Public Pool

The lifeguards are pummeling dummies
on the deck, pinching their noses, tilting chins,
and giving them full-kisses. The dummies lie
armless and legless, failing to rise despite
this inspiration. They are mostly Caucasian
but two African-American, mostly adults
but one poor plastic baby. In this rational
central Pennsylvania town, home to a university,
the mothers drive Volvo station wagons, breastfeed
in public, and adopt Asian children. The kids
practice stride-dives off the side. Even those

born in Korea are called "Katie" and "Melissa,"
flat-chested little sparks unextinguished
by chlorine. The guards teaching them are
college students, fleshy and impervious. The
plumpest yells to a friend, "I'm too sexy for this pool!"
I trail my father-in-law to the bathhouse,
struggling to keep balance on the slick cement.
He stands in the shower, eighty-six years old,
gray and lank, ass collapsed and bony,
penis a naked creature, a modest virtue. I can't
imagine him creating my wife. It's been
two decades since I married her, had three children
and lost one. The stingy showers have
spring handles which shut off when let go of.
Soon the disinfectant fumes get my eyes.
Out in the summer sun
two pregnant swimmers are taking laps.

SHARON OLDS
Poem to Our Son After a High Fever

When what you hear speeds up, again,
and gets too loud, and I call the doctor,
and I'm waiting for her to call back,
I think of the skin of your throat, greenish
as the ice at the edge of the pond when it starts to melt,
and the back of your neck, sometimes mottled as the
moss found on the north sides of trees.
I think of the insides of your wrists, their
dusty ivory waxy glow like
saints' candles fallen in the detritus
behind the altar, where the mice live
and propagate, feeding their young on the
crumbs of the Host like little rough pieces of light,
I think about the faint layer of grime all over your body
as if you'd been dredged with the soil of the earth
like a sacred object, and how light catches on each
facet of grit so you gleamed with a rubbed
haze. They held you as you came forth from me
in slow pulses, one, two, three—

head, shoulders, all—your feet like the
flukes of a tail as they lifted you up,
flecked with random blood bits,
like a child freckled with crumbs after a long journey,
fallen asleep next to a train window,
the fields of ice going by in the evening,
the way your brain falls asleep a few times a day now for a few minutes
and everything seems to be going fast and loud.
I picture your brain, like a blue-grey cauliflower,
the leaves, with their veins, wrapped around the stem and the heart,
I think of your navel, small rose
always folded, I think of your penis, its
candor and virtue, I picture your long
narrow feet and your bony chest and your
clever hands, you let them lie in your lap
when the episode comes, you wait for it to be over.
I think of every part of your body,
thought being a form of prayer,
but it's hard to think of your face, the globe
forehead, the speckled cheeks, the mouth
tensed, and the eyes—I can hardly stand
to see the courage there, the calmness of the
fear, as if you are prepared to bear
anything.

FRANK O'HARA
The Day Lady Died

It is 12:20 in New York a Friday
three days after Bastille day, yes
it is 1959 and I go get a shoeshine
because I will get off the 4:19 in Easthampton
at 7:15 and then go straight to dinner
and I don't know the people who will feed me

I walk up the muggy street beginning to sun
and have a hamburger and a malted and buy
an ugly NEW WORLD WRITING to see what the poets
in Ghana are doing these days
                              I go on to the bank
and Miss Stillwagon (first name Linda I once heard)
doesn't even look up my balance for once in her life
and in the GOLDEN GRIFFIN I get a little Verlaine

for Patsy with drawings by Bonnard although I do
think of Hesiod, trans. Richmond Lattimore or
Brendan Behan's new play or *Le Balcon* or *Les Nègres*
of Genet, but I don't, I stick with Verlaine
after practically going to sleep with quandariness

and for Mike I just stroll into the PARK LANE
Liquor Store and ask for a bottle of Strega and
then I go back where I came from to 6th Avenue
and the tobacconist in the Ziegfeld Theatre and
casually ask for a carton of Gauloises and a carton
of Picayunes, and a NEW YORK POST with her face on it

and I am sweating a lot by now and thinking of
leaning on the john door in the 5 SPOT
while she whispered a song along the keyboard
to Mal Waldron and everyone and I stopped breathing

ROBERT FROST
The Wood-Pile

Out walking in the frozen swamp one gray day,
I paused and said, 'I will turn back from here.
No, I will go on farther—and we shall see.'
The hard snow held me, save where now and then
One foot went through. The view was all in lines
Straight up and down of tall slim trees
Too much alike to mark or name a place by
So as to say for certain I was here
Or somewhere else: I was just far from home.
A small bird flew before me. He was careful
To put a tree between us when he lighted,
And say no word to tell me who he was
Who was so foolish as to think what *he* thought.
He thought that I was after him for a feather—
The white one in his tail; like one who takes
Everything said as personal to himself.
One flight out sideways would have undeceived him.
And then there was a pile of wood for which
I forgot him and let his little fear
Carry him off the way I might have gone,
Without so much as wishing him good-night.
He went behind it to make his last stand.

It was a cord of maple, cut and split
And piled—and measured, four by four by eight.
And not another like it could I see.
No runner tracks in this year's snow looped near it.
And it was older sure than this year's cutting
Or even last year's or the year's before.
The wood was gray and the bark warping off it
And the pile somewhat sunken. Clematis
Had wound strings round and round it like a bundle.
What held it though on one side was a tree
Still growing, and on one a stake and prop,
These latter about to fall. I thought that only
Someone who lived in turning to fresh tasks
Could so forget his handiwork on which
He spent himself, the labor of his ax,
And leave it there far from a useful fireplace
To warm the frozen swamp as best it could
With the slow smokeless burning of decay.

Influence and Mastery

I'm not sure I can say much on this topic since what I feel from other poets isn't exactly influence and what I feel about my own work certainly isn't mastery (more like sweaty struggle relieved by strokes of good luck). When I first started writing, my poems sounded very much like bad imitations of Walt Whitman, T. S. Eliot, Wallace Stevens, and e. e. cummings (usually one at a time, but sometimes mixed in an unhappy party). Since then, I've gone my own way, and when I write it feels as though I'm listening to a voice that isn't always coming through very well. Either I'm trying to clear my mind so I can hear the voice coming from within, or the voice is outside and I feel I've grabbed part of its shirt and I'm fighting to pull it through the window.

My attitude toward other poets now is one of appreciation. I've picked poems by three poets with whom I feel an affinity, and I'll try to explain what that affinity is. Perhaps you could say they are influencing me. But I feel more that I'm watching them deal with similar problems, and appreciating the beauty of their solutions.

I have a very wide range of taste in poetry. For example, I still love the verbal lushness of Stevens though I no longer write anything like him.

The poems I now write, and those I feel closest to, are fairly direct and plain. They have a strong visual sense. Usually they describe a single scene or a related set of scenes, perhaps with some connecting narrative. The role of the speaker in these poems is to move through the scene, describing it and trying to find some meaning in it. I don't like poems in which the poet, from outside the scene, imposes a meaning either through abstract statement or allegory. For the most part, I hold to Pound's dictum that "the natural object is always the adequate symbol."[1] The voice of the speaker should seem honest, personal, confiding. Obviously, I'm attracted to the confessional poets. It doesn't bother me, though, to realize that the honesty of the voice is artificially constructed or even to learn that the revelations of the poem don't match the author's life. A poem may be a pack of factual lies and still be honest in its stance. Finally, I like poems that exhibit complete trust in the reader, draw the reader into the poem, and allow the reader to do much of the poem's work of finding meaning.

This particular poetic tradition goes back at least as far as Wordsworth. I guess that I like this poetry for its capacity to duplicate experience. I admit, though, that this poetry depends on its own conventions and isn't any more truthful than the extravagant wordplay of Stevens or even the pompous didacticism of someone like Arthur Hugh Clough. But I don't care for Clough either as poet or man; and after awhile, Stevens begins to seem too mono-tonal, too much the stuff of weekends.

The topic of all three poems I've picked, as well as mine, is mortality. It is a common topic for the sort of poetry I've described, but it is one of the most difficult, as well, since death is one experience that can't be reported (unless you move frankly into fantasy like Emily Dickinson). Poetry that remains in the realm of ordinary experience can only intimate mortality, since death is beyond language or symbolization by any natural object. So the poet is faced with the problem of conveying that which the ground rules of the style say can't be conveyed.

The living poet with whom I feel most kinship is Sharon Olds. I still remember being stopped by her *Poem to Our Son After a High Fever* when I first read it in the *New Yorker*. Like my other poets, she quickly establishes a sense of immediacy by using the present tense. (Frost actually uses the past tense but makes it seem present by not going outside that moment.) All three poets invite the reader to join in by admitting to a condition of "quandariness." Olds is waiting for the doctor to call back, and O'Hara is trying to decide which presents to buy. We watch Frost making up his mind with "I will turn back from here./ No, I will go on farther—and we shall see." These lines are obviously a rhetorical ploy, since by the time the poem is written, the decision has been made (if there actually even was such a decision), but the lines are effective nonetheless. In my own case, I wait awhile to introduce "I" but hope the reader senses and participates in my "quandariness" as I survey the pool, puzzling over the mortality of the people there.

What stopped me, when I first read Olds's poem, was the word "penis." I pay my respects, as it were, by lifting this word along with the accompanying "virtue," whose Latin root—"manliness"—is brought out by the proximity of these words. The shock of "penis," though, has little to do with eroticism. It is used tenderly, unashamedly, and with the realization that every part of the body is perishable. The poem's perspective is secular, and it is probably this deconsecration that drives both the style and the impossible wish to get beyond the style. Here the saints' candles have fallen behind the altar. There is no transubstantiation of the Host; it is used only as food to nourish the baby mice. Any continuation of life is imagined strictly through the terms of procreation. But both the individual who procreates and the body parts used for it fall amongst the detritus. Where there is no longer a hope of rebirth, the only possible form of prayer is to write poems revering the physical in its frailty. The final crux of this poem is Olds's move to the consciousness of her son, the courage in his eyes as, trapped in the flesh she and her husband gave him, he bears the ominous "anything" expressed in the single word of the last line. A loving parent's realization not just of the mortality of the child, but also of the child's own realization of that mortality, is close to devastating. And the devastation falls on both parents, as indicated by the title, which addresses the husband even as the poem itself speaks to the son.

This poem is slightly longer and more ornate than Olds's usual work. I'm not sure of the precise setting. Perhaps the speaker is standing by the phone, waiting for the return call, as she imagines her sick son's body. In most of her poems, Olds uses only a few figures of speech, but here she uses many, drawing comparisons for each body part to heighten the visual effect and to get in the religious (or rather non-religious) theme since the saints' candles and church mice aren't literally there.

In O'Hara's poem, there are no noticeable figures. The scene is New

York City on July 17, 1959, as the speaker does a series of errands on his lunch hour. Following the tenets of O'Hara's essay "Personism," the poem is grounded in a concrete and particular viewpoint, without being especially personal.[2] We do, in fact, learn quite a bit about the speaker. He is fairly well off, literate, and hip. But we don't get the intimacy of Olds. Nor do we get the expression of any strong feeling until the very end. Most of the poem appears to consist of a casual listing of small, ordinary, almost insignificant activities. Perhaps none of these details is meant to be symbolic, but as I read the poem, I sense that the speaker has dying on his mind from the outset. The name "Stillwagon" seems ominous, as does the question of the speaker's balance. The speaker also seems to be opposing themes of liberation (the Bastille, newly independent Ghana) and the quotidian (Hesiod's *Works and Days,* the newspaper, the lunch hour itself). Thus the last stanza comes as a surprise, but it is not unanticipated. The concluding words "stopped breathing" give a jolt somewhat similar to Olds's "anything." "Stopped breathing" makes you think of death, of Lady Day dying, of "everyone and I" inevitably dying. But it also refers to the electrifying, time-suspending effect of Billie Holiday's singing on her audience. O'Hara's poem leaves the reader with some still unresolved questions. Is daily life deadening? Should we try to liberate ourselves from it? Can art do so? What is the relation between art and death, both of which take your breath away?

Frost's symbol-finding as he walks through his scene is a bit more obvious, though he is characteristically sly about what it all means. His speaker is anxious about erasure. The scene is so monotonous that he can't identify the place and begins to doubt his own presence. His foot occasionally falls through the snow. He ridicules the bird who thinks the speaker is after him. But the reader sees that the bird's "little fear" is similar to the speaker's own anxiety. Both perceive a threat, take it personally, and will end up forgotten. Similarly, the reader sees beyond the speaker's interpretation that the woodcutter has turned to new tasks. The more probable explanation for his not coming back is that he has passed away. The final truth of the poem is the "slow smokeless burning of decay," which hits as hard as the last lines of Olds and O'Hara. Since the reader can see more than the speaker, we come to the conclusion that the speaker isn't quite identical with Frost as author. However, by a further turn, we can guess that the poem itself is Frost's woodpile, his attempt to "mark or name a place" so as "to say for certain I was here." And he realizes the attempt is futile. Just like the cord of maple, *The Wood-Pile* will eventually disappear.

I'm reluctant to explain my own poem, whereas I have no shame in analyzing these others. I guess I don't want to spoil the fun by shutting down the interpretive interaction between reader and writer—which would be the case in commenting on my own work, though not in my reading the work of others. Suffice it to say, I follow the same procedures just described, make some metaphors, find some symbols. *At the Public Pool* is based closely on actual occurrence. In writing it, I felt particularly fortunate to find the symbol of the shower handles, though less fortunate to be subject to the fate they represent.

Poetry that is visual and "realistic," as these poems are, must treat language as transparent. It must assume no distance between word and referent. But poetry must also pay attention to form, and these poems, including mine, do so, though in deliberately subtle ways. Olds uses long lines, many of them enjambed, and long sentences, many with comma splices, extending phrases like "I think" or "I picture" into lines that produce a rushing rhythm, mimicking the child's illness, even up to the jolt of the dash and the phrase "I can hardly stand" near the end of the poem. She ties the poem together with alliteration and assonance and certain key repetitions. The pond ice which is like the neck at the beginning of the poem returns as fields of ice seen through the window of a train. The blood bits like crumbs return with the speckled cheeks. The Latinate "detritus" prepares us for a Latinate reading of "virtue." The "clever hands" prepare the transition from thinking about the boy's body to realizing his consciousness. O'Hara uses the shorter lines of a list but gets continuity and flow by using conjunctions in the place of punctuation. He ties together his collection of discrete errands with references to things French (Bastille day, Verlaine and Bonnard and Genet, Gauloises and Picayunes) and things African (Ghana, *Les Nègres,* Lady Day herself). Frost writes a meditative blank verse but disguises it with his caesuras. He unites the poem with repeated sounds, especially sibilants. The progression of his poem is linear, following the walk of the speaker and flight of the bird, but (as I've noted) these two come to mirror each other, then to reflect the author himself.

In my poem, I try for a casual, conversational rhythm until near the end. I use a lot of repeated sounds, mainly plosives and sibilants, which I hope aren't very noticeable. Close to the beginning, I throw in a small joke ("failing to rise despite this inspiration") to soften the poem before we get to the serious matters later on. Olds uses this same strategy with her baby mice eating the Host; O'Hara with his "practically going to sleep with quandariness"; and Frost with the silly bird worrying about its tail. I mean my observations at the beginning to appear almost random (and not even mine initially), but they all prepare for what is coming. The unrevivable dummies really do represent the people. The poor plastic baby is my lost child. Like Olds, I dwell on the question of whether sexual reproduction means our survival. I believe my closing lines seem more upbeat than those of Olds, O'Hara, or Frost. But whether they are indeed, I'll leave to the reader to decide.

JANE HIRSHFIELD

Jane Hirshfield was born in New York City in 1953. She received her undergraduate degree in 1973 from Princeton University, where she was an independent major in Creative Writing and Literature in Translation. Her books of poetry include *Alaya* (The Quarterly Review of Literature Poetry Series, 1982), *Of Gravity & Angels* (Wesleyan University Press, 1988), *The October Palace* (HarperPerrenial, 1994), and *The Lives of the Heart* (HarperPerrenial, 1997). Hirshfield's most recent book is *Given Sugar, Given Salt* (Harper-Collins, 2001). She is also the author of a book of essays, *Nine Gates: Entering the Mind of Poetry* (HarperCollins, 1997), and the editor and co-translator of two anthologies of women's writing, *Women in Praise of the Sacred* (HarperCollins, 1994) and *The Ink Dark Moon* (Scribner, 1988). She is the recipient of fellowships from the Guggenheim and Rockefeller Foundations, and winner of the Poetry Center Book Award as well as the Bay Area Book Reviewers Award. Her poetry, which has appeared in the *New Yorker,* the *Atlantic,* the *Nation,* the *New Republic,* and other literary periodicals, has been anthologized in *Best American Poems* and in the Pushcart Prize compilation. Hirshfield has taught at the University of California at Berkeley and at the University of San Francisco, and is on the core faculty of Bennington College's M.F.A. Writing Seminars.

Skipping Stones

There are certain poems I have long thought of as "pebbles": small, a little intractable, lithic in their singleness of perception. Like an actual pebble, cold until warmed by an exterior heat source; like an actual pebble, unwavering in outlook and replete in simple thusness. The conception of this term, I'm sure, bows more than a little in the direction of Zbigniew Herbert's famous poem; but I recognized the type long before reading his *Pebble*, which is, in any case, a bit more extended a meditation than the examples I consider archetypal. I first encountered one such poem in fifth-year Latin when I read Catullus's *Odi et Amo* and discovered the almost elemental directness of speech that marks certain classical lyrics:

CATULLUS
Odi et Amo
Translated from the Latin by Jane Hirshfield

> I hate and I love.
> Ask, if you wish, why this is so—
> I can't say.
> But I feel it and I am in torment.

Now as then, the poem's effectiveness puzzles. Its straightforward reportage of emotion goes against the semi-canonical "show, don't tell." Everything seems said, everything appears to be on the surface. From where, then, does the wrenching arise, the interior motion that caused Frank Bidart to place into his free translation of this poem the writhing of a hooked fish?

The mysterious sense that there is a movement in *us* as we read is for me one mark of the pebble in poetry: the poem seems to hold still, and yet the reader moves. The poem has set it up this way: in a good poem, something must give, and so if the poet's situation does not alter, we do, in encountering it. Contradiction appears in Catullus's opening statement, and in the poet's apparent confession of a psychological powerlessness that mirrors his powerlessness as lover. But contradiction and lack of power are not the poem's ultimate destination. Rather, we feel, in the end, the sureness of the poet's stance before the unbearable: *this* I feel; *this* I am; *this* I say. In his few words, the dilemma of the one whose love is not quite returned—that most flickering and elusive of states—is durably set down and so preserved, "as if," as we sometimes say, "written in stone."

I fell in love with small poems early. The first book I purchased on my own, at age nine or so, was a little *haiku* collection, organized by season. That early attraction to the image poems of Japanese literature continued to play itself out in my life, first in my undergraduate studies and, later yet, in undertaking *The Ink Dark Moon*, a co-translation of Japanese *tanka* by the two foremost women poets of the classical age. It played itself out, as well, in my developing sense of the lyric, instilling in me a virtually kinesthetic recognition of the way that good poems move at their core and the way various arrangements of image and statement—and image *as* statement—work to make that happen.

Yet most Japanese poems, whether *haiku* or the slightly longer *tanka*, are not precisely "pebbles." Most work by an almost diametrically different means: reading a *haiku*, one enters into the image as into a transparence. Encountering Basho's crow on an autumn branch at nightfall, self and crow become one: the fragrance and color of austere solitude unfold from within the reader's own being. Nor is a poem of simple aphorism a pebble: here the full meaning is handed over directly, and the aesthetic pleasure comes from the craftedness of the saying. Reading a pebble-poem, one feels more as though one has walked into a wall; the reverberations of the impact are the route to its re-engagement with the self.

Pebbles are almost always descriptive, whether of inner or outer conditions; they can also be prescriptive. Didactic poetry has not been valued much in recent decades, yet I am quite drawn to it, both the overt kind and the covert. We may dislike it, in truth, less than we sometimes say: Dickinson's poems, read happily by laypersons, practicing poets, and academics alike, are full of instructive statements. I like being bossed around by a poem good enough to succeed at doing it, and I also like Horace's account of poetry's twin intentions, "to delight and to instruct." Horace as a poet gave me an early shiver of both those ends in his lyric presentations of *carpe diem*, including this one:

HORACE
Odes I, 11
Translated from the Latin by Burton Raffel

Leucon, no one's allowed to know his fate,
Not you, not me: don't ask, don't hunt for answers
In tea leaves or palms. Be patient with whatever comes.
This could be our last winter, it could be many
More, pounding the Tuscan Sea on these rocks:
Do what you must, be wise, cut your vines

And forget about hope. Time goes running, even
As we talk. Take the present, the future's no one's affair.

The poem's toughness of surface is what marks it as a pebble, and differ-
ent though it is from Catullus's small lyric, it too contributed to my de-
veloping sense of the type. Here was a poem whose intellectual concepts
were couched in the powers of the verbal imperative, yet whose emotion
was cached within coolness. Again, a degree of self-contradiction is at the
poem's axis. The advice is sincere enough, the philosophy genuinely meant
to be lived by . . . and yet, and yet. The skin of the poem is cool, but who
would arrive at these detached conclusions except by heat of tears? Every
Epicurean and Stoic, every student of Zen, begins with the bedrock experi-
ence of transience and suffering. Those who truly live in the moment need
not be reminded to do so; those who have no propensity for hope need
not be told to forego it.

An example of a covertly didactic pebble is this poem by Bertolt Brecht:

BERTOLT BRECHT
The Lovely Fork
Translated from the German by John Willett

When the fork with the lovely horn handle broke
It struck me that deep within it
There must always have been a fault. With difficulty
I summoned back to my memory
My joy in its flawlessness.

The poem seats itself strongly in simple depiction: the fork, and then the
self's response to its revealed nature, are held up to an objective scrutiny.
Here again is the outward coldness and detachment essential to the peb-
ble. (As Herbert put it: "Pebbles cannot be tamed/ to the end, they will
look at us/ with a calm and very clear eye.") If our hopes of perfection,
of nobility of being (in an object, in a person) are dashed, well then, they
are dashed, Brecht's poem proposes; and the shattered fact of our own prior
innocence must also be considered in the full daylight of that disclosure.

It may be that another reader would take from this poem another read-
ing. While that risk applies to all poems, it is particularly true for pebbles:
they supply a set of data, leaving the reader to draw conclusions as he or

she will. It is in the reader, after all, that the poem finds its human life. "I feel a heavy remorse/ when I hold it in my hand/ and its noble body/ is permeated by false warmth," wrote Herbert of his pebble—and in these lines, too, several possible conclusions inhere, depending on what levels of irony and earnestness one attributes to the poem. Read on the literal level, Herbert's words would mean one thing, on the political level, another. Yet I believe both readings to be fully true to the poem's intentions.

Pebbles tend to have a worldly sophistication; they require a taste for classical irony. This, too, differentiates them from the *haiku,* whose sophistication is metaphysical in nature. Underneath the surface acceptance of implacable fate, the pebble-writer has his or her opinions, and more—by the amount of restraint that is required to keep it in check, we recognize, often enough, an almost overwhelming measure of unspoken, perhaps unspeakable, feeling.

C. P. CAVAFY
Hidden Things
Translated from the Greek by Edmund Keeley and Philip Sherrard

From all I did and all I said
let no one try to find out who I was.
An obstacle was there distorting
the actions and the manner of my life.
An obstacle was often there
to stop me when I'd begin to speak.
From my most unnoticed actions,
my most veiled writing—
from these alone will I be understood.
But maybe it isn't worth so much concern,
so much effort to discover who I really am.
Later, in a more perfect society,
someone else made just like me
is certain to appear and act freely.

The obvious context for Cavafy's poem is his homosexuality, alluded to throughout his works both directly (though never by name) and indirectly. Omnipresent in his work are persons marginalized by history and custom: even his emperors walk away from their thrones like actors stepping out of costume. The axis of the poem is again an act of self-contradiction hiding out in the open, like a night-active insect made visible only by black light. However poignant the poem's concluding prediction, the fact of the obstacle stands at its center. The imagination of future freedom exists only to point backward to the truth of what now is; it is ultimately the portrait of the one who speaks and acts under a present, terrible constraint that breaks the heart. And heartbreak, whether of greater or lesser magnitude, is the true business of the pebble-poem, accomplished discreetly, by subterfuge, in words spoken so quietly they travel almost in silence.

Articulation creates us, both our own speaking and the articulations of others. A young woman both sentimental and romantic learned other modes of pleasure and other modes of self-sustaining not only from the simple recalcitrance of the objective world but also from the vertiginous tempering found in the words of poems. I have never thought of poems as "art," but as life: reading a good poem is as integral to my life's course as any other experience. For the part of us that is sponge, poems are water, and a living sponge is inseparable from what it has taken in. If I have written pebble-like poems of my own, it is not only because I developed a taste for the flavor of river-smoothed rock. The influence of an aesthetic becomes an influence of character; the rhythms and sensibilities of the poems one loves infuse the person one becomes.

The collection for which these thoughts were set down is devoted to "influence and mastery," but of mastery I have little to say. The world of temporal existence consents to let us walk with it for a while, clumsily or less clumsily, then shrugs us off. We have no more mastered anything than a flea can master the elephant it rides on. It is possible that the flea may perhaps master itself a little; if the flea is a writer, this may at times manifest itself in sentences useful for others. But it is not for the flea to judge, or know.

In the context of poetic transmission, "mastery" may perhaps mean the process of making a poetic gesture so thoroughly one's own that one is able not simply to imitate the beloved music or word-dazzle or insight, but to bring it forth newly from within. Here again, it is not for the poet to judge whether this has occurred. Better the chastening remembrance that all poetry, all language, lives in the realm of convention—that a certain sound made by breath and lips and teeth means to us what it does, or that a metrical rhythm or pattern of rhyming means to us what it does, because we speak and listen within an immense, mutually created field of extant knowledge. To till this shared field of language with some exuberance, and with as much fidelity to a life's portion of losses and joys as we can manage, is what we do, master and ordinary poet alike. And it is good, also, to recall a few sentences set down in a prologue by Jorge Luis Borges, that consummate master: "After all these years I have observed that beauty, like happiness, is frequent. A day does not pass when we are not, for an instant, in paradise. There is no poet, however mediocre, who has not written the best line in literature, but also the most miserable ones. Beauty is not the privilege of a few illustrious names. It would be rare if this book did not contain one single secret line worthy of staying with you to the end."[1]

Perhaps a discussion of the pebble is not the place to examine poetic mastery in any case. The pebble is a modest form, cloaking itself in the simplicity of straightforward speech. Never baring its teeth, it is more sketch than oil painting, more tune plucked out one note at a time than symphonic arch. Its hopes, though real, are unassertive; its obeisance to the actual is large. And precisely for that reason I have found this lineage of small, skipped stones immensely heartening, in times of happiness and discouragement alike.

I finish by skimming a few pebbles of my own across the water—

Minotaur

Once a minotaur,
a secret revealed becomes a rock,
a tree, a cow like any other.
Only the one who once held it, seeing it
thus diminished, strokes the rough bark or small ears,
leans against the silent, cold surface with sorrow,
remembers it in its former, fearsome glory.

Speed and Perfection

How quickly the season of apricots is over—
a single night's wind is enough.
I kneel on the ground, lifting one, then the next.
Eating those I can, before the bruises appear.

Moment

A person wakes from sleep
and does not know for a time
who she is, who he is.

This happens in a lifetime
once or twice.
It has happened to you, no doubt.

Some, in that moment,
panic,
some sigh with pleasure.

How each kind later envies the other,
who must so love their lives.

CLAUDIA KEELAN

Claudia Keelan is the author of three collections of poetry: *Refinery* (Cleveland State University Center, 1994), *The Secularist* (University of Georgia Press, 1997), and *Utopic,* which won the 2000 Beatrice Hawley Award from Alice James Books. Her essay "Against the Poetry of Witness" won the Robert D. Richardson Award for the best essay published in the *Denver Quarterly* in 1997. A native Californian, she received her M.F.A. from the University of Iowa Writers' Workshop in 1985 and has lived and taught in Boston, Kentucky, Tennessee, and Utah. She now lives in Las Vegas with her husband, the poet Donald Revell, and her son, Benjamin Brecht Revell.

Tool

The one I wanted to teach

                        proved to be my teacher:
Christ's sermon on the mount,

             Buddha, with the lamb on his shoulder,

                  love at heart.
The one I wanted to teach

                     silenced spirit,
dharma guru   wind erasing all edge.
No one follow me.
The slaughter house is in the heart I pass.

Beautiful spots in that place & there countless are killed,
my idea of devotion.
Follow ideas: Christ's sermon on the mount,
Buddha, with the lamb on his shoulder.
    Love at heart
    requires understanding.
The slaughter in the heart I pass,
knows no other method.

EMILY DICKINSON
288

I'm Nobody! Who are you?
Are you—Nobody—Too?
Then there's a pair of us!
Don't tell! they'd advertise—you know!

How dreary—to be—Somebody!
How public—like a Frog—
To tell one's name—the livelong June—
To an admiring Bog!

881

I've none to tell me to but Thee
So when Thou failest, nobody.
It was a little tie—
It just held Two, nor those it held
Since Somewhere thy sweet Face has spilled
Beyond my Boundary—

If things were opposite—and Me
And Me it were—that ebbed from Thee
On some unanswering Shore—
Would'st Thou seek so—just say
That I the Answer may pursue
Unto the lips it eddied through—
So—overtaking Thee—

WALT WHITMAN
Excerpts from *Song of Myself*

6

A child said *What is the grass?* fetching it to me with full hands;
How could I answer the child? I do not know what it is any more than
    he.

I guess it must be the flag of my disposition, out of hopeful green stuff
    woven.

Or I guess it is the handkerchief of the Lord,
A scented gift and remembrancer designedly dropt,
Bearing the owner's name someway in the corners, that we may see
    and remark, and say *Whose?*

Or I guess the grass is itself a child, the produced babe of the
    vegetation.

Or I guess it is a uniform hieroglyphic,
And it means, Sprouting alike in broad zones and narrow zones,
Growing among black folks as among white,
Kanuck, Tuckahoe, Congressman, Cuff, I give them the same, I receive
    them the same.

And now it seems to me the beautiful uncut hair of graves.

Tenderly will I use you curling grass,
It may be you transpire from the breasts of young men,
It may be if I had known them I would have loved them,
It may be you are from old people, or from offspring taken soon out of
    their mothers' laps,
And here you are the mothers' laps.

This grass is very dark to be from the white heads of old mothers,
Darker than the colorless beards of old men,
Dark to come from under the faint red roofs of mouths.

O I perceive after all so many uttering tongues,
And I perceive they do not come from the roofs of mouths for nothing.

I wish I could translate the hints about the dead young men and
        women,
And the hints about old men and mothers, and the offspring taken soon
        out of their laps.

What do you think has become of the young and old men?
And what do you think has become of the women and children?

They are alive and well somewhere,
The smallest sprout shows there is really no death,
And if ever there was it led forward life, and does not wait at the end to
        arrest it,
And ceas'd the moment life appear'd.

All goes onward and outward, nothing collapses,
And to die is different from what any one supposed, and luckier.

52
The spotted hawk swoops by and accuses me, he complains of my gab
        and my loitering.

I too am not a bit tamed, I too am untranslatable,
I sound my barbaric yawp over the roofs of the world.

The last scud of day holds back for me,
It flings my likeness after the rest and true as any on the shadow'd
        wilds,
It coaxes me to the vapor and the dusk.

I depart as air, I shake my white locks at the runaway sun,
I effuse my flesh in eddies, and drift it in lacy jags.

I bequeath myself to the dirt to grow from the grass I love,
If you want me again look for me under your boot-soles.

You will hardly know who I am or what I mean,
But I shall be good health to you nevertheless,
And filter and fibre your blood.

Failing to fetch me at first keep encouraged,
Missing me one place search another,
I stop somewhere waiting for you.

Without Sovereignty

The Colorado River wends its way through many western states, influenced by underground valleys and canyons, its direction at any given point dictated by the physical reality of the course it must take. Whatever it has become by the time it meets the ocean is a result of that course—acid rain, motor oil, garbage, fish, and grass, arriving in a confluence of water that occurs only for an instant before it is dispersed into the larger body of the Pacific.

Influence, as the river reveals, has a physical cause and is labile. It crosses categories and moves backward and forward in time. The negative capability I first heard defined in the letters of John Keats brought me back to the faith outlined in the Sermon on the Mount:

> But when thou prayest enter into thy closet and when thou hast, shut thy door. . . .
> When ye pray, use not vain repetitions as the heathen do: for they think that they shall be heard for their much speaking.[1]

In the Sermon on the Mount, Jesus advocated versions of what I'll call negative virtue, a wholly unnatural acceptance of pain, solitude, and otherness as the way to honor. Inside the closet, without the misguiding comfort of Congregation, the seeker is instructed to begin alone and anew. Likewise, Keats understood that negation of self would bring him closer to the whole. In this century, the Sermon on the Mount reemerged in the civil movements of Mohandas Gandhi and Martin Luther King and in their efforts to destabilize the status quo. The passive resistance they espoused involved a concept of self in service to a society *of which their opponents would ideally be part.* As King explained,

> What is the nonviolent resister's justification for this ordeal to which he invites men, for this mass application of the ancient doctrine of turning the other cheek? Things of fundamental importance to people . . . have to be purchased with their suffering. . . . This can only be done by projecting the ethic of love to the center of our lives.[2]

Formally, a poetics dedicated to finding the words anew each time might insist that the body of the poem, the shape it comes to be, arrives not from an already-negotiated self, nor from *a priori* forms. In such a poem, mastery is a paradox, since the poem annihilates all former paradigms of sovereignty in favor of the uncharted Now. In such a poem, poet, subject, and reader are labile and the measure of success is how all three are changed by the mutual recognition that there is no self. I look for versions of this dynamic in all that I read and am instructed not only by its evidence, but also by its absence.

> I'm Nobody! Who are you?
> Are you—Nobody—Too?
> Then there's a pair of us!
> Don't tell! they'd advertise—you know!
>
> How dreary—to be—Somebody!
> How public—like a Frog—
> To tell one's name—the livelong June—
> To an admiring Bog!

Emily Dickinson's much quoted *288* stays with me, not because it succeeds in outlining the relationship I've been talking about, but because it fails to do so. The Other for Dickinson was, of course, the grand Master, and much of her incredible poetry details the ecstatic pain of pursuing election. For though, as she writes elsewhere, "I'm ceded—I've stopped being Theirs—," she remains, to my mind, the ultimate Protestant, charting one soul's passage to eternity. While many of her poems—*My Life Had Stood a Loaded Gun, He Fumbles at Your Soul, The Soul Selects her Own Society,* etc.—detail the great price exacted for such faith, *288* revels in the negative power of choosing anonymity in a world that privileges fame. I like it because it is playful, while intensely angry. Make no mistake, however: *288* is a poem absolutely empowered by a singular sense of self, a self admittedly dedicated to the pursuit and possession of grace but still firmly entrenched in the Somebody advanced in all of Emily Dickinson's poetry: an unaccompanied Soul who foregoes the "bog" for the celestial regions "he" might inhabit.

Unlike her transcendental countryman Walt Whitman, Dickinson never sees nature as real by itself but, rather, as a metaphor illuminating her relationship to the human world. In *288,* Dickinson celebrates the lack of connection she elsewhere mourns, and "Nobody," instead of becoming a transparency through which others are reached, becomes a persona for the "right" sort of pilgrim. The poem taught me to beware the kind of self-abnegation that hopes to be rewarded.

What has been lauded as the unconventionality of her prosody seems to me masterful in the most conventional of senses: her attenuated experiments with syntax, punctuation, and capital letters, a kind of Braille through which we find her. I'd be mistaken, however, if I thought Dickinson didn't understand the nature of her choice. *881* reckons the costs of self-abnegation with heartbreaking accuracy:

> I've none to tell me to but Thee
> So when Thou failest, nobody.
> It was a little tie—
> It just held Two, nor those it held
> Since Somewhere thy sweet Face has spilled
> Beyond my Boundary—
>
> If things were opposite—and Me
> And Me it were—that ebbed from Thee
> On some unanswering Shore—
> Woulds't Thou seek so—just say
> That I the Answer may pursue
> Unto the lips it eddied through—
> So—overtaking Thee—

Bound to "Thee" and "Thee" alone, the lover/pilgrim experiences nature only as the objective correlative of her love and entrapment. Now that "Thee" has "spilled Beyond [her] Boundary," the speaker briefly questions the dynamic existing between them, wondering if "Me it were—that ebbed from Thee . . . Would'st Thou seek so." Her query isn't in earnest, however, because she is determined in advance, as always, to "pursue" the "Thee" she seeks.

When Whitman writes at the end of *Song of Myself,* "I bequeath myself to the dirt to grow from the grass I love,/ If you want me again look for me under your boot-soles," he gives us what only great poetry can give us: not merely the acceptance but the *love* of annihilation as a natural and life-giving process. Beginning with the minuscule atoms that we are here to share, Whitman's joyous *Song of Myself* enacts a chaotic reciprocity that refuses to unify point of view, proving that "I" is indeed another. I began this essay with a paragraph describing the passage of the Colorado River, and while the description might seem to depict a metaphorical relation between that river's course and the particular relation between influence and mastery I've posited here, it was intended to show that influence is, in fact, the physical by-product of things that make passage together. Whitman's *Song of Myself* taught me this, beginning with the atom and the natural world, and moving on to himself together with the human world and then to the dust we become. Like Dickinson, Whitman's power as a poet relies on negative affirmations. But where Dickinson's radical negativity foregoes the world to create a circumference that successfully encloses her personae in their pursuit of God, Whitman's negation invites an inclusiveness that foregoes nothing in his pursuit of radical democracy. In section 6, the poet's inability to answer the child's query "[w]hat is the grass?" leads him to a tender meditation that is all the more beautiful for its tentativeness. Each of his attempts to answer the question enlarges the frame in which he sees the possibilities of grass, until he ventures that grass must be "a uniform hieroglyphic . . . [g]rowing among black folks as among white,/ Kanuck, Tuckahoe, Congressman, Cuff." The democratic ideology Whitman advances becomes all the more astounding by the end of the section, when he realizes that the equality he invites is also *physically* true: when he sees the end of death in the continuity of the grass:

> I wish I could translate the hints about the dead young men and women,
> And the hints about old men and mothers, and the offspring taken
>   soon out of their laps.
>
> What do you think has become of the young and old men?
> And what do you think has become of the women and children?
>
> They are alive and well somewhere,
> The smallest sprout shows there is really no death,
> And if ever there was it led forward life, and does not wait at the end
>   to arrest it,
> And ceas'd the moment life appear'd.
>
> All goes onward and outward, nothing collapses,
> And to die is different from what any one supposed, and luckier.

As I hear "virtue" and "verity" in the green ("vert") of the grass, so I believe Whitman's generosity begets his genius. As translator, he reads a world that has already been authored, and, as translator, he is free to see the unbroken chain of existence in which all beings participate and are, by that participation, released. The poem is bound to Blake's notion of Generation, and Whitman's mastery exists in a reverence for that process, over against self-knowledge. Uncertain to the end, *Song of Myself* posits the possible world, poet, and reader as mutually bound together:

> The spotted hawk swoops by and accuses me, he complains of my
>   gab and my loitering.
>
> I too am not a bit tamed, I too am untranslatable,
> I sound my barbaric yawp over the roofs of the world.
>
> The last scud of day holds back for me,
> It flings my likeness after the rest and true as any on the shadow'd
>   wilds,
> It coaxes me to the vapor and the dusk.
>
> I depart as air, I shake my white locks at the runaway sun,
> I effuse my flesh in eddies, and drift it in lacy jags.
>
> I bequeath myself to the dirt to grow from the grass I love,
> If you want me again look for me under your boot-soles.
>
> You will hardly know who I am or what I mean,
> But I shall be good health to you nevertheless,
> And filter and fibre your blood.
>
> Failing to fetch me at first keep encouraged,
> Missing me one place search another,
> I stop somewhere waiting for you.

Incapable by nature of either pure grief or pure ecstasy, I am unable to process the world without immediate knowledge that the opposite of what I am feeling is equally true. It's a ridiculous way to live, but there you have it. My mind is not singular in the manner of Dickinson, and the joyful stance Whitman strikes, as he faces down death, embarrasses and likewise eludes me. You might say my spirit is as tortured as Dickinson's, but my sense of justice promotes Whitman ahead of all other poets living or dead. I was eight years old when Martin Luther King was killed at the Lorraine Motel in Memphis, and the loss and rage I felt then, that I still feel, led me to Gandhi. His writing helped me in my most recent book, *Utopic,* where I had been trying to find a way to use the pronoun "I" plurally. I had written a whole series of poems that broke rules of tense and case hoping to evolve a method of composition that allowed opposites to coexist without disintegration and, if possible, with love. I knew that the poem I wanted to make would dismantle much of what I'd previously imagined as "poetry," and there was pain in that recognition. I'd begun to understand, in the writing of *Utopic,* that I had to go where the writing took me, regardless of the company I might or might not bring with me. I'd thought that I'd wanted to write poetry from the necessity of suffering Otherness, but *Tool,* the last poem of the book, taught me—at last, or perhaps for the first time—what I thought I already knew: I wasn't important. I wrote *Tool* after reading an account by Gandhi of a scene on a train in which his exhaustion causes him to rebuke a young man who has traveled far to see him, because the young man isn't wearing *khadi,* the handspun cloth Gandhi advocated as essential to Indian economic autonomy. The man goes away offended, and Gandhi knows he has sacrificed a potential worker for an unyielding adherence to doctrine. A few hours later, another young man comes, again from a long distance, and Gandhi finds the new language with which to speak. He writes, "The one whom I wanted to teach proved to be my teacher." It struck me that the poems I'd written so far in *Utopic* had been so intent on destabilizing the singular function of the letter "I" that they had inadvertently made "I" a character. Failing to create transparency, I, too, had been developing a script that called attention to the materiality of language, when what I'd wanted was to call attention to the selflessness that makes possible a secular paradise. Strangely, by avoiding the real self-investigation available in the act of saying "I," I had disregarded my own culpability and withheld the ethic of love, which is the first step to Utopia. The books and poems I love teach me this, and while I haven't yet mastered the art of being Nobody, poets such as Whitman have taught me not to be embarrassed as I try.

YUSEF KOMUNYAKAA

Yusef Komunyakaa is the author of *Neon Vernacular: New and Selected Poems 1977–1989* (Wesleyan University Press, 1993), for which he won the Pulitzer Prize in 1994, and *Thieves of Paradise* (Wesleyan University Press, 1998), a finalist for the 1999 National Book Critics Circle Award. He has recently published *Blue Notes: Essays, Interviews & Commentaries* (University of Michigan Press, 2000); *Pleasure Dome: New and Collected Poems, 1975–1999* (Wesleyan University Press, 2001); and *Talking Dirty to the Gods* (Farrar, Straus, and Giroux, 2000), a finalist for the 2001 National Book Critics Circle Award. Komunyakaa was commissioned by Northwestern University to write the libretto for *Slip Knot,* a collaboration with composer T. J. Anderson. Other jazz-related releases include *Love Notes from the Madhouse* (8th Harmonic Breakdown, 1998) and lyrics on *Thirteen Kinds of Desire,* sung by singer and composer Pamela Knowles (Cornucopia, 2000). His poem on Charlie Parker's life is featured on *Testimony* (Australian Broadcasting Corporation, 1999). A professor in the Creative Writing Program at Princeton University, Komunyakaa has been appointed to the Council of the Humanities and was also recently elected Chancellor of the Academy of American Poets. In March 2001, he won the Ruth Lilly Poetry Prize.

The Millpond

They looked like wood ibis
From a distance, & as I got closer
They became knots left for gods

To undo, like bows tied
At the center of weakness.
Shadow to light, mind to flesh,
Swamp orchids quivered under green hats,
Nudged by slate-blue catfish
Headed for some boy's hook
On the other side. The day's
Uncut garments of fallen chances
Stumbled among flowers
That loved only darkness,
As afternoon came through underbrush
Like a string of firecrackers
Tied to a dog's tail.
Gods lived under that mud
When I was young & sublimely
Blind. Each bloom a shudder
Of uneasiness, no sound
Except the whippoorwill.
They conspired to become twilight
& metaphysics, as five-eyed
Fish with milky bones
Flip-flopped in oily grass.

We sat there as the moon rose
Up from chemical water,
Phosphorous as an orange lantern.
An old man shifted
His three-pronged gig
Like a New Guinea spear,
So it could fly quicker
Than a frog's tongue or angry word.
He pointed to snapping turtles
Posed on cypress logs,
Armored in stillness,
Slow kings of a dark world.
We knelt among cattails.
The reflection of a smokestack

Cut the black water in half.
A circle of dry leaves
Smouldered on the ground
For mosquitoes. As if
To draw us to them, like decoys
For some greater bounty,
The choir of bullfrogs called,
Singing a cruel happiness.

Sometimes I'd watch them
Scoot back into their tunnels,
Down in a gully where
The pond's overflow drained . . .
Where shrub oak & banyan
Grew around barbed wire
Till April oozed sap
Like a boy beside a girl
Squeezing honeycomb in his fists.
I wondered if time tied
Everything to goldenrod
Reaching out of cow manure for the sun.
What did it have to do
With saw & hammer,
With what my father taught me
About his world? Sometimes
I sat reading *Catcher in the Rye,*
& other times *Spider Man*
& *Captain Marvel.* Always
After a rain crawfish surfaced
To grab the salt meat
Tied to the nylon string,
Never knowing when they left
The water & hit the bottom
Of my tincan. They clung
To desire, like the times
I clutched something dangerous
& couldn't let go.

ROBERT HAYDEN
The Diver

Sank through easeful
azure. Flower
creatures flashed and
shimmered there—
lost images
fadingly remembered.
Swiftly descended
into canyon of cold
nightgreen emptiness.
Freefalling, weightless
as in dreams of
wingless flight,
plunged through infra-
space and came to
the dead ship,
carcass that swarmed with
voracious life.
Angelfish, their
lively blue and
yellow prised from
darkness by the
flashlight's beam,
thronged her portholes.
Moss of bryozoans
blurred, obscured her
metal. Snappers,
gold groupers explored her,
fearless of bubbling
manfish. I entered
the wreck, awed by her silence,
feeling more keenly
the iron cold.
With flashlight probing
fogs of water
saw the sad slow
dance of gilded
chairs, the ectoplasmic
swirl of garments,
drowned instruments
of buoyancy,
drunken shoes. Then

livid gestures,
eldritch hide and
seek of laughing
faces. I yearned to
find those hidden
ones, to fling aside
the mask and call to them,
yield to rapturous
whisperings, have
done with self and
every dinning
vain complexity.
Yet in languid
frenzy strove, as
one freezing fights off
sleep desiring sleep;
strove against the
cancelling arms that
suddenly surrounded
me, fled the numbing
kisses that I craved.
Reflex of life-wish?
Respirator's brittle
belling? Swam from
the ship somehow;
somehow began the
measured rise.

ELIZABETH BISHOP
The Fish

I caught a tremendous fish
and held him beside the boat
half out of water, with my hook
fast in a corner of his mouth.
He didn't fight.
He hadn't fought at all.
He hung a grunting weight,
battered and venerable
and homely. Here and there
his brown skin hung in strips
like ancient wallpaper,
and its pattern of darker brown

was like wallpaper:
shapes like full-blown roses
stained and lost through age.
He was speckled with barnacles,
fine rosettes of lime,
and infested
with tiny white sea-lice,
and underneath two or three
rags of green weed hung down.
While his gills were breathing in
the terrible oxygen
—the frightening gills,
fresh and crisp with blood,
that can cut so badly—
I thought of the coarse white flesh
packed in like feathers,
the big bones and the little bones,
the dramatic reds and blacks
of his shiny entrails,
and the pink swim-bladder
like a big peony.
I looked into his eyes
which were far larger than mine
but shallower, and yellowed,
the irises backed and packed
with tarnished tinfoil
seen through the lenses
of old scratched isinglass.
They shifted a little, but not
to return my stare.
—It was more like the tipping
of an object toward the light.
I admired his sullen face,
the mechanism of his jaw,
and then I saw
that from his lower lip
—if you could call it a lip—
grim, wet, and weaponlike,
hung five old pieces of fish-line,
or four and a wire leader
with the swivel still attached,
with all their five big hooks
grown firmly in his mouth.
A green line, frayed at the end

where he broke it, two heavier lines,
and a fine black thread
still crimped from the strain and snap
when it broke and he got away.
Like medals with their ribbons
frayed and wavering,
a five-haired beard of wisdom
trailing from his aching jaw.
I stared and stared
and victory filled up
the little rented boat,
from the pool of bilge
where oil had spread a rainbow
around the rusted engine
to the bailer rusted orange,
the sun-cracked thwarts,
the oarlocks on their strings,
the gunnels—until everything
was rainbow, rainbow, rainbow!
And I let the fish go.

The Lure

> The sea was without color, and it was without anything that I had known
> before. It was still, having no currents. It was warm as freshly spilled blood,
> and I moved through it as if I had always done so, as if it were a perfectly
> natural element to me . . . nothing lived here. No plant grew here, no
> huge sharp-toothed creature with an ancestral memory of hunter and
> prey searching furiously for food, no sudden shift of wind to disturb the
> water. How good this water was. How good that I should know no fear.
> —Jamaica Kincaid, *At the Bottom of the River*

Bogalusa means "dark water." I grew up with water, even inundations of
it, because the city did not cut the necessary ditches to route the water out
of our neighborhood. Whenever the rains fell, water loomed up around
us. For us children, water brought joy and excitement. I loved the rise and
fall of water; I loved its magic, how it coaxed life out of things. I learned
it killed as well. My early imagination was linked to water; I was claimed
by its dualities.

A few lifetimes away from Bogalusa, after Vietnam and monsoons that meant the difference between life and death, I came to Robert Hayden's *The Diver* and Elizabeth Bishop's *The Fish*. I felt that I had been claimed again by familiar terrain—or rather, familiar waters. These poems capture, with cinematic beauty, the experience of weaving through an underworld that is nocturnal, shadowy, wet, and prehistoric.

In *The Diver*, Robert Hayden's "[f]reefalling, weightless" "manfish" is immediately unfaithful to the "easeful" beauty of the watery realm because he arrives, with his human mind, as an outsider to that easy, pale, abstracted romanticism. This creature brings a perception that contraposes what is instinctual, and he disturbs that otherness which seems to deepen by his mere presence. The diver experiences contrast, tension, and unnaturalness. He doesn't possess a natural ease; even his descent "as in dreams of/ wingless flight" seems uncontrolled, almost beyond his power. Corseted in his wetsuit, he is submerged among the unevolved: among ancient plants and animals.

Is "the dead ship" the *Titanic,* a white whale of a ship captured by this bright, otherworldly domain? This symbolist poem is crammed with numerous signals: from the plunging short lines of the diver's descent to its carefully realized last line. Its beauty elicits the kind of horror embedded in near silence. The "manfish" who evolves from fish doesn't feel the ease of nature; he is an outsider, there to clock and measure what lives in the "fog of water" with his flashlight. Ultimately, he is there to behold death.

Removed from his own terrestrial world, a world ruled by laws of gravity, he comes into focus as an artful contradiction, as one who seems himself to have glimpsed human existence through a distant lens and who now delves into this watery haven and grave. In many ways, he is an artist as well as an explorer or scientist. This seeker and seer, close to bliss (art) and death, attempts to ease into this "easeful" kingdom of fluid images and illusions. There is also a sexual easing down into mystery, penetrating a watery psyche.

The Diver encapsulates a descending, downward meditation that seems as if it is a step toward a spiritual connection, and "the/ measured rise" out of this place where one loses oneself suggests an ecstatic experience— a deeper baptism that is a journey to the abyss of death. The "manfish" becomes a witness. He is willing to be alone with this otherness that borders on a godlike existence: this immersion in and connection to the invincible other.

The sea itself is hypnotic, a place where "one freezing fights off/ sleep desiring sleep," and a place that mirrors the symbolic and makes the human mind sway to its reflective appearances.

This metaphorical place is a theater of gesture and affectation—a path of ritual where one comes to glimpse oneself, to enter another domain in order to test the self in a larger arena. A godlike artist transforms the darkness, shining his flashlight, until he must rise slowly or risk dying.

Elizabeth Bishop's *The Fish* isn't exactly a plunging into the psyche as much as it is the dredging up of a mystery. This fish is a living art object that represents both life and struggle—a symbol within a symbol. This "tremendous fish" exists in a man-made version of hell. We could say that Bishop's repeated pronouns—I, my—are pronouns of audacity and conjure the illusion of ownership.

The fish is also an ugly angel: "the coarse white flesh/ packed in like feathers." It is as if the fish, alive in death, rises out of the corrupted water to transcend this nether world. The first two lines suggest transcendence and fate in the fish's non-resistance: "He didn't fight./ He hadn't fought at all." Having spent his whole life fighting to exist, the fish seems prepared for something that surpasses any overt act(ion). There is a beauty in his ugliness: "He was speckled with barnacles,/ fine rosettes of lime,/ and infested/ with tiny white sea-lice. . . ."

Bearing scars and emblems alike, this fish is both a thing—a collection of near misses—and a matrix of suffering, a symbolic saint who experiences torment and, finally, absolution. He is an old warrior. And in this sense, the fish is of Biblical or mythic proportions; his presence is not unlike a diminished, "brown" Moby Dick. Embodied so, he exemplifies wisdom through experience—knowledge incarnate. Because human beings measure themselves against him, he appears to be semi-human. As a philosophical poem, *The Fish* compresses a treatise on ontology and free will through its imagistic, subtle language of understatement.

The fish seems at first to represent chance but then exceeds chance and grows into something larger, something harder to encompass. Though seemingly debased by clusters of unattractive similes, this distillation of meaning has the bearing of benevolence. He seems to have given himself to the narrator; he is the offering of a troubled presence. In this sense, his inaction becomes an act(ion). He becomes a rainbow: beautiful, imbued with the positive, a symbol of redemption. Is this what prompts the narrator to expel the "tremendous fish" from "the boat"?

The two poems give me the means, a tonal approximation through imagery and music, to embrace what I know from experience. They assist me in journeying back to the mystery of places and times of meditation when I believed I could transcend almost anything. As I stood at the edge of a millpond, my imagination entered the water's depths, and I populated it with bright creatures. Now, decades later, I realize that the essence of nature was there, and, no matter how defiled by chemicals, the millpond was also a splendid province for a dark-skinned boy who reveled within a good, strong imagination.

DANA LEVIN

Dana Levin was born in Los Angeles, California, in 1965. She attended Pitzer College, where she studied English and writing as an undergraduate. She received her M.F.A. in creative writing from New York University. Levin's first book of poetry, *In the Surgical Theatre* (American Poetry Review, 1999), won the Honickman First Book Prize from the *American Poetry Review,* the 2000 Witter Bynner Prize from the American Academy of Arts and Letters, and the Great Lakes Colleges Association New Writers Award. A recipient of a National Endowment for the Arts fellowship in poetry, Levin teaches creative writing at the College of Santa Fe. She is currently at work on a second poetry manuscript.

Bridge of Light

Bridge of light.
    They can't see it.
Arcing over the browned-out room, sheets in a heap
    on the floor—
Stale. Curtains drawn.
    Smell of damp ashes and beer—
Bridge of light.
    The little soulsperms wriggling inside it, waiting, waiting
to see—

His breath, sour. Breathing a word in her ear—
Stubble of his chin
    raking her cheek, as he pulls her arms
around him—
    Until she unfurls.
Until they slide out of the heavy
    latitude of sleep,
like two snakes dropping from a stick—
    And the bridge

is getting brighter and brighter with the friction of sex,
    he with his curly head between her legs,
he with his throbbing prick in her mouth,
    the bridge getting brighter and brighter with sex—
And the little soulsperms
    are hot and itching to descend, whispering and jockeying to *see*
as he turns on top of her,
    the heat between her legs coiling up and reaching

for the bridge,
    humming without heat or sympathy, bright, indelible, over the whole
mud-toned room,
    hiss of light as her body arcs, hiss of light as the souls
begin their descent,
    flaming down
to the door of light opening between their bodies
    as he drives her into the floor—

and the soul, the lucky soul—

will be born
    into fire—

the flesh one, in which their hands were forged,
that will burn the bridge of light from its eyes.

WILLIAM BLAKE
Excerpts from *The Marriage of Heaven and Hell*

A Memorable Fancy

As I was walking among the fires of hell, delighted with the enjoyments of Genius; which to Angels look like torment and insanity. I collected some of their Proverbs: thinking that as the sayings used in a nation, mark its character, so the Proverbs of Hell, shew the nature of Infernal wisdom better than any description of buildings or garments.

When I came home; on the abyss of the five senses, where a flat sided steep frowns over the present world. I saw a mighty Devil folded in black clouds, hovering on the sides of the rock, with corroding fires he wrote the following sentence now perceived by the minds of men, & read by them on earth.

How do you know but ev'ry Bird that cuts the airy way,
Is an immense world of delight, clos'd by your senses five?

The Proverbs of Hell

Prisons are built with stones of Law, Brothels with bricks of Religion.
The pride of the peacock is the glory of God.
The lust of the goat is the bounty of God.
The wrath of the lion is the wisdom of God.
The nakedness of woman is the work of God.
Excess of sorrow laughs. Excess of joy weeps.
The roaring of lions, the howling of wolves, the raging of the stormy
    sea, and the destructive sword. are portions of eternity too great
    for the eye of man.
The fox condemns the trap, not himself.
Joys impregnate. Sorrows bring forth.
Let man wear the fell of the lion. woman the fleece of the sheep.
The bird a nest, the spider a web, man friendship.

The selfish smiling fool. & the sullen frowning fool. shall be both
    thought wise. that they may be a rod.
What is now proved was once, only imagin'd.
The rat, the mouse, the fox, the rabbet; watch the roots, the lion, the
    tyger, the horse, the elephant, watch the fruits.
The cistern contains: the fountain overflows
One thought. fills immensity.
Always be ready to speak your mind, and a base man will avoid you.
Every thing possible to be believ'd is an image of truth.

The eagle never lost so much time. as when he submitted to learn of
the crow.

The head Sublime, the heart Pathos, the genitals Beauty, the hands &
feet Proportion.
As the air to a bird or the sea to a fish, so is contempt to the
contemptible.
The crow wish'd every thing was black, the owl, that every thing
was white.
Exuberance is Beauty.
If the lion was advise'd by the fox. he would be cunning.
Improvement makes strait roads, but the crooked roads without
Improvement, are roads of Genius.
Sooner murder an infant in its cradle than nurse unacted desires
Where man is not nature is barren.
Truth can never be told so as to be understood, and not be believ'd.
Enough! or Too much

A Memorable Fancy

The ancient tradition that the world will be consumed in fire at the
end of six thousand years is true. as I have heard from Hell.

For the cherub with his flaming sword is hereby commanded to leave his
guard at [the] tree of life, and when he does, the whole creation will be con-
sumed, and appear infinite. and holy whereas it now appears finite & corrupt.

This will come to pass by an improvement of sensual enjoyment.

But first the notion that man has a body distinct from his soul, is to
be expunged; this I shall do, by printing in the infernal method, by corro-
sives, which in Hell are salutary and medicinal, melting apparent surfaces
away, and displaying the infinite which was hid.

If the doors of perception were cleansed every thing would appear to
man as it is, infinite.

For man has closed himself up, till he sees all things thro' narrow
chinks of his cavern.

The Garden of Love

I went to the Garden of Love,
And saw what I never had seen:
A Chapel was built in the midst,
Where I used to play on the green.

And the gates of this Chapel were shut,
And Thou shalt not. writ over the door;
So I turn'd to the Garden of Love,
That so many sweet flowers bore,

And I saw it was filled with graves,
And tomb-stones where flowers should be:
And Priests in black gowns, were walking their rounds,
And binding with briars, my joys & desires.

Excerpt from *The Book of Thel*

The eternal gates terrific porter lifted the northern bar:
Thel enter'd in & saw the secrets of the land unknown;
She saw the couches of the dead, & where the fibrous roots
Of every heart on earth infixes deep its restless twists:
A land of sorrows & of tears where never smile was seen.

She wanderd in the land of clouds thro valleys dark, listning
Dolours & lamentations: waiting oft beside a dewy grave
She stood in silence. listning to the voices of the ground,
Till to her own grave plot she came, & there she sat down.
And heard this voice of sorrow breathed from the hollow pit.

Why cannot the Ear be closed to its own destruction?
Or the glistning Eye to the poison of a smile!
Why are Eyelids stord with arrows ready drawn,
Where a thousand fighting men in ambush lie?
Or an Eye of gifts & graces, show'ring fruits & coined gold!

Why a Tongue impress'd with honey from every wind?
Why an Ear, a whirlpool fierce to draw creations in?
Why a Nostril wide inhaling terror trembling & affright
Why a tender curb upon the youthful burning boy!
Why a little curtain of flesh on the bed of our desire?

Infant Sorrow

My mother groand! my father wept.
Into the dangerous world I leapt:
Helpless, naked, piping loud;
Like a fiend hid in a cloud.

Struggling in my fathers hands:
Striving against my swadling bands:
Bound and weary I thought best
To sulk upon my mothers breast.

Strong Water

William Blake did not write on paper. He engraved his poems directly into plates of copper, using vinegar, baysalt, and salt armoniack rather than ink; using chalk, blade, quills, brushes rather than a pen. His words bit into the page: they were actors, not ethereal products, though Blake believed his poetry to be divinely inspired. Perhaps one can say that for Blake, poetry was born in spirit and then embedded in matter, effectively changed by that process.

That words act, that they act through meaning, that through meaning they change reality—today these are, for many, unfashionable, even naïve, beliefs. Yet poetry, as one of the few, if not last, remaining art forms not driven by the market, has enormous freedom and capacity to tell the truth. Is the truth that language is oppressed by reference and syntax and must be liberated? No, the truth is that human beings suffer under all kinds of oppressions, not the least of which is being a human being who suffers. In such a televised, narcoticized culture as America, it is astonishing that there is any art form left that might wake one up to the awareness of suffering and offer, perhaps, a relief from it.

An art—an "infernal method," as Blake calls it in *The Marriage of Heaven and Hell*—is "in Hell salutary and medicinal, melting apparent surfaces away." It is this melting away of surfaces that first drew me to Blake's work: what was he finding underneath? Angels in the trees. The spirit of his brother at the moment of death rising to the ceiling, "clapping its hands for joy." The agency of the soul. His sense of the *meat* of the spiritual realm, that it was inextricably woven into the fabric of the everyday, led to his most wonderful and original statements. He writes, about his "Vision of the last judgment," "What, it will be Question'd, when the Sun rises, do you not see a round Disk of fire somewhat like a Guinea? O no, no, I see an Innumerable company of the Heavenly host crying Holy, Holy, Holy is the Lord God Almighty."[1]

What saves the passage from dull splendor is the inclusion of the guinea. What saves Blake's belief in a new Jerusalem from utopian cliché is that he saw it located in London—not the London of wizards and credulous kings, but the eighteenth-century city, with its foul lanes, bawds, and revolutionary pamphlets, what he called "a Human awful wonder of God!" In this London, as Peter Ackroyd relates in his engaging biography, *Blake* (from which most of the biographical material in this essay comes), Blake can witness a drunk woman "reeling up the Street" and see "material reality as a refuge from 'The Hermaphroditic Satanic World of rocky destiny.'"[2]

Is it any wonder his neighbors called him Mad Blake? Or Poor Blake, from his kinder, more successful artistic colleagues. After all, he lived during the first throes of scientific discovery and political democracy, when science was revelatory and certain, when democracy was bloody and revolutionary, and when there were periodic riots over the price of bread. What is fantastic about Blake is that he caught the revolutionary fervor and applied it to the human soul, without for a minute forgetting, indeed reminding us always, that "the Corner of Broad Street weeps."

This essay is to be, in part, about mastery. As a master of craft, Blake's music was deceptively simple—at times it seems his lyrics settled for easy rhyme and sing-song rhythm. Sometimes he could not (or would not?) even maintain a simple abcb schema, as in *The Garden of Love,* when the last stanza unravels into the rhythm of limerick and then unravels out of that. Yet it is the unraveling that defines Blake's poetic control and invention. I am fascinated by how this poem mimics the unraveling of love as sweet permission and the consequent binding of it to forbidden sin; how Blake's life showed an unwavering adherence to a visionary and poetic impulse that unraveled out of the strictures of burgeoning Enlightenment thinking and Puritan belief; how Blake even unraveled the tight yarn of eighteenth-century poetry, using, in *The Marriage of Heaven and Hell,* proverbs and slogans from political tracts, the most popular publications of his day, to publish a call to his own kind of revolution. He was a master of image, invention, and appropriation. Stubborn, pugnacious, energetic, idiosyncratic, his mastery was that of constant fidelity to inner vision—one of the essentials, and one of the struggles, of great poetry.

Blake's prophetic rage, his belief in the action of the soul, his visions of angels, his assertion that "without Contraries is no progression"—all of these have had a profound affect on my own work. I too believe in the soul and in the agency of an invisible psychic realm; I too believe that words act, that they can reflect and affect life. But we live in an age in which the pioneering empiricism of Blake's day has cemented itself against anything that cannot be visibly proven; in which the incendiary affect of the political tract has been replaced with hostility, cynicism, and suspicion, not just toward the political but also towards language itself. This is the primary situation I struggle with whenever I sit down to write.

Bridge of Light is predicated on a Hindu idea of conception: that when two people make love all the possible souls that might incarnate through them gather, watching, feeling the vibe, if you will. What finally calls one soul out of the millions to the fertilized egg is the quality of the relationship between its parents: the more enlightened the love, the more enlightened the child conceived.

Well.

It wasn't so much the *idea* of this that struck me as the *vision* of the top of the seen world coming off as you were having sex and an entire aethiric audience watching, judging. A kind of spiritual voyeurism. It delighted me. What surprised me, as I began writing the poem, was how much the idea behind the vision—the moralism of it—infiltrated the poem. Words like *stale, sour, raking, snakes.* The light *hissing.* I started feeling uneasy: was I judging? What was I judging? When I got to *mud-toned* I thought, Now this is really enough—you've got to change that. *Darkened? Dull brown?* But no, no, it was *mud.* Sigh. What to do with raging moralism in a relativistic age? All the public figures I hated pounded it out in fistfuls.

Blake's method of writing was corrosive both in execution and thought. Underneath its "apparent surfaces" are not only angels and spirits but also aspects of human behavior, thought, and feeling that we prefer to ignore. As Thel cries out in *The Book of Thel,* "Why cannot the Ear be closed to its own destruction?" Blake reveled in opening that ear. It is the part of him I love best and took in most: wanting to open the closed ear. Wanting the words to bite into the page. Should I have been surprised at the adamancy of the poem I was writing?

But was it really sex I was judging? What a terrible thing! It took weeks to accept my discomfort with *throbbing prick*—but how else to say it? *Erect penis? Red member?* In time, I thought the poem was not so much about the "badness" of loveless sex as it was about the perils of being a human being: the terror of parents; the terror of the world. I was fascinated by a vision of the moment of the soul *deciding* to be born. And what a surprise it was in for—such suffering, in the body. And yet it is so eager to come down—a mystery.

I think often, though not exclusively, of Blake's poem *Infant Sorrow* in this context. It seems a very true poem to me. I admire that Blake wrestles birth away from being caged in a cliché of joy. That is not to say that the birth of a child is not joyful—but often we use ideas and words of joy and happiness to gloss over suffering. And then we come to believe in that gloss. We wonder what's wrong when happiness doesn't feel as we think it should. In this respect, I've found I am most motivated to write by the impulse to erase the gloss. To "cut the dark caul." And might a truer joy vibrate underneath? A joy that is not a panacea?

There were many other things that plagued me in the writing of this poem: the fear of melodrama, countered by my love of a baroque staginess; the fear that a reader might find the poem offensive, pornographic, which only inflamed my rage to stay true to what I saw. And then Blake saying, "Without Contraries is no progression." And then Blake saying, "If the doors of perception were cleansed." Using aqua fortis—strong water.

LISA LEWIS

Lisa Lewis was born in Roanoke, Virginia, in 1956. She received her B.A. from Virginia Intermont College and her M.F.A. in creative writing from the University of Iowa. She also holds a Ph.D. in English from the University of Houston. Her books of poetry are *The Unbeliever* (University of Wisconsin Press, 1994) and *Silent Treatment* (Penguin, 1998). Lewis lives in Stillwater, Oklahoma, and directs the creative writing program at Oklahoma State University. She is currently at work on another book of poems.

Media

I keep trying to get my friend on the phone but the line's busy.
Pretty soon she'll be putting her little boy to bed; there's no use
Calling then. She lies next to him till he drifts off; usually
She does too. They tuck into his bunk bed like darner's pins
Gathering the eastern horizon, so far below where the sun
Comes up the wrinkle doesn't show in the southern plains.
That's where I'm pacing my living room, thinking about
What I'd like to tell my friend, mostly what another friend
Has said, and what I think will happen next in the drama
That shouldn't even interest me, it's just petty, local intrigue—
Really, what must my friend think? It probably looks like
I'm desperate—the word people use to ward off terror

Of making it to middle age without someone so long reliable
It's merely predictable when he comes on to the boss
Or the boss's secretary after just one drink at the Christmas
Party. "What is she, desperate?" I used to sneer, sizing up
A pairing that reminded me of my secret fear I'd have to
Marry someone who asked me, not someone I wanted.
That was a marriage and divorce ago. I'd say they were
Like waves breaking on a beach except I never glistened
White like a beach and no one searched me for treasure.
I knew nothing of despair when I saw it everywhere
And shrank until it passed me by. It takes being found out
As the one with the bruise or fontanel, the terrifying
Vulnerability the stab of a thumb could pulp, to use up
The time, or the shelter, or the light by which to see.
Tonight, though, getting directions isn't the problem.
Despair looms like a mountain closing in on a highway—
No, wait, it's the other way around, a fast-moving sedan
Heading for the tunnel entrance bored in the forested slope—
And I'm going to have to wait here forever as car after car
Crashes in what turns out to be an optical illusion, there's
No tunnel entrance and no tunnel and the highway sent us
All here by accident so no one can be held accountable
For those many deaths, their inevitability, or the loneliness
Of the dying, who know the day they're born their fate
Awaits them here in this carefully laid trap; they live
Toward impact, fierce to force away anyone who might
Come near to offer a little kindness, maybe a touch, before
Flame the size of a broken heart starts straight up through
The moving image, the film ends, and the crowd goes home.
My world of solace is as distant as ever, spinning away
With me on it, waving my spindly arms, a light year every
Beep of the busy signal, my friend's words, her very breath
Punctuating cycles of madness, misery, loneliness and despair,
So far away nobody could possibly know about it, let alone
Care, even when they're well within earshot, I'm even talking
Directly to them, explaining as calmly as I know how.

JOHN MILTON
Excerpt from *Samson Agonistes*

Samson Out, out *Hyæna*, these are thy wonted arts,
And arts of every woman false like thee,
To break all faith, all vows, deceive, betray,
Then as repentant to submit, beseech,
And reconcilement move with feign'd remorse,
Confess, and promise wonders in her change,
Not truly penitent, but chief to try
Her husband, how far urg'd his patience bears,
His vertue or weakness which way t'assail:
Then with more cautious and instructed skill
Again transgresses, and again submits;
That wisest and best men full oft beguil'd
With goodness principl'd not to reject
The penitent, but ever to forgive,
Are drawn to wear out miserable days,
Entangl'd with a poysnous bosom snake,
If not by quick destruction soon cut off
As I by thee, to Ages an example.

Dalila Yet hear me *Samson*; not that I endeavour
To lessen or extenuate my offence,
But that on th'other side if it be weigh'd
By it self, with aggravations not surcharg'd,
Or else with just allowance counterpois'd,
I may, if possible, thy pardon find
The easier towards me, or thy hatred less.
First granting, as I do, it was a weakness
In me, but incident to all our sex,
Curiosity, inquisitive, importune
Of secrets, then with like infirmity
To publish them, both common female faults:
Was it not weakness also to make known
For importunity, that is for naught,
Wherein consisted all thy strength and safety?
To what I did thou shewdst me first the way.
But I to enemies reveal'd, and should not.
Nor shouldst thou have trusted that to woman's frailty:
E're I to thee, thou to thy self wast cruel.
Let weakness then with weakness come to parl
So near related, or the same, of kind,
Thine forgive mine; that men may censure thine

The gentler, if severely thou exact not
More strength from me, then in thy self was found.
And what if Love, which thou interpret'st hate,
The jealousie of Love, powerful of sway
In human hearts, nor less in mine towards thee,
Caus'd what I did? I saw thee mutable
Of fancy, feard lest one day thou wouldst leave me
As her at *Timna*, sought by all means therefore
How to endear, and hold thee to me firmest:
No better way I saw then by importuning
To learn thy secrets, get into my power
Thy key of strength and safety: thou wilt say,
Why then reveal'd? I was assur'd by those
Who tempted me, that nothing was design'd
Against thee but safe custody, and hold:
That made for me, I knew that liberty
Would draw thee forth to perilous enterprises,
While I at home sate full of cares and fears
Wailing thy absence in my widow'd bed;
Here I should still enjoy thee day and night
Mine and Love's prisoner, not the *Philistines*,
Whole to my self, unhazarded abroad,
Fearless at home, of partners in my love.
These reasons in Love's law have past for good,
Though fond and reasonless to some perhaps;
And Love hath oft, well meaning, wrought much wo,
Yet always pity or pardon hath obtain'd.
Be not unlike all others, not austere
As thou art strong, inflexible as steel.
If thou in strength all mortals dost exceed,
In uncompassionate anger do not so.

JOHN ASHBERY
Excerpt from *A Wave*

One idea is enough to organize a life and project it
Into unusual but viable forms, but many ideas merely
Lead one thither into a morass of their own good intentions.
Think how many the average person has during the course of a day,
    or night,
So that they become a luminous backdrop to ever-repeated
Gestures, having no life of their own, but only echoing
The suspicions of their possessor. It's fun to scratch around

And maybe come up with something. But for the tender blur
Of the setting to mean something, words must be ejected bodily,
A certain crispness be avoided in favor of a density
Of strutted opinion doomed to wilt in oblivion: not too linear
Nor yet too puffed and remote. Then the advantage of
Sinking in oneself, crashing through the skylight of one's own
Received opinions redirects the maze, setting up significant
Erections of its own at chosen corners, like gibbets,
And through this the mesmerizing plan of the landscape becomes,
At last, apparent. It is no more a landscape than a golf course is,
Though sensibly a few natural bonuses have been left in. And as it
Focuses itself, it is the backward part of a life that is
Partially coming into view. It's there, like a limb. And the issue
Of making sense becomes such a far-off one. Isn't this "sense"—
This little of my life that I can see—that answers me
Like a dog, and wags its tail, though excitement and fidelity are
About all that ever gets expressed? What did I ever do
To want to wander over into something else, an explanation
Of how I behaved, for instance, when knowing can have this
Sublime rind of excitement, like the shore of a lake in the desert
Blazing with the sunset? So that if it pleases all my constructions
To collapse, I shall at least have had that satisfaction, and known
That it need not be permanent in order to stay alive,
Beaming, confounding with the spell of its good manners.

ELIZABETH BISHOP
Excerpt from *Crusoe in England*

When all the gulls flew up at once, they sounded
like a big tree in a strong wind, its leaves.
I'd shut my eyes and think about a tree,
an oak, say, with real shade, somewhere.
I'd heard of cattle getting island-sick.
I thought the goats were.
One billy-goat would stand on the volcano
I'd christened *Mont d'Espoir* or *Mount Despair*
(I'd time enough to play with names),
and bleat and bleat, and sniff the air.
I'd grab his beard and look at him.
His pupils, horizontal, narrowed up
and expressed nothing, or a little malice.
I got so tired of the very colors!
One day I dyed a baby goat bright red

with my red berries, just to see
something a little different.
And then his mother wouldn't recognize him.

Dreams were the worst. Of course I dreamed of food
and love, but they were pleasant rather
than otherwise. But then I'd dream of things
like slitting a baby's throat, mistaking it
for a baby goat. I'd have
nightmares of other islands
stretching away from mine, infinities
of islands, islands spawning islands,
like frogs' eggs turning into polliwogs
of islands, knowing that I had to live
on each and every one, eventually,
for ages, registering their flora,
their fauna, their geography.

Just when I thought I couldn't stand it
another minute longer, Friday came.
(Accounts of that have everything all wrong.)
Friday was nice.
Friday was nice, and we were friends.
If only he had been a woman!
I wanted to propagate my kind,
and so did he, I think, poor boy.
He'd pet the baby goats sometimes,
and race with them, or carry one around.
—Pretty to watch; he had a pretty body.

And then one day they came and took us off.

Media

The three poems I'd like to claim as my influences in the writing of *Media* (and most of the rest of my work) are all too long to cite in their entirety: John Milton's *Samson Agonistes*, John Ashbery's *A Wave*, and Elizabeth Bishop's *Crusoe in England*. I almost always write in longer forms. I write narrative, meditation—argument, really; it can't be done in a few lines, and sometimes the whole point is to go on a while anyway. So although I read and learn from a great many poets who are more lyrical or imagistic —or who just write shorter poems—the connections I could make between their work and mine would be difficult to explain and perhaps not as informative as the seemingly obvious points to be made about the relationship between long poems and my poem *Media,* which works as many of my longer poems do.

Samson Agonistes first influenced me as a doctoral student at the University of Houston, when I wrote a seminar paper on its prosody. The project required scanning that long poem in its entirety. I did it twice, to make sure; and there was a lot to make sure of in Milton's iambic variations, substitutions, and so-called "feminine" endings. It took a long time to complete the scansion, longer still to come up with a thesis and write the paper. But I learned how Milton worked lengthy syntactical structures and argument into pentameter lines whose metrical irregularities have a logic of their own. Because I was so close to the poem—scanning the lines and describing each one in the margins of my copy: how many feet, which ones inverted, which syllables elided, and so on—it seemed that it was the time itself, the hours devoted to scanning lines, that made the language so real yet so seemingly malleable, like clay that could be fired into bricks, notched and mortared into a wall, solid as a poem. I saw, as if for the first time, parts of speech, grammar, syntax, the line as a unit, line breaks, enjambment. I saw how a line is built. That exercise influenced everything that I have written since. If nothing else, the project made me measurably more confident about rhythm and its Miltonic subtleties—not a bad way for a poet to feel even if she's not interested in making her own poems adhere to such rigid formal structures.

I chose to excerpt a passage in which Samson accuses Dalila. The choice of that accusation and her response is my idea of a joke about Milton's characterization of gender: it is still a wonder to me that the meter de-accentuates the "lie" in the middle of her name. But I don't mean that it's funny. In fact, it is infuriating to understand that the argument between Samson and Dalila recurs even today, and that the story of Samson and Dalila is part of the reason why. There's no question that Milton understands the familiar terms and positions of this argument: that men don't stay at home enough, don't care enough about women and love, are forever fascinated by stamping the world with their mark in public ways, and, finally, that women who seek to keep men at home are actively treacherous and should be punished with far more severe force than women use against men. Milton understands, as well, that women, finding their wishes circumscribed, are susceptible to manipulations from outside, which only seems to confirm what men fear about women in the first place. Every now and then, someone observes this understanding in Milton and attempts to argue that he was a "feminist" of sorts. Surely those people are simply out of their minds.

I don't think of myself as influenced by other writers at all in the sense of being "changed" or "shaped" or "ordered": the subjects I write about are drawn from my own experience, even if it's the experience of something I have read or heard in conversation. That assertion may seem in one way naïve and in another paradoxical. But the nature of my experience has left me bereft of whatever naïveté I might have preferred to retain and has put in its place political paradoxes that I had to learn to think clearly about, like a surgeon separating twins born sharing one skull. Recalling my education as a poet, I have a sense of myself trying to get handy enough with the control of form to shoehorn my ideas and clumsy language into something that could pass muster as "poetry." That's one reason why Milton became important for me as a formal "master."

But *Media* looks a lot less like *Samson Agonistes* than it does *A Wave* by John Ashbery. The passage I've quoted for the purposes of this essay deals specifically with thought and expresses it as a "luminous backdrop to ever-repeated gestures." Both formally—in its line length and its willingness to move freely in a more discursive mode—and in subject and tone —in the ironic self-referentiality that Ashbery is known for—I see a relationship between this poem and *Media*. The optical illusion of a tunnel in a mountainside that drivers crash into over and over, a repeated death experienced by the "I" in *Media*—I won't say "speaker" because the "I" in this poem understands the possibility of her extinction too much to care especially about such classroom-as-parlor etiquette—echoes Ashbery's rendition of thought itself, characterized here in deflatingly ironic terms, as a kind of structure that could be violently dismantled and transformed into a series of partial realizations and manifestations:

> Then the advantage of
> Sinking in oneself, crashing through the skylight of one's own
> Received opinions redirects the maze, setting up significant
> Erections of its own at chosen corners, like gibbets,
> And through this the mesmerizing plan of the landscape becomes,

At last, apparent. It is no more a landscape than a golf course is,
Though sensibly a few natural bonuses have been left in. And as it
Focuses itself, it is the backward part of a life that is
Partially coming into view. It's there, like a limb.

In his handling of an abundance of ideas as a backdrop or landscape, Ashbery switches from one image to another. I do less of this with my false tunnel, a metaphor for obsessively self-destructive ideas that become obsessively self-destructive actions. But the urge to describe thought in terms of an illusory "landscape" is much the same. So is the pressure to expand the line so that it contains an excessive volume of words. Yet the words are chosen generously, not randomly, and, in my case, on the assumption that to communicate ideas and their emotional resonances, only generosity will do. What I'm calling "emotional resonances" are seemingly more important to most of my work than to most of Ashbery's. However, in *Media,* I think I've distanced the speaker—that is, me, since the "I" who is speaking this essay rejects the assumption that one must speak of "speakers" to understand or practice the concept of "distance"—from emotion, and the reader as well, in much the same way Ashbery does. Passing the metaphorical baton often and swiftly can alter the reader's perspective on the emotional action, if only because having to "think" about what one is "feeling" in order to feel it at all tends to cool everything down a few degrees and to isolate the irony inherent in that action.

I've saved Elizabeth Bishop for last because I have the most ambivalent —and most intense—relationship with her work; and I know exactly why, too. To be a young woman who wants to be a poet, reading the male poets, sitting in workshops run by male poets, taking the ideas and the craft very seriously but hesitating to point out the obvious in class or even sometimes in your own thoughts is to play what appears to be a "man's game." Oh, I'm going back a few years now, not that many, really, less than fifteen, though now I run workshops myself and we do talk about women poets —and sometimes I'm even taken to task for discussing the dead white males too much. But I notice that most magazines still publish more men than women, more men's books get reviewed, and there's a noticeable difference in the way people talk about the poets of the two (is that all?) genders. For the most part, we still make stereotypical assumptions about the sexes, and if I feel ambivalent about Elizabeth Bishop, it's likely for the same reason I felt ambivalent about my mother. Women of the past often seem, to later generations of women, inhibited or held back, no matter how well they worked within the limitations they faced. When I read Bishop I feel tremendously glad that she has been such an obvious influence on virtually every poet who came after her, the men as well as the women, but also a little annoyed that someone with all that ability didn't use it to bring more attention to the social realities that limited someone of even her powers. I don't mean to imply that I can guess or know that what mattered to Bishop would be the same as what matters to me "as a woman" or that there are necessary and essential subjects for women poets. But I do recognize that if experience is shaped by possibility, then the experience of women is shaped by the possibilities available to them in a world ordered by men. Imagination may offer a release from the limitations of worldly experience, but it can't and probably shouldn't totally evade a world in which a narrowly defined order has remained all too much the norm for everyone and in which distinctions in individual lives and attitudes are thought to happen against that backdrop. I am referring to that rumbling against women poets who do deal specifically with so-called "women's issues": I've even heard the term "chick poem." That rumbling makes me wonder if it's easy for everyone to embrace Bishop's work because she's one woman who doesn't make us face those issues, who doesn't incite those rumblings or solicit responses to them. In that way she can seem to prove, to those with a secret antifeminist agenda, that women really don't need to remind us of those issues and experiences, or that practice of a precise craft can leave aside the discussion of gender and sexuality that makes so many of us uneasy. I dislike making that kind of remark, since I don't wish to be misunderstood as unrealistically critical of Bishop; I mean rather to invite a more self-critical attitude in Bishop's readers, including, of course, myself.

Crusoe in England has always resonated most for me among all of Bishop's poems. I first read it when I was still an undergraduate, and I rather dismissively wondered why a woman would want to occupy a man imaginatively at all. Nonetheless, it seemed significant that the man was Crusoe and that he clearly feels something deeper and more voluptuous for Friday than I ever understood him to feel when I read the novel. Now the poem seems to me a code or, rather, a code within a code and a code for women only. It seems to designate the boundaries of what we can say about the social limitations imposed on us—and not necessarily imposed by men, since part of the constraint is to encourage women to enforce those limitations on themselves. Bishop, in all her poems, and especially in the "persona" of this fictional character, this cultural icon of male adventure and resourcefulness in the face of fear, loneliness, and crisis, reveals how gracefully poetry seems to yield itself to such a male voice. Yet in this poem it is hard to overlook the parallel between Crusoe's isolation and the isolation of the woman poet, especially since Bishop's fascination with the clarity and specificity of every object the world has to offer correlates to Crusoe's observations. I know Crusoe's dream of being made to live on island after island, examining every last item of flora and fauna, in an exile so complete that it only takes a little human companionship to make it bearable. Questions of sexual preference further complicate Bishop's rendition of Crusoe, namely his fondness for Friday; and it is interesting that Crusoe wishes him a woman. It would be simplistic to assume a direct correlation between the poet and the speaker, as if Bishop were somehow "cross-dressing" in *Crusoe in England;* yet in another way it would be worse not to, assuming a naïve relationship between author and fictional character.

When I wrote *Media,* very little of what I've said here was conscious in my thoughts. I was only caught up in my frustrations of the moment: the upset that had made me try to get my friend on the phone in the first place; the need to be told I was right in my thinking by someone who trusts my judgment. Unable to get my first choice, I sat down to write a poem. Writing is another way I remind myself that I know what I'm doing, that I'm "right," despite what others might believe. That's "mastery," isn't it? To be good enough at something that performing it is a way of reminding oneself that one is "right," "good," worthy of staying alive and of being taken seriously? I've taken my time; I've studied; I've remembered and forgotten; I've stored away a lot of details that no longer have to "occur" to me in order to inform my thinking. And now, for me, writing poetry masterfully is like driving a car or riding a horse: it's complex and subtle, and no matter how good you are, you have to keep working to get better or you start getting worse. The first line of *Media* is long because it's a sentence, a "mouthful." The conversational tone, similar to—given permission by—*Crusoe in England,* is established in the phrase "keep trying to get": "get" is a word I won't use in a poem unless it's embedded in a conversational idiom, and it appears in the section of *Crusoe* I've excerpted as well. "Pretty soon," at the beginning of line 2, gets me deeper into the conversational. Once I established that conversational tone, and it was established by line 2, I can't say I had problems to resolve in the writing of *Media*. I was simply wounded by the events of the day and frustrated at not being able to talk about them or my loneliness. That made me even angrier. The absurdity of it made me angry; it made me think of dirty tricks, of my own meanness, my calling women "desperate" because they reminded me of my own dread of isolation. What an absurd fate, what a mockery of my own idea it would be if someone designed and constructed a highway to lead into a false tunnel, all those drivers seduced into believing they're going into a safe place, believing that they'll emerge in the light on the other side, but it's a ruse, they die, they pile up, there in the mountains where maybe nobody will even find the bodies. . . . When I wrote *Media* I wasn't thinking consciously of what parts of speech to use or what parts of speech to break lines on or where in the lines to place the caesurae or how often to move to metaphor or image. In my rush to say what was bothering me, to put a shape to it, to finish it off the way I wanted it for once, I also couldn't stay pleased for long with any particular word or phrase. It was only later that night when I'd finished a draft that I realized I liked it. It's shorter than most of my work, but it moves in much the same way, with a frame, a series of images, and a lengthy metaphor for thought that seems to me not "taken from" Ashbery but perhaps given permission by his poem to exist. There are poets who consciously strive to imitate in order to learn, as I enjoyed learning from *Samson Agonistes,* and who write with other people's poems on the desk beside them. I can see all sorts of good reasons for such exercises. But I've never performed them myself.

"Mastery" is not a word that I use readily to describe what I do, at least not in public, where I fear I would be taken too seriously, like someone who wants to be elected President. But if "mastery" means anything in practical terms about my attitude and work as a poet, it describes my sense when writing—or, at least, when writing well—that I have the luxury to pay as much attention to what I'm saying as to how I'm saying it. "Mastery" is an ability to handle the language and the imagined experience in the poem; it is the poet's ability to say what she wants in such a heightened way that the reader is induced to join with her in the experience of the poem. It's a tall order; or maybe it's just that the word, "mastery," makes me think it is. I can't end this essay without remarking that I hardly feel that I can apply "mastery" to myself without making some kind of joke about it, since it describes a tradition that has not generally included "me." But despite my recognizable political loyalties, I am not one who would rid the world of the concept of "mastery." It's not inherently oppressive to recognize and respect expertise. The source of oppression lies elsewhere—in a failure to observe and acknowledge expertise in the "wrong" hands, for instance. I want to give credit for "mastery" where it is due, defining it, as I have above, as knowing what to do and when to do it, not all the time, but at least part of the time—a modest notion of "mastery," perhaps, but a realistic one.

LAURENCE LIEBERMAN

Laurence Lieberman was born in Detroit, Michigan, in 1935. He was a double major in English and pre-med at the University of Michigan and studied medicine briefly, choosing instead to pursue graduate work in English at the University of California at Berkeley. He taught at the College of the Virgin Islands for four years before moving to Urbana, Illinois, in 1968 to teach poetry writing. He has since remained with the University of Illinois as a professor in the department of English and as founding editor of the poetry books program at the University of Illinois Press. Lieberman frequently returns to the Caribbean, a region that informs much of his writing, to teach and to write. In 1986, he helped to found *Caribbean Writer* magazine. Lieberman has published twelve books of poetry, most recently *Compass of the Dying* (University of Arkansas Press, 1998), *The Regatta in the Skies* (University of Georgia Press, 1999), and *Flight from the Mother Stone* (University of Arkansas Press, 2000). He has written three books of criticism, including *The Achievement of James Dickey* (Scott, Foresman & Co., 1968) and *Beyond the Muse of Memory: Essays on Contemporary American Poets* (University of Missouri Press, 1995). Lieberman was awarded two recent grants for his ongoing cycle of poetry books dealing with Caribbean cultures: Associate in the Center for Advanced Study at the University of Illinois for the Fall 2000, and a Fellowship in a Second Discipline for Spring and Fall of 2001. He and his wife, Bernice, have three children, Deborah, Mira, and Isaac, and four grandchildren, Mariah, Dylan, Jesse, and Ayla.

Voice to Voice

The macaw does his full lineup of tricks
to please Chico. These two magic-
makers, man and bird,
have teamed up
before. You can read the glimmers of rapport
in their eye-
flash simpatico. When young Chico
hums a brief tune,
his feathered mimic chatters
back; tongue clicks

rouse like-sounding throaty squawks. Tuning
up, they could be an ensemble
of two instruments, as
far removed
as cello and bassoon, say, but the crazily mis-
matched voices
flirt with each other, toying
with near octaves.
Then, after many little shifts
of fine cueing,

they groove in sync. Chico signals by finger
wave, and the wide-faced parrot
(its owlish skull broader
than its wing-
folded torso) hops on jointed-twig toes across
the cyclone
fence cage mesh, twirls, and hangs
upside down. Next,
he wags that inverted oval
of wry face back

and forth, abrupt swings like the pendulum
of a Grandfather Clock. *Now dance,*
O dance, says glad Chico,

and Macaw
obeys, bobbing up and down, while revolving big
lowered beak
     in narrow circles—he keeps time
     with his mentor's
finger snaps, blithe shut-winged
live metronome

       dangled in place. His yellow stripes flare out,
         clashing wildly with his feathers'
               royal blue sheen, flamy
                  yellow bands
     circling his eyes. He shrieks joy from cage roost,
                 he and Chico
       intertwined in voice-to-voice relay
              act. It's a shared
         zingy high—man to bird margins
            wane and vanish. . . .

The Pull of the Sentence

When questioned about her "literary antecedents" in an interview, Marianne Moore's first spontaneous reply was—none, "so far as I know."[1] Certainly, she hadn't adopted her "style of writing" from any prior poets. When further pressed to consider whether any "prose stylists" had helped her to find her "poetic style," she promptly reversed her disavowal and rattled off a litany of quotes from Doctor Johnson, Edmund Burke, Sir Thomas Browne, Sir Francis Bacon, etc. It seemed as if all of these exemplars of best style were touchstones in the flow of her own compact prosody, drawn from an inexhaustible stockpile of succinct, exquisite writing, handily tucked away in her memory-vault. Her catalogue of mentors crested with an allusion to Henry James, who was in many ways her chief literary forbear: "In Henry James it is the essays and letters especially that affect me."[2] In her own brilliant essay, she declares James a most "characteristic American" and praises his mind for "reaching westward, southward, anywhere, everywhere . . . incapable of the shut door in any direction."[3] This passage resonates in the quote from James that ends her poem *New York:*

It is not the plunder,
but "accessibility to experience."[4]

Finally, when asked by Donald Hall in the same interview, "what is the rationale behind [your] syllabic verse?" she replied, somewhat cryptically, "I am governed by the pull of the sentence as the pull of a fabric is governed by gravity."[5]

Though I have been correctly targeted by critics and reviewers as a poet who often writes in stanza patterns that are syllabically arranged like those of Marianne Moore, perhaps a more significant common denominator between my work and hers would be a near-dogged preoccupation with "the pull of the sentence" across the intricately patterned verse mosaic to create a fabric of stanzas, so to say, and I suspect that my prosody —like Moore's—may well be grounded more in those enigmatic miracles of syntax that abound in the sweeping long sentences of Henry James's style than in any direct poet-ancestors. My own continuing fascination with the matchless long syntactical prodigies of "the Master" dates back to 1954 (a full year before I wrote my first poetry) when I took a class on Henry James taught by Austin Warren, to whom I later paid tribute in my poem of homage:

. . . Sentences of Henry James
He spoke inflated the unused ear of my mind like a third lung air
Found in my second wind of hearing a better place
To stream I took one step from hearing to breathing one
Step the trained ear flowering into voice
Shaking loose. . . .

Warren's recital of James's works proved spellbinding beyond measure, for the sensual contractions, dilations and oscillations of those serpentine clauses found a permanent niche in my mind's ear. To this day, it seems that I'm always swayed by the subliminal tugs, the nearly musculo-skeletal pulls, of those Jamesian sentences whenever I come to shaping the elaborate stanzas of my poems—eerily, those endlessly churning word-chains I first heard in Warren's vocalizations may have incised a permanent lodging in my nervous system.

To speak directly about the process of writing my poem *Voice to Voice,* I began by taking rather sketchy notes in an unlined, pocket-sized tablet that I carry with me whenever I travel. I usually work in this notebook at the end of a day of adventures, before retiring for the night. I wrote the first draft of the poem, poring over these notes, six or seven months after I returned home from my weeks of travel in Guyana. For some years, most of my early drafts for poems have been written in prose, or a very rough free verse with little attention paid to line or formal units of any kind. I tend to work at a number of first drafts with various pieces, in rotation, before I set about to carve out a shape for any one poem of the sequence. This poem was the last of a cycle of six short animal portraits that emerged from one afternoon visit to the Georgetown Zoo, escorted by my guide Chico.

In composing early prose drafts, I am on the alert for pockets of thickly textured or musically dense phrasing as well as little challenging knots of uncertain syntax that I know will take much sorting out and rearranging when I come to shape the poem into lines and stanzas. I may experiment with five or six stanzaic patterns before I hit upon the one syllabically arranged mix of lines that rings true for this particular welter of poetic raw materials. As I put one trial stanza after another to the test, I'm excitedly on the lookout for the one configuration of lines that may best enable me to solve the difficulties posed by what seem to be intractably long sentences that must be looped and interlaced about the stanzaic prototype. When I stumble upon a stanza that works, it seems to take off with a strange life of its own, as if it had been incipient in the rough gathering of unfocused words and clauses. But more often than not, it is the lumbering, entangled sentences that point the way to my choice of form. The pull of the cumbersome right sentence, like the pull of a shaman's divining rod, leads the way to my architecting of stanza shapes.

Now, it occurs to me that something of the normal drive and propulsion of prose, its energy and forward push, is retained by Moore's poetry (whether she writes in stanzas or free blocks of verse), and hopefully mine as well, since our aesthetic is so rooted in prose rhythms. Perhaps more on this account than the shared discipline of syllabics, I feel my debt to Marianne Moore's art most profoundly. Even so, I mustn't make light of my frequent practice of adapting syllabic stanza patterns roughly identical to Moore's in my poetry. I still recall the exhilaration, mixed with guilt, that

I felt when I completed my poem, *God's Measurements.* The poem describes my family's encounter with the Giant Buddha of Nara, Japan, and was my first work to transpose directly the essential stanza mold of my favorite masterwork in Moore's oeuvre, *The Pangolin,* a poem that begins as pure animal depiction and climaxes in an astonishing surprise portrait of Man, the human animal. The poem, following a familiar circuit from many of her most distinguished works, begins by scrutinizing a little-known exotic creature displaced from a remote foreign land and works its way round by deft surprise shifts to an utterly novel vision of our human nature. To borrow her form for the Buddha poem was my way of paying tribute. And my descriptive piece also sets out simply to picture the giant sculptured Ikon; although, shifting to a dialogue between myself and my small son, bestride my shoulders, about the precise nature and possible dimensions of God, our God, anyone's God, the poem ultimately addresses an awakening to the awesome spiritual responsibilities of fatherhood.

MARIANNE MOORE
The Buffalo

> Black in blazonry means
> prudence; and niger, unpropitious. Might
> hematite—
>   black, compactly incurved horns on bison
>   have significance? The
>   soot-brown tail-tuft on
>   a kind of lion-
>
>   tail; what would that express?
> And John Steuart Curry's Ajax pulling
> grass—no ring
>   in his nose—two birds standing on his back?
>
>   .   .   .   .   .   .
>
>   The modern
> ox does not look like the Augsburg ox's
> portrait. Yes,
>   the great extinct wild Aurochs was a beast
>   to paint, with stripe and six-

foot horn-spread—decreased
    to Siamese-cat-

    Brown Swiss size or zebu-
shape, with white plush dewlap and warm-blooded
hump; to red-
    skinned Hereford or to piebald Holstein. Yet
      some would say the sparse-haired
    buffalo has met
      human notions best—

    unlike the elephant,
both jewel and jeweller in the hairs
that he wears—
    no white-nosed Vermont ox yoked with its twin
      to haul the maple-sap,
    up to their knees in
      snow; no freakishly

    Over-Drove Ox drawn by
Rowlandson, but the Indian buffalo,
albino-
    footed, standing in a mud-lake with a
      day's work to do. No white
    Christian heathen, way-
      laid by the Buddha,

    serves him so well as the
buffalo—as mettlesome as if check-
reined—free neck
    stretching out, and snake tail in a half-twist
      on the flank; nor will so
    cheerfully assist
      the Sage sitting with

    feet at the same side, to
dismount at the shrine; nor are there any
ivory
    tusks like those two horns which when a tiger
      coughs, are lowered fiercely
    and convert the fur
      to harmless rubbish.

> The Indian buffalo,
> led by bare-leggèd herd-boys to a hay
> hut where they
> > stable it, need not fear comparison
> > > with bison, with the twins,
> > indeed with any
> > > of ox ancestry.

Marianne Moore's remarkable poem *The Buffalo* is yet another work in the bestiary mode of *The Pangolin;* it traces the historic ancestry of all modern oxen back to the ancient European aurochs. She surveys several species of bison from a range of countries and historic eras, pointing, at last, to the American Indian buffalo, which she finds cause to prize among all of its ancestral species (it "need not fear comparison/ . . . with any/ of ox ancestry"). She composed this piece by brooding over a multifarious array of oxen as depicted in paintings in historic museums, photos in newspaper clippings, woodcuts, lithographs, ceramic seals from India, and the writings of the nineteenth-century American travel author Bayard Taylor. Her ardent sense of cultural partisanship, an oblique form of American patriotism, is the point of arrival—as if to suggest that an artist best proves his or her national loyalty by having toured afar and returned to home base reinvigorated to espouse and praise local heroes. Thus, her apotheosizing of our indigenous buffalo. Her favorite compatriots, James, Eliot, and Pound, had paid their dues by putting in their most seminal years of artistic fruition abroad, while Moore's chief travels were restricted to a few foreign zoos and local libraries.

A couple of Moore's better commentators have singled out the buffalo poem as one of those exquisite syllabic constructs in which the workings of her form—visual as well as rhythmical—seem most poignantly to express the subject. I wholly concur with that assessment. In my poem *Voice to Voice,* too, I believe that the visual mosaic of stanzas helps to express—to articulate in a swirling of pieces—the subject, and especially the movements of the macaw.

In her foreword to the 1961 *Reader* she compiled of her poetry and prose works, Marianne Moore replies to a question often addressed to her: "Why an inordinate interest in animals and athletes? . . . They are subjects for art and *exemplars* [my italics] of it, are they not?" Like many of her other animal personae, her favorite ox—the American buffalo—is portrayed as an artist-exemplar of sorts. And so, too, is my "magic-maker," the macaw. The bird is more the accomplished artist, Chico perhaps only the accompanist.

Moore's stanza form in this poem is one I find to be especially supple and arresting. The succession of such stanzas revolving down the page enhances the illusion that these oxen drawn from various historical and geographical sites are marching across the poetry screen in lively series. The geometric stanza shape, roughly a three-quarters moon configuration, may seem to resemble an ox's head, open-mouthed and chewing to one side. (My own variation on this stanza unit appears in my poem *Swimming Pool Pastoral,* which depicts a cow falling into a hotel's unfenced outdoor pool near a pasture in Antigua.)

Far more relevant to the buffalo poem's innovative structure than the visual shape of the stanza, I feel, is the interweaving of the long periodic sentences around the line grids. The syntax is like musculature, and the punctuation of those long sentences, highlighted by the frequent shrewd timing of semicolons, suggests the indomitable force of hereditary succession in animal species, the unstoppable unfolding across time of new species built upon old. The momentum of this unbroken genetic lineage is driven home by Moore's habit of letting the ongoing clause charge across all of the breaks between stanzas. The units are cemented together in multi-linked series, and the stanza breaks operate more as hinges or bridgework in the syntactical chain rather than as the conventional hiatus between units. This effect of the sentence dominating the stanzas, the sentence *pulling* its weight across and between the units alike, is intensified by the single monosyllabic words that begin those long sentences, dangling at the end of a line, as in stanza 3, line 3 ("Yes"), stanza 4, line 4 ("Yet") and stanza 6, line 5 ("No white"). The sharp break with this pattern comes in the final unit, the only unit in the poem in which the sentence is coterminous with the stanza. The American Indian buffalo is now compacted into this one last stanza sentence as if to emphasize, by implication of style, that this species of oxen has somehow managed to gather up the many diverse strengths of its ancestors into the one most noble stock, the stock that "has met/ human notions best." And thus, here we see how *the pull of the sentence* has commandeered the weave of this verse fabric.

Likewise, in my poem *Voice to Voice,* I feel that the vivacity of the syllabic unit really comes into its own in stanzas 3 and 4, where the two long sentences that describe the dance of the macaw about the "cyclone/ fence cage mesh" become most naturally intermingled with the full skeletal graph of the verse units. The sentence wraps itself around the stanzaic maze like vines: the sinuous wave-motion of varying long and short lines seems to mimic, stylistically, the macaw's "jointed-twig toes" curling upon the bars of cage wire. Thereby, my weavings of sentence syntax around the line matrix—the word grids—from stanza to stanza do appear to express the action of my subject. The silhouettes of the stanzas form units like the geometric floats of a Calder mobile; the stanzas themselves waggle and sashay through the poem like the struts of a dancing bird.

How, then, does my form as a whole articulate the poem's content? Perhaps the alternating right-justified and left-justified stanzas may suggest the lead voice tossed back and forth between man and bird. Mirror-image stanza forms, like ego and alter-ego, evoke the mystery of antiphonal voices which grow before our eyes to resemble each other more and more, until they merge in a surprise communion. Both sound and sight—the syncopation of syllabic rhythm and the visual impact of the mirror-image pairings of stanzas—drive home the message. (To be sure, it's nothing quite so direct as conforming the shape of the stanza to the physical subject, the typographical realism, so trendy in the sixties and seventies, of concrete poetry.)

To speak of the comparative pace of delivery in Moore's poem versus mine, *The Buffalo* proceeds with the halting stop-and-go rhythm of a meditative discourse. Her taut and chiseled measure allows for frequent pauses to reflect on the evolution of species. Slow ruminations of intellect are perhaps a characteristic timbre for this writer. *Voice to Voice*, in contrast, sprints across the field of action to make its narrative canvas. My stanza line-flux is a fluent, springy medium which, from time to time, approaches the slack and easy measures of common speech, a pitch of voice and fleetness of cadence that perhaps tilts more toward the lithe prosody, say, of a poem like D. H. Lawrence's *Butterfly*.

D. H. LAWRENCE
Butterfly

Butterfly, the wind blows sea-ward, strong beyond the garden wall!
Butterfly, why do you settle on my shoe, and sip the dirt on my shoe,

Lifting your veined wings, lifting them? big white butterfly!

Already it is October, and the wind blows strong to the sea
from the hills where snow must have fallen, the wind is polished with
    snow.
Here in the garden, with red geraniums, it is warm, it is warm
but the wind blows strong to sea-ward, white butterfly, content on my
    shoe!

Will you go, will you go from my warm house?
Will you climb on your big soft wings, black-dotted,
as up an invisible rainbow, an arch
till the wind slides you sheer from the arch-crest
and in a strange level fluttering you go out to sea-ward, white speck!

Farewell, farewell, lost soul!
you have melted in the crystalline distance,
it is enough! I saw you vanish into air.

Lawrence was the first master of works portraying animals with ut-
most fidelity to the singular traits of each living creature. Virtually all the
best animal poems in the language of our time owe an obvious debt to
him, from Kinnell's *Bear* to Roethke's *Meadow Mouse* to Dickey's *Sheep
Child*. Lawrence's best poems in the genre have achieved the status of
enduring classics: *Snake, Tortoise Shout, Whales Weep Not*. But even the
more modest scale of *Butterfly* exhibits the relish this author takes in dis-
covering the innate beauties of each animal species he encounters and in
enthralling the reader with these luminous details.

In the graceful, tender poem *Butterfly,* Lawrence addresses a personal
chant, almost a missive, to the lovely winged being that has, auspiciously,
landed on his shoe. All of the lines are beautiful clean strokes of rhythm.
Lawrence's spare, lean style is so light of touch, so natural in its litany of
repetitions, it could be pacing the flaps of those butterfly wings: "Will you
go. . . . Will you climb. . . . Farewell, farewell, lost soul!" Lawrence's medium
is streamlined, pared down to barest essentials. The near-weightlessness
of the insect is mirrored by the buoyant surge of the lines; and the plain
transparency of language captures the essence, the velvety softness, of those
"veined" see-through wings. In so gentle a voice, in the easy lilt of its
cadence, we can almost hear the creature "sip the dirt on my shoe."

This poetry not only describes the butterfly's delicate moves—its progress, wind-tossed, from the shoe out to sea—it simultaneously enacts those motions with its suppleness of verse rhythms. The wavelike undulations of Lawrence's free verse tellingly express the shuffling to-and-fro flight of the butterfly, and, indeed, this painterly author loves to evoke the complex physical actions of animals with his rhythm and syntax, even transcribing the sexual interactions of mating goats, tortoises, whales. His handling of the subtle variations in line length, swerves in phrasing, and surprise shifts of caesuras are all modulated to keep pace with the creature's physical processes. Frame by frame, each phase of the action is highlighted, as in a movie. Lawrence's animal depictions more closely approach the art of film than any other poet of his period. In *Butterfly,* the most striking example of this power to suggest intricate or sudden body movements with his versification is the finish of the third stanza:

> Will you climb on your big soft wings, black-dotted,
> as up an invisible rainbow, an arch
> till the wind slides you sheer from the arch-crest
> and in a strange level fluttering you go out to sea-ward, white speck!

These lines seem to weave a zigzag counterpoint like the wind-pocket that suddenly propels the winged "white speck" in a violent upsweep. The last two lines release the tightly coiled energy like a verse slingshot, and the reader can sense those helpless wings "fluttering" in the wind that carries them off.

In my poem, perhaps I most follow Lawrence's lead in exploring a language that limns the singular macaw. I take from Lawrence the interest in capturing the very thrust of the animal's movements with verse rhythms and musical turns of phrase. Despite my boxy verse diagrams, the patterned skeletal word grids, I like to think that I approach a Lawrentian teetering on the verge of rhythmic sprawl, hopefully tucked up and reined in by the network of line breaks and somewhat porous stanza overflow. Though he crafts in free verse and I work with formal syllabic units, the flow of my cadence, like his, aspires to the swift tempo of a speaking voice and the pace of the physical body, a tempo I hope will transcribe into the line graph of my stanzas the illusion that the living bird twists and flutters before a reader's eyes.

Perhaps no other modern poet more openly proselytized the strategy of stealing from other poets than Theodore Roethke. In his essay "How to Write Like Somebody Else," he formulates a method of successful versus failed thieveries.[6] Mastery, as he defines it, is not so much a matter of hiding your debts to other writers, your *influences,* as one perhaps of pushing far enough into the other poet's labyrinth of visions and devices to come out the other side with a unique idiom, as if by occult metamorphosis. Perhaps Roethke could afford to be more overt and shameless in his thefts than others, since his signature of stylistic originality was never in doubt, from early on in his career. Imitating the masters as a formal mode—not just in apprenticeship, but throughout one's life—was surely at the core of Roethke's practice of teaching, and since the roster of his students includes many wonderful poets, James Wright, Richard Hugo, Carolyn Kizer, and David Wagoner among them, his explicit pedagogy for teaching both one-self and students cannot be easily discounted. In the text of his most am-bitious poems, he would digress to cry out for help from a mentor ("Be with me, Whitman, maker of catalogues")[7] or to slyly confess his literary pilferings ("I take this cadence from a man named Yeats;/ I take it, and I give it back again:/ For other tunes and other wanton beats/ Have tossed my heart and fiddled through my brain").[8] In his essay he shrewdly dis-claims Yeats's influence on this poem, partly to disarm any over-zealous critic–detective, but also to emphasize that an authentic writer subtly braids multiple influences into a work. As a reader of Roethke, I've come to dis-cern that he struggled with the style of each author-mentor in phases, milking each one for all he's worth. I count Eliot, Dylan Thomas, Lawrence, Whitman, and Yeats chief among those recognizably percolating in Roethke's most mature work.

THEODORE ROETHKE
The Geranium

When I put her out, once, by the garbage pail,
She looked so limp and bedraggled,
So foolish and trusting, like a sick poodle,
Or a wizened aster in late September,
I brought her back in again
For a new routine—
Vitamins, water, and whatever

Sustenance seemed sensible
At the time: she'd lived
So long on gin, bobbie pins, half-smoked cigars, dead beer,
Her shriveled petals falling
On the faded carpet, the stale
Steak grease stuck to her fuzzy leaves,
(Dried-out, she creaked like a tulip.)

The things she endured!—
The dumb dames shrieking half the night
Or the two of us, alone, both seedy,
Me breathing booze at her,
She leaning out of her pot toward the window.

Near the end, she seemed almost to hear me—
And that was scary—
So when the snuffling cretin of a maid
Threw her, pot and all, into the trash-can,
I said nothing.

But I sacked the presumptuous hag the next week,
I was that lonely.

We cannot approach a tragicomic poem like *The Geranium* without taking into account Roethke's childhood absorption in the greenhouses kept by his father, Otto. Indeed, Roethke first struck out for greatness, arguably, in his pungent early lyrics that hint at the ghostly near-human otherness lurking in flowers, plants, even moss, or a gardener's "cuttings" for transplant, works justly celebrated by Kenneth Burke's brilliant essay coining the catchword phrase "vegetal radicalism," later echoed by "magical realism" in describing the visionary hyperreality of Marquez and other South American novelists.[9] Given this mystical backdrop, we may ascribe full credulity to the speaker, who treats the final days of his relationship to the potted geranium, "limp and bedraggled," as a romantic love affair. The geranium is a larger-than-plantlife persona who comes, more and more, to resemble her companion's sickly and aging mistress. For all its overtones of parody, its witty burlesque parade of images, this work may be apprehended as no less a true love poem than Shakespeare's *My Mistress' Eyes Are Nothing Like the Sun*. Love poems to flowers, as well as those to birds, are genuinely erotic for Roethke. *All Morning*, his Whitmanesque catalogue of favorite birds near his home in Seattle, is surely one of his most enduringly eloquent love poems. *The Geranium,* though far less ambitious a work, is perhaps unique in Roethke's oeuvre in its full personification of plant as paramour.

My piece *Voice to Voice,* too, is a love poem of sorts, in its commingling of twin spirits, human and animal. But more relevant to my poem, perhaps, is the spooky moment near the finish when Roethke writes that the geranium "seemed almost to hear me." The flower is invested with a haunting extrasensory power that may carry over into the near-human receptivity of the macaw in my work. Both poems explore a subtly varied interchange between human and non-human life forms verging on an eerie and supernatural dimension.

Roethke's humor is expressively deployed in a rich assortment of details describing the grungy dross of the man's life spattered in layers upon the plant's leaves and petals, the geranium pot's having been relegated to the lowly status of ashtray, wastebasket, or spittoon. Man and flower, via these hybridizing images, seem to be engaged in a collaborative descent into squalor and decadence; together, they resemble an old couple fallen into chronic alcoholism.

While comic verve and wit dominate the main trajectory of the work, the poem's wry trance accrues in the hallucinatory clarity of its details, which suggest as much by their musical overtones as by their realistic portrayal of the ghostly intermingling of human and plant lives. Roethke's luminous intensity in rendering these details was a powerful influence on the detail-work in my poem. I came to believe in the language of preternaturally sharp and clear observation. Just the vivid outlines of the thing itself, drawn in heightened relief and described with lucidity, might hint of a magical world that resonates in sensual particulars. Roethke's piercingly raw and memorable details, then, are the single aspect of his poems that inspired me to trust the graphic picturing of Chico and the macaw going through their stagy routines together in *Voice to Voice.*

When I first came to read Hart Crane, I was struck by the flashes of wildly vivid language, exotic words and phrases that leapt from the page and boldly translated pictures of the modern city—machinery, buildings, auto traffic, bridges—with a clarity and immediacy that verged on the sudden closeness of photographs. The language, though novel and unfamiliar at first hearing, seemed to capture the feel and texture of everyday city objects and scenes with amazing freshness and utter verisimilitude. The flair and tactility of this vocabulary recalled Hopkins and Keats, but it added its own unique patina of grittiness: the soot and ash and rust and grime of the mechanized workplace seemed to cling to the words like mildew. This language reeked of the subway, the aircraft hangar, the factory, the ghetto as no poetry before it had done, hence the rough-hewn glistening majesty of *The Bridge.*

Crane grafted an equally new-minted idiom, this one palpitating and visceral, onto the classic pentameters of his groundbreaking sea poems, *Voyages.* These compact and hypersensory fantasias were the single most imposing precursors for my cycle of poems exploring the underwater world of the coral reefs. Certainly, my poetry of skin diving and spearfishing in the West Indies drew more lavishly on Crane's influence than Walcott's, though Marquez's fiction would later become for me a prodigal guide and model.

HART CRANE
The Air Plant
Grand Cayman

This tuft that thrives on saline nothingness,
Inverted octopus with heavenward arms
Thrust parching from a palm-bole hard by the cove—
A bird almost—of almost bird alarms,

Is pulmonary to the wind that jars
Its tentacles, horrific in their lurch.
The lizard's throat, held bloated for a fly,
Balloons but warily from this throbbing perch.

The needles and hack-saws of cactus bleed
A milk of earth when stricken off the stalk;
But this,—defenseless, thornless, sheds no blood,
Almost no shadow—but the air's thin talk.

Angelic Dynamo! Ventriloquist of the Blue!
While beachward creeps the shark-swept Spanish Main
By what conjunctions do the winds appoint
Its apotheosis, at last—the hurricane!

The setting for Crane's poem and mine may suggest other crossover links and parallels. We'd both taken repeated voyages to the Caribbean and South America prior to crafting these brief descriptive lyrics. Crane had most recently been subjected to a fierce life-threatening hurricane while visiting his grandmother's plantation on the Isle of Pines, and he evidently wrote this piece and others in a state of manic joy after having survived the havoc of the storm. He also found the hurricane a fitting emblem for psychic storms that ravaged him. I, on the other hand, had forsaken a long-planned speedboat trip down rivers in Guyana's interior, my safari derailed by a bout of dysentery, and confined my wayfaring that day to a visit to the Georgetown Zoo, accompanied by my native guide Chico. An ex-farmer, he had a remarkable *simpático* with many of the indigenous caged animals: snakes, monkeys, wildcats, birds, etc. *Voice to Voice* is part of a continuing cycle of poems about the zoo animals I encountered that day.

Various images in Crane's poems such as *The Air Plant* and *Voyages* provided leverage for my image-making strategy in a number of recent poems dealing with Caribbean wildlife. The most prodigious and compelling images in Crane's island and sea poems are those which seem to salute the living entity—whether plant, animal, or the ocean itself—in its perceived totality, as if rediscovered in pristine grandeur by the witnessing eye of the poet:

> —And yet this great wink of eternity,
> Of rimless floods, unfettered leewardings . . .
> Take this Sea, whose diapason knells
> On scrolls of silver snowy sentences. . . .
> (from *Voyages, II*)

> This tuft that thrives on saline nothingness,
> Inverted octopus with heavenward arms . . .

> Angelic Dynamo! Ventriloquist of the Blue!
> (from *The Air Plant*)

Whereas in the sea poems, brief passages of literal description are quickly superseded by visionary leaps and songlike rhapsodizing, in *The Air Plant,* the poet's eye stays riveted to the fascinating details of botanical exotica, and Crane's direct observation of nature retains the upper hand until the ecstatic outcries and revelation of the final stanza. In this poem, particularly, Crane was sufficiently beguiled by the actual particulars of the living organism to hold in reserve his accustomed impulse to reach for a symbolic mythos. The image of the parasitic and seemingly ethereal air plant, a medium through which the powerful gusts of a hurricane may pass without dismembering its tentacled shape, comes to embody the limitless power of human imagination surging through the meager vessel of a poet's brain and nervous system.

This work feels much more akin to my own recent practice than Crane's usual mystical pitch. In my poem, perhaps I catch some of Crane's childlike awe in the sheer act of observation. Though *Voice to Voice* is, provisionally, a linear narrative of events, my images are arranged spatially as well, and the visual seesawing of the stanza form gives the scenic gyrations predominance over the temporal structure. A second level of my story, if you will, is playing itself out through the unfolding of picture and process. In both *The Air Plant* and *Voice to Voice,* a consecutive chain of images generates the central drama. Both works are plainly descriptive, but Crane's piece hits the reader's ear as a metaphor from the start, while my poem may seem merely one-dimensional and storyish in the opening stanza or so. Crane's language is far more innovative, his line texture more densely compact, yet I feel that the true subject of both works is the visionary or extrasensory underpinning of overt sensory details and events. Each poem, in its way, moves into the Beyond by finding roots of the timeless, the eternal, in plainly observed concrete facts.

Finally, I seem to take fire from Crane's eclectic, hybrid images and from his swift and adroit shifts between plant, animal, and human traits. His metaphoric image-leaps are masterful and unrestrained. The plant is an "inverted octopus" and "a bird" by turns: the first a visual parallel, the second an uncanny overlapping of nervous systems ("of almost bird alarms"). The plant "tentacles" are like human bronchial tubes, as the air plant seems to breathe like a human ("pulmonary to the wind"); and then, too, the human metaphor invests the plant with the power of speech ("the air's thin talk . . . Ventriloquist of the Blue"). Somewhat comically, though, Crane faults the plant for its failure to feel wounds as an animal might, for it "sheds no blood." If it seems to have lungs, to draw breath, why not a heart and blood vessels and circulatory system as well? Following Crane's lead, I risk a wide spectrum of images, playing freely over a field that includes musical instruments, the pendulum of a clock, a metronome, and hybrids of bird and plant ("hops on jointed-twig toes").

In its final stanza, Crane's poem *The Air Plant* sweeps from the literal to the symbolic, from the physical attributes of the plant to a spiritual ascension. My work runs a narrower gamut, shifting from vocal images to physical gyrations, from song to dance, from ear to eye in a kind of birdy pyrotechnics; the range of my narrator's perspective never strays very far from sense perception. In fact, the full color portrait of bird-persona is saved for the last stanza. The deeply mysterious interplay and communion between Guyanese man and macaw, whose beings are "intertwined" in the final lines, perhaps draws more on my readings of Lawrence and Roethke than any glimmerings drawn from Hart Crane.

THOMAS LUX

Thomas Lux is Director of the M.F.A. Program in Poetry at Sarah Lawrence College, where he has taught since 1975. He is the author of *The Glassblower's Breath* (Cleveland State University Poetry Center, 1976), and *Sunday* (1979), *Half Promised Land* (1986), *The Drowned River* (1990), *Split Horizon* (1994), and *The Street of Clocks* (2001), all published by Houghton Mifflin. Winner of the 1995 Kingsley Tufts Poetry Award and the Alice Fay di Castagnola Award, Lux has also been awarded three grants from the National Endowment for the Arts as well as a Guggenheim Fellowship. He lives in Bronxville, New York.

Grain Burning Far Away

The wheat fields blaze again, the great waving plains
of them, on fire again, the black burn-line lapping
the gold grain, nature's delete button eating
each letter of each stalk. Over that short mountain
to the north: barley fields ignite
and to the south, across the salt marshes, acres
and acres of oats
crackle and smoke
and, it is reported from the east, the long green marches of corn
sawed off at the ankles

by heat. All the flora's, in fact, on *fire:* onion fields fried
underground, not one turnip unscorched, every root
vegetable, every bulb, each peanut on the planet boiled
in the soil. Trees burn
like matches, but faster, orchids die
when the fire's still a mile away. Seaweed, too, burns
and the great kelp beds
from the top down like candle wicks; spinach, in cans,
when opened, is ash. Moss melts,
hedgerows explode, every
green thing on earth
on fire and still each smoke-jumper snug,
asleep, undisturbed, the fire station's pole cold,
palmless, the fire extinguisher fat
with foam. Hear it snap,
the red angry fire,
hear it take the air and turn it into pain,
see the flame's blue, bruised heart
waver, never waver, waver.

On Influence

Influenced? Indeed, deeply, and even imitative, as a young writer. And
probably influenced still. I hope still influenced, in the way I mean it here:
learning something, being taught. It's a good thing. Every once in a while
I run into a student or newer writer who will say, when I ask her what
she's reading or which poets or poems he loves: "I don't like to read that
much, I don't want other writers to influence my style." Although I am
normally a very patient teacher, one glad to help anyone willing to learn,
this kind of statement will illicit from me a response something along the
lines of: But you don't *have* a style. Then I say something like: That's how
you learned to put your socks on—somebody influenced you by doing it
for you or you watched your father put his socks on and you imitated him.
It's how one learns. There is no way to become a writer unless one first
loves the writing of others. You read something that does something to
you that nothing else ever did, and you want to try to do that yourself. Is
there, or was there ever, on this planet, a writer who was not also a prodi-

gious reader? If this kind of logic and common sense fails to register with the new writer, I point to the door.

I have a theory: the first books you fall in love with, the first poems you read—this is an experience like falling in love for the first time with another. Maybe you'll read better books in the future, just like maybe you'll find a better match after your heart is first broken or you are careless with another's heart, but the *feeling,* the aches and joys, the exhilaration, the intensity, the aliveness of it, is never the same.

I was always a reader, even as a young child, but not until high school did I begin to read with a kind of hunger or urgency. Mostly novels. I read virtually all of Dostoyevsky the summer between my freshman and sophomore years in high school. I remember sitting in the high school gymnasium during orientation that September and wondering if anyone else was thinking about Raskalnikov. I was not aware that contemporary poetry existed. I knew and loved some poems by Robert Frost and Dylan Thomas, but that's where the English textbooks ended. I assumed that every poet on earth but Mr. Frost, who read a poem at Kennedy's inauguration and was clearly not long for this world, was dead. I don't think I'd even entered a bookstore, let alone a bookstore that carried poetry. Most of the novels I read were bought from a rack of paperbacks in the local drugstore. I remember driving home once—it was probably about 1965—from a larger town about 20 miles away. I'd found a copy of the New Directions edition of Pound's *Selected Poems.* I can still see it sitting on the seat beside me in my '57 Chevy. I'd never heard of Ezra Pound but knew I had to buy the book.

A few years later, in college in Boston, I walked into a bookstore that actually had a poetry section. Just recently I came into contact with a girlfriend from that time. I asked her what I was like then, hoping she'd say something like "wild" or "rakish." She said: "I'm not sure—you were always reading."

I did read a lot, and I tried to write. The most obvious influences at first were the poems on the back of Bob Dylan albums. But a miracle, for me, happened in my junior year of college: a living, breathing, published poet was hired to teach poetry writing. Her name was Helen Chasin, and she'd won the Yale Younger Poets Prize a year or two before for her book, *Coming Close.* She was in her late twenties, drop-dead beautiful, and the best teacher I ever had. She was the perfect teacher for a young poet: she was tough—sloppiness and sentimentality never flew with her, she insisted we learn the basics of the craft, and she was generous and encouraging. I was in her class for two years. Influence? Probably more than the three specific poets and poems I'm going to talk about shortly. She taught me to *work*, that poems were made things, that writing was rewriting. She taught me that to work on a poem, to apply the pressure of craft, was to honor and respect the impulse, the passion, the "lump in the throat" that made me want to write the poem in the first place.

The three poets I want to cite as direct influences are Hart Crane, Bill Knott, and James Wright, all of whom I "discovered" during these years, roughly 1967–69. I'll start, as I have listed them alphabetically, with Crane. When I first read his great poem *Voyages* I didn't have the slightest idea what it was about. I did know that it had great emotional intensity, a rich, knotty music, and that it was a love poem. I couldn't consciously identify it at the time, but I was also greatly moved—literally and figuratively— by his syntax. Whenever I read particular parts of this poem aloud I got (and still get) the chill down my spine, the happy adrenal rush—my more prosaic equivalent to Dickinson's feeling as if the top of her head were taken off or Housman's cutting himself while shaving. Sections II, III, and V are my favorites. Here is II:

HART CRANE
Voyages, II

—And yet this great wink of eternity,
Of rimless floods, unfettered leewardings,
Samite sheeted and processioned where
Her undinal vast belly moonward bends,
Laughing the wrapt inflections of our love;

Take this Sea, whose diapason knells
On scrolls of silver snowy sentences,
The sceptred terror of whose sessions rends
As her demeanors motion well or ill,
All but the pieties of lovers' hands.

And onward, as bells off San Salvador
Salute the crocus lustres of the stars,
In these poinsettia meadows of her tides,—
Adagios of islands, O my Prodigal,
Complete the dark confessions her veins spell.

Mark how her turning shoulders wind the hours,
And hasten while her penniless rich palms
Pass superscription of bent foam and wave,—
Hasten, while they are true,—sleep, death, desire,
Close round one instant in one floating flower.

Bind us in time, O Seasons clear, and awe.
O minstrel galleons of Carib fire,
Bequeath us to no earthly shore until
Is answered in the vortex of our grave
The seal's wide spindrift gaze toward paradise.

I still love this poet, this poem of his, and many others by him—not quite as breathlessly as at one time, but in a deeper and more abiding way. I love the way this poem starts, the dash reminding us that it contradicts the last line of section I: "The bottom of the sea is cruel." Calling the sea "this great wink of eternity" is such a richly textured metaphor: it's a visual pun (the horizon's slight bend, and the shore, mimics an eye, a wink.) I like the many connotations of wink, but especially, in this case, the-joke's-on-us wink. This image is a huge, yet fresh, evocation of the Big Abstract. I like all the noises: the sounds, the singing s's and e's, and ahs, how the fourth line, for example, as I scan it, is anapest, iamb, trochee, trochee, masculine ending. In other words, he gets us leaning one way, and then bang, bang, bang, he moves us another. The b and d sounds in that line are like tack-hammer blows that ground it and darken it. All throughout Crane's work, one finds stunning textures of metaphor and mouth-music. A similar kind of music, but in a different place in the line, sets up the visionary leap that is the section's last line: "The seal's wide spindrift gaze toward paradise." (There's a whole story about the word choice "spindrift" here—look it up in John Unterecker's or Paul Mariani's wonderful new biography of Crane.) Every poet, young or old, should shout for joy that Hart Crane wrote the lines: "Hasten, while they are true,—sleep, death, desire,/ Close round one instant in one floating flower." Did this poet influence me? Oh, I hope so.

I believe I was a sophomore in college when a literature teacher read us some poems from a first book called *The Naomi Poems* by a poet still in his twenties named Bill Knott. Actually, Knott wrote his first book under the pseudonym of Saint Geraud (1940–1966). They were very short poems, and the teacher only read three or four. Afterwards he said, "Knott is a *fine* poet." I'd never heard anyone emphasize the word "fine" in such a way. He was saying exceptional, utterly the real thing, and he said it with a verve, a pleasure I can still hear exactly today. Compared to Crane, Knott's poems in this book were spare, less dense, and more direct, but with little flares of surrealism or what was called at the time the "deep image." I found in these poems a great tenderness and purity, a distillation and a level of imagination that rivals the best lyric poems and fragments from the classical Greek. He was probably the first poet who showed me one could address political or social issues in poems without being a windbag, a polemicist, or a whiner. Take this poem (called *Poem*) about the death of a child:

BILL KNOTT
Poem

> The only response
> to a child's grave is
> to lie down before it and play dead.

That poem can be put in the context of the Vietnam War, as can this poem (from Knott's second book, *Autonecrophilia*), *Ignorance 1967*:

Ignorance 1967

> I don't understand anything
> so
> if you understand something
> explain it to me
> but real slow
> and use one-syllable corpses.

How about this one called *Widow's Winter*:

Widow's Winter

> Outside,
> the snow is falling into its past . . .
> I do want this night to end.

In the fireplace
a section of ash caves in.

The day you were buried
birds went over,
south,
thick enough to carry someone.
They took my gapes of breath
—their fuel?
We are together in some birds, who fail.

I didn't even want to look at your grave,
its heroic little mound
like the peck of dirt we hope to eat in our life.

Its utter clarity is heartbreaking; its tone, diction, line breaks, all perfect. These poems are deeply mysterious and lucid at the same time. The snow is falling into its past, oh Lord, the snow is falling into its past. Did Bill Knott influence me? Abso-fucking-lutely. He still has one of the best ears in the business; he is an absolute original, one of the best love poets of all time, *and* such a brilliant writer of sonnets that most people don't even know he writes sonnets! He once showed me a notebook—we were on a subway in NYC going uptown on the Lexington Avenue line—in which he had written and rewritten a few lines of a poem he was working on dozens and dozens, maybe hundreds of times, trying to get it right.

Say you are a relatively intelligent person and you love an art form. Do you take as your example an aesthetic that says it's all poured down your arm from heaven, first word best word, just write what you feel, Tommy, or might you be wiser to emulate and be influenced by aesthetic values greatly informed by craft, close attention, and the willingness to *work*?

The last poet I would like to thank for writing the poems he wrote is James Wright. The two books of his I read first were his third and fourth collections: *The Branch Will Not Break* and *Shall We Gather At The River*. Around the time that I was so lost in these books—lost in their tremendous grief and their tremendous heart—I visited my parents back on the farm. I noticed in the paper that James Wright was going to be on an educational TV program. That particular station came in only faintly and with a great deal of snow. It was on late at night, and I sat about a foot from the screen so I could just make out Wright's head and shoulders. The sound was fine. He read some of my favorite poems. For me, this beat Elvis or the Beatles! I was still only familiar with a handful of contemporary poets, and seeing James Wright (sort of) and hearing him was a quiet and deep thrill. One of the poems I most loved is *The Jewel:*

JAMES WRIGHT
The Jewel

There is this cave
In the air behind my body
That nobody is going to touch:
A cloister, a silence
Closing around a blossom of fire.
When I stand upright in the wind,
My bones turn to dark emeralds.

Perhaps the cave in the air behind his body in the poem moved me because it acknowledged a certain kind of loneliness that I (and many young men) had which we were both terrified of and proud of because we believed it set us apart from others. I loved the defiance of that speaker, that even in his loneliness he is going to "stand upright" in the wind, and when he does his bones will turn to emeralds. And now, as a much older man, I still love this poem and its utterance, the "how" of its utterance, its mystery and its absolute clarity. By mystery, I do not mean obscurity, and I especially do not mean arbitrariness. I'm not sure which I find more tedious, but at least a poem that is genuinely obscure will yield somewhat if you're willing to seek exegesis and go to school on it, whereas if you try to explicate a poem that is arbitrary, you will more often merely follow the lazy self-indulgence and trivial arrogance of that poet's rambling psyche. True mystery is imbued with the human: you get the poem's intent, its "meaning," its "ulteriority" (as Mr. Frost called it in his letters),[1] you get it by "testing it on your pulse" (as Mr. Keats put it in his letters).[2] Other ways James Wright influenced me, taught me? His lineation, his compassion, his willingness to risk sentimentality to achieve true sentiment, his impeccable ear.

May my influences continue. May there be new ones. May the old ones never cease.

JANE MEAD

Jane Mead was educated at Vassar College, Syracuse University, and the University of Iowa. She is the author of *A Truck Marked Flammable* (a State Street Press chapbook, 1990), *The Lord and the General Din of the World* (Sarabande Books, 1996), and *House of Poured-Out Waters* (University of Illinois Press, 2001). A recipient of fellowships from the Lannan and the Whiting Foundations, Mead is currently poet-in-residence at Wake Forest University in Winston-Salem, North Carolina.

Three Candles
And A Bowerbird

I do not know why
the three candles must sit
before this oval mirror—

but they must.—
I do not know much
about beauty, though

its consequences
are clearly great—even
to the animals:

to the bowerbird
who steals what is blue,
decorates, paints

his house; to the peacock
who loves the otherwise
useless tail of the peacock—

the tail *we* love.
The feathers *we* steal.
Perhaps even to the sunflowers

turning in their Fibonacci
spirals the consequences
are great, or to the mathematical

dunes with ripples
in the equation of all things
wind-swept. Perhaps

mostly, then, to the wind.
Perhaps mostly to the bowerbird.
I cannot say.

But I light the candles
and there is joy in it.
There is joy in the mirror—

joy in all of it.

LOUISE GLÜCK
The Wild Iris

At the end of my suffering
there was a door.

Hear me out: that which you call death
I remember.

Overhead, noises, branches of the pine shifting.
Then nothing. The weak sun
flickered over the dry surface.

It is terrible to survive
as consciousness
buried in the dark earth.

Then it was over: that which you fear, being
a soul and unable
to speak, ending abruptly, the stiff earth
bending a little. And what I took to be
birds darting in low shrubs.

You who do not remember
passage from the other world
I tell you I could speak again: whatever
returns from oblivion returns
to find a voice:

from the center of my life came
a great fountain, deep blue
shadows on azure seawater.

WILLIAM CARLOS WILLIAMS
Danse Russe

If I when my wife is sleeping
and the baby and Kathleen
are sleeping
and the sun is a flame-white disc
in silken mists
above shining trees,—
if I in my north room
dance naked, grotesquely
before my mirror
waving my shirt round my head
and singing softly to myself:
"I am lonely, lonely.
I was born to be lonely,

I am best so!"
If I admire my arms, my face,
my shoulders, flanks, buttocks
against the yellow drawn shades,—

Who shall say I am not
the happy genius of my household?

WALLACE STEVENS
The Snow Man

One must have a mind of winter
To regard the frost and the boughs
Of the pine-trees crusted with snow;

And have been cold a long time
To behold the junipers shagged with ice,
The spruces rough in the distant glitter

Of the January sun; and not to think
Of any misery in the sound of the wind,
In the sound of a few leaves,

Which is the sound of the land
Full of the same wind
That is blowing in the same bare place

For the listener, who listens in the snow,
And, nothing himself, beholds
Nothing that is not there and the nothing that is.

JAMES WRIGHT
The Life

Murdered, I went, risen,
Where the murderers are,
That black ditch
Of river.

And if I come back to my only country
With a white rose on my shoulder,
What is that to you?

It is the grave
In blossom.

It is the trillium of darkness,
It is hell, it is the beginning of winter,
It is a ghost town of Etruscans who have no names
Any more.

It is the old loneliness.
It is.
And it is
The last time.

Influence, Process, Mastery:
The making of a poem

> And artists in their work sometimes intuit
> that they must keep transforming, where they love.
> —Rainer Maria Rilke, *Requiem*

Like most writers, I have found apparently satisfactory ways to speak of influence and mastery, briefly and without dishonesty. I answer, for example, the question about influence, which comes up casually and with great frequency, by naming poets whose style is clearly evident in my own, just as I will as part of this essay. This is not so difficult to do, and the chances of being completely wrong are minimal. Likewise, the little I know about mastery can be made into a small but respectable package.

Given here the challenge of discussing in more depth these subjects, I find myself most interested, however, in *felt* certainties about the process of writing a poem and in the influences that exert themselves upon that process—subjective certainties. I am not a person who likes this state of affairs. My early education was in economics and philosophy; Descartes and Adam Smith were the heroes of my young adulthood, not so much for the content of their beliefs as for the elaborate rational structures they used to support those beliefs. I am someone who likes to disassemble mystery and rebuild it brick by brick into something that seems, then, fully explained. For years I resented my own eventual realization that what one is then left with is simply a pile of bricks: I am a die-hard convert to the fact of mystery, and like most converts, my respect for the object of my conversion is immense.

Having said all that, I will begin where the most mysterious of these subjects, that of influence, is *least* mysterious—where it is evident in technique. As I suggested above, I believe that even here a writer can only make a good guess. My sense is that only those poems that have been absorbed deeply, physically, make any real impact: to be influenced by a poem, one must fall in love with it and be changed by it. The writer, thus changed, may produce poems that are noticeably shadowed by that which changed her. But since influence happens only through this deep absorption, it cannot necessarily be traced directly. The literary influences that bring themselves to bear on the process of revision—on the writer's attempt to master the technical difficulties presented by a given poem—are not always apparent, even to the writer. Still, they may reveal themselves to the maker who chooses to look: in the break of a line, in qualities of voice as they are embodied in diction, pacing, syntax; in very specific elements of a poem, I can often hear, *in retrospect,* the echo of another poet.

I emphasize the retrospective nature of this recognition because it is fundamental to the difference between influence and emulation, the former of which is driven indirectly and by love, the latter, directly and by admiration or envy. Writing a poem is a way of taking (and simultaneously losing) possession of some part of one's self, and, as a result, the poem is born with the sense of utter originality. Influence sneaks up on one while one is completely engaged in writing and revising one's own poem. Emulation, while a valuable exercise, never produces poems, for imitations lack the fundamental energy of originality, the very energy that blinds a writer to his influences while they may be quite apparent to others. Yet when I reflect, it seems a given that every technical decision I make in a poem must surely be influenced to some degree by my reading. Sometimes this is more apparent than at other times, but the originality in a poem lies in the unique set of technical choices one makes and in the unique struggle one undergoes with the poem's content—a struggle which begins in the pre-literary life of the poem.

Like many writers, I tend to obsess about certain elements of craft for years at a time and to absorb what I read through the lens of those obsessions. To begin with an example of this very basic level of influence, I'll start with the syntactical structure of *Three Candles/And A Bowerbird,* which draws on two very different kinds of poems, one represented here by *The Wild Iris,* the other by *Danse Russe.*

The Wild Iris is an embodiment of the speaker's thought process and so depends on simple syntax to imitate the motions of the mind: the shifts in tone indicate that one part of the poem is said in response to the preceding section. It is not apparent that the speaker, at the beginning of the poem, has a destination; we overhear a musing. The poem moves from description to a kind of abstraction that is textured by voice, grounded in the sense we have of it being thought (i.e., process) and idea (i.e., destination) only by extension. Look, for example, at the voice shifts between the third and fourth stanzas and between the fifth and sixth stanzas—this process of moving toward knowledge or realization does not lend itself to complex syntax. Complex syntax does not build, it presents.

This use of syntax in *The Wild Iris* is in obvious contrast to a poem like *Danse Russe,* in which the entire poem is shaped around a single "if . . . then" swoop, although the "then" is only implied in the stanza break—where the thought itself breaks toward its conclusion. The poem is held in its syntax as if in a net. It's a tidy poem, and it knows where it is going from the start. It will not be distracted—it has committed itself from the beginning to the overall rhythm and timbre of the thought. Paratactic syntax, hypotactic syntax: simple syntax, layered syntax: enactment, explanation. Every poem commits itself to these strategies in some variation and degree.

I realized early in the writing of *Three Candles/And A Bowerbird* that extended syntax and anaphora were going to be basic to the structure of the poem: the things in the poem were pieces of an idea. In early drafts I can see myself smoothing out the arch of this idea, which begins in the third stanza with "its consequences/ are clearly great . . . " and continues into the ninth stanza, keeping itself in order through the repetition of "to the," which is further complicated from the sixth stanza on with the additional repetition of "perhaps." Clearly, this poem owes a debt to poems that proceed in the manner of Williams's poem, using syntax to assemble the parts of the poem into the order of an idea.

However, I also notice that there is a frame to my poem that is indebted to the sense of syntax I have acquired from reading poems such as *The Wild Iris.* The first three lines are a statement; they do not, syntactically, commit the poem to a destination. In that first stanza break, there's a little shrug in which the poem decides that the question implied in the first stanza is not going to be the one explored by the poem (i.e., *why* is one number preferable to the other? *Why* is the oval necessary?). The "why?" is embedded in a statement; it is not asked, but accepted; and thus the question is transformed into belief. With the colon at the end of the third stanza, the poem shifts into its more layered sentence structures and commits itself to the single idea it will explore in depth. The last two stanzas revert back to the *modus operandi* of the first. The final realization, that there is joy in these things, arrives by way of a small leap—it is not a logical extension of the thought that the poem has been developing but is structured more like *The Wild Iris.* It is the product of pausing, then taking a clean step forward.

Seen one way, my poem is made of technique and as such is made from other people's poems. Syntax is just one example. A related example would be the use of image—the commitment to one's place on a spectrum that runs from purely literal description to purely symbolic use of the image, neither of which extremes is particularly satisfying. For the great extent to which the images are drawn from my reading, *Three Candles/And A Bowerbird* is unusual for me. In the poem, the images are not elaborated upon but used in the service of developing an idea that has been foregrounded by the syntax. I think of *The Snow Man* as the archetypal example of a poem in which image attaches itself more firmly to idea than to an exploration of actual appearances. In *The Snow Man* the idea appears to require the image, whereas in *The Wild Iris,* where the speaker moves from careful description to realization, the image seems to bring to mind the thought. Not surprisingly, given the distinction I've already made between the syntax in the central section of my poem and that of the frame, the image with which *Three Candles/And A Bowerbird* begins is drawn from my life. The poem begins with the real and then engages at the level of idea.

A more nebulous manifestation of literary influence has to do, paradoxically, with learning to recognize and trust one's own originality. *Three Candles/And A Bowerbird* darted out in the way a poem does when I have a sudden recognition of the authority of a particular voice above all other competing voices. In this way, it owes a debt to all those poems I have read which have taught me to recognize authenticity of statement and authority of music, qualities that cannot be defined by interpretation or prosody. It is processed not so much by the mind as by the body, which learns to distinguish true from false rhythms—the meant from the merely said. These lessons are absorbed by a writer from a smaller arena than that of her chosen inheritance; they do not spring from translations and are tied most often to the rhythms of relatively recent English.

All of the poems I have included here fall into this most difficult to define and yet most sublime category of influence: they have taught me how to recognize the truth in my own poems and to trust that truth will conform to music, as Richard Hugo would say. Glück's poem, though, may best illustrate this reliance upon voice. Even taking into account that the speaker is an iris, much of what the poem says depends upon the utter believability of voice to be interesting, the authority of a somber pacing and music. To my ear, "At the end of my suffering there was a door. Hear me out: that which you call death I remember" are intellectually engaging sentences but not seductive enough rhythmically to be deeply convincing. The line breaks and the stanza breaks transform these statements into wholly felt truths.

> At the end of my suffering
> there was a door.
>
> Hear me out: that which you call death
> I remember.

This is an example of how important pacing is to authority of voice. One learns, from reading this kind of poem, to hear the true and to strive, in all decisions regarding technique, to emphasize the truth one recognizes in one's own voice. I like to think that my own line breaks, while much more enjambed, create a similar authority; I *know* that the line breaks are necessary to the voice and that this particular voice enabled me to write the poem.

The Life is an example of a poem that, were it not for its strong, authoritative rhythms, might lose my attention; for the images are so symbolic that they lack the advantage of being visually engaging. In making a decision, such as the one I made in the first line of my own poem to avoid the contraction and say "I do not know why . . . ," it does me no good to scan the two options, or to apply some rule about using lots of stresses when one is making a firm statement. But it does me a world of good to have fallen in love once, long ago, with a poem called *The Life* by James Wright. Am I thinking about that poem as I make my decision? It could not be further from my mind, but I have learned Wright's poem physically and by heart. In this way, as one creates one's own poems, a thirteenth-century definition of "influence" as an emanation from the stars feels more apt than any other.

A poem's first influences are non-literary and can be traced back to that addictive moment when the life of the mind, the life of the heart, and the life of the body in the world come together unpredictably at a point that is the poem. My poem about the bowerbird was influenced by my reading and thinking, which also provided much of the substance of the poem. However, it was only when I was made alert to my surroundings by the intrusion of terrible weather that the body, through fear, and the heart, through desire for safety, came awake. A poem becomes possible when the intellect is balanced and challenged.

On June 29, 1999, a great straight-line wind swept across much of Iowa. Trees that had survived a hundred years of prairie winds were split apart by heavy snows and ice storms; barns, roofs, silos, and parts of houses were carried into the air and smashed. At the airport five miles from my cottage outside the town of Hills, the winds were clocked at 148 miles per hour, tornado-force winds with longer duration and a wider path of destruction. Since I have no basement, I crouched in the closet with my head against the chimney, my small dog under me, my large dog to one side, and to the other side my unfortunate houseguest, a friend from the first grade who last visited me in Iowa during the flood of 1993. As my tall trees came down around us, it was hard to know how much of the house we were losing, and once or twice a complete lift-off seemed inevitable.

All this interrupted an increasingly resonant mulling. I'd been reading Joseph Campbell's *Historical Atlas of World Mythology,* in which he chronicles man's developing sense of the mysterious, and was thinking about our reluctance to believe that animals might possess a similar capacity for wonder. I'd also been reading a compilation of anecdotes related to these same topics: Jeffrey Moussaieff Masson's *When Elephants Weep.* He discusses, in one section, the difficulty of distinguishing a sense of aesthetics in animals from behavior that might have distinct survival value, and the examples he uses, bowerbirds and peacocks, appear in my poem.

This all resonated with and took on the weight of my long-standing fascination with the overlap between the mysterious and the mathematical orders. The Fibonacci numbers I mention in the poem are one such example. Fibonacci, "son of the simpleton," known to his peers in thirteenth-century Pisa as "the Blockhead," was the first to discover the numerical sequence, produced by the addition of the two previous numbers in the sequence, hence 1, 2, 3, 5, 8, 13, and so on. That sequence patterns a huge array of phenomena, from the numerical relationship between the clockwise and counter-clockwise spirals of seeds in a sunflower (they will be successive Fibonacci numbers) to the laws of phyllotaxis to the "golden spiral" of the chambered nautilus to the architectural proportions most pleasing to the human eye—the golden mean of Greek architecture and art and, later, Leonardo Da Vinci's "divine proportion."[1]

We are surrounded by shapes, both natural and man-made, that bear some relation to the Fibonacci sequence. If man and the rest of nature answer to a common numerical sequence, then it is a very small step to assume that the human sense of aesthetics is similar to that of other animals, each based on the same natural relationships. Discussing the mysterious in terms of the mathematical collapses our categories of the scientific and religious into a single mystery.

I had much of this material for the poem on hand before the storm hit. The pressure necessary to the making of a poem was already beginning to build, as these ideas fermented in relation to one another. I had, so to speak, a poem in mind. Then we had the storm: the world insisted upon its grasp on the body. And the body, alert with fear, brings to one's thinking all that it knows about music.

When it became clear that we would not have electricity for days, I bought candles and, for the bedroom, two glass cups to hold them so it wouldn't matter if I fell asleep without blowing them out. I put them on the dresser, in front of the mirror, hoping to create more light. I find the oval of this mirror exceptionally lovely (my guess is that there's a Fibonacci number in there somewhere), and so while I sat in bed reading, it began to drive me nuts that I'd bought two candle holders and not the more symbolically resonant and, to my eye, aesthetically pleasing three. I was in the presence of a potentially powerful but flawed image. Of course, it also drove me nuts that it drove me nuts, and so on—perhaps within the body's fear of chaos and ruin lies the heart's desire for order and sanctuary. Why would one feel fear and longing when one could just think in circles? From this battle came the necessity for the poem: a necessity answered at first by intellectually competent but completely unauthoritative false starts. I hope that this poem has some authority in its music and rhythm, its voice. Certainly it began with my recognition of the superiority of one particular voice: a voice informed by the heart and body as well as the mind. Elation: the poem is off, and one begins the struggle to master the material, a struggle that involves an absorption in technique and therefore influence. Your entire self is involved here, if the poem is to be a good one. For me, the terror of how the parts war with one another is less powerful than the delight in how they are momentarily focused on the same project. How hard it is to turn toward the poem. How impossible to turn away.

Draft by cumbersome draft, one struggles with a poem. If you are lucky, you finally get it to the mat with as few flaws as you can manage. For a misguided moment you might even think that you have mastered it. Soon you realize, though, that if the poem is good, you yourself have much to learn from it, and if the poem is not so hot, then surely it has successfully resisted your struggle. Mastery exists only as a momentary illusion, but one's desire for it is unquenchable, so we write. And we keep on writing. We write because mastery does not exist.

JACK MYERS

Jack Myers was born in Lynn, Massachusetts, in 1941. He received a B.A. in English from the University of Massachusetts and an M.F.A. in writing at the University of Iowa Writers' Workshop. He has published seven books of poetry, including *As Long as You're Happy* (Graywolf Press, 1986), selected by Seamus Heaney as the National Poetry Series Open Winner, and his most recent publications, *OneOnOne* (Autumn House Press, 1999) and *The Glowing River: New and Selected Poems* (Invisible Cities Press, 2001). Myers compiled Volume I of Leaning House Records' compact disc recording, *Leaning House Poets*. He was also the co-editor, along with Roger Weingarten, of two anthologies of poetry, *New American Poets of the 80's* (Wampeter Press, 1984) and *New American Poets of the 90's* (Godine, 1991). In 2002, Harcourt Brace will publish *The Poet's Workshop: A Field Guide to Poetic Technique*. Myers lives in Mesquite, Texas, teaches at Southern Methodist University, and is the father of four children. He is married to Thea Temple, Executive Director of a literary center in Dallas called The Writer's Garret.

The Wisdom of Not Knowing

It sounds self-evident to say that art, like any human activity, is a by-product of life. But if you could poll young writers who are fervently in the midst of learning their craft, many would admit that they feel as though their lives just happen to occur, with them as unconscious inhabitants, while they're absorbed in plumbing the mysteries of the creative process and their art (derived from heightened perceptions!). It can take almost a lifetime for good writers to finally "get things" in normal, commonsensical order. As Charles Olson wrote: "I have had to learn the simplest things/ last. Which made for difficulties."[1] But when artists and seekers finally do learn the simplest things, they do so with considerably more conscious understanding and appreciation than those folk who weren't exceptional enough to get the main thing backwards in the first place.

I'm attempting to make an analogy here between how life and art, which imitates it, unfold in an upward spiral, beginning with: 1) *not knowing,* which is actually an all-knowing, unconscious bliss; to 2) merely *knowing* through the gaining of knowledge; to 3) *knot knowing,* which is the acceptance of the gifts of difficulty, uncertainty, contraries, and dual consciousness; and finally to 4) *Not Knowing,* a return to the first level of *not knowing* but, this time, at a higher level of consciousness that accepts paradox, a consciousness within which skill, knowledge, and mastery have been absorbed and subsumed into one's being like a person's signature gait.

I'm talking about a magical blinding here, not a romancing of the poet. Great writers are alchemists and wizards for whom time and distance, matter and energy, spirit and consciousness are as mutable as dreams and as solid as highways. Over imagined distances of time and space, artists are able *to produce real and profound changes in human perception, and, in fact, change how people act.* "The power to produce effects over great distances without having to be there physically" is Webster's definition of the word *influence.* Interestingly, the word originally referred to the flowing in of an ethereal fluid or power from the stars that affected the characters and actions of people. Over the millennia, poets have influenced, instructed, and mentored other poets, just as many craftspeople teach their apprentices.

No one knows your soul. Not even you. If, as an artist, you think you do, you're either in the wrong business or you're not looking hard enough. We only feel we know who we really are when our soul resonates with something of a kindred nature outside of it. For me, early on, the sonic booms and verbal orchestrations of Dylan Thomas's poetry (he had no idea what words meant when he was little, and that phenomenological, abstract aspect of his work comes across brilliantly) put me blissfully to sleep every night. Later on, the shocking psychosexual confessions in Anne Sexton's work bottle-rocketed me onto a level where I could finally find my subject: me. But at that time my work was, well, not very intelligible, except to me sometimes. "When the pupil is ready, the Teacher will appear," a

Chinese saying goes; and that's when the work of Richard Hugo came roaring to my attention as if by coincidence. Aside from knowing how to write accessibly and powerfully, Dick's main contribution to my poetic education, as our student-teacher relationship blurred into a friendship, was in showing me, through who he was, that *there is no dividing line between life and art.* One is as one is. And one's work will either reflect that or it will reflect the struggle against it.

After I had crawled out of The Foggy Swamp of Sodden Meanings, I bumped into the breathtakingly rarefied, strange pastel poems of W. S. Merwin's *The Lice.* His softly surreal work furthered the project of integration I had begun with Dick Hugo by showing me that the walls I had constructed between the worlds of waking and dreaming, ego and unconscious, and body and soul, were permeable. His poem *The Child* not only exemplifies this double-layered kind of connecting consciousness, but it also happens to be a beautifully lyrical and humbly surrendering contemplation—a prayer, really—which I came to know *by heart:*

W. S. MERWIN
The Child

Sometimes it is inconceivable that I should be the age I am
Almost always it is at a dry point in the afternoon
I cannot remember what
I am waiting for and in my astonishment I
Can hear the blood crawling over the plains
Hurrying on to arrive before dark
I try to remember my faults to make sure
One after the other but it is never
Satisfactory the list is never complete

At times night occurs to me so that I think I have been
Struck from behind I remain perfectly
Still feigning death listening for the
Assailant perhaps at last
I even sleep a little for later I have moved
I open my eyes the lanternfish have gone home in darkness
On all sides the silence is unharmed
I remember but I feel no bruise

Then there are the stories and after a while I think something
Else must connect them besides just this me
I regard myself starting the search turning
Corners in remembered metropoli
I pass skins withering in gardens that I see now
Are not familiar
And I have lost even the thread I thought I had

If I could be consistent even in destitution
The world would be revealed
While I can I try to repeat what I believe
Creatures spirits not this posture
I do not believe in knowledge as we know it
But I forget

This silence coming at intervals out of the shell of names
It must be all one person really coming at
Different hours for the same thing
If I could learn the word for yes it could teach me questions
I would see that it was itself every time and I would
Remember to say take it up like a hand
And go with it this is at last
Yourself

The child that will lead you

   This is wisdom earned by knowing what one does not know, and then
the entering into not knowing in order to find the gold in the shadow.
   As I think about this poem's influence on me, in hindsight, it seems
it was a road sign pointing to my subsequent involvement in Jungian studies
and therapy, a branch of psychoanalysis highly amenable to many artists
because of its emphasis on universal cultural symbols. And then, over the
next hill—hairpin curves, dips in road, slippery when wet—my struggle
to become more integrated through Jungian therapy inevitably led me to
a renewed sense of spirituality through Gnostic studies and Eastern and
Middle Eastern poetry and literature. These works greatly affected the style
of my poetry writing with their aesthetic of water: simple, clear surfaces,
boundless depths, and paradox.
   Nor does it surprise me now that the next strong influence over my
work was the work of American literary legend, prodigal son, and ascetic
Zen sojourner, Jack Gilbert. Gilbert, in a self-imposed exile from his native

City of Steel, Pittsburgh, sought to master the art of saying a thing by not saying it. Once a Zen archer has mastered accuracy through rigorous practice and meditation, when he can no longer miss the bull's-eye unless he tries, he continues his practice without the bow and arrow. I feel sure that the combination of freedom and severity in Jack Gilbert's writing has been wrested from his relentless practice of making spare, calligraphic verbal strokes over and over in an effort to capture essences. Picasso did this, too, in his minimalist pen-and-ink sketches. This is much deeper than style. It is a matter of character and spirit: who one is and how one wants to be. Look at the way *To See If Something Comes Next* weighs whether or not it's possible for the grief-stricken self to ever flow again:

JACK GILBERT
To See If Something Comes Next

There is nothing here at the top of the valley.
Sky and morning, silence and the dry smell
of heavy sunlight on the stone everywhere.
Goats occasionally, and the sound of roosters
in the bright heat where he lives with the dead
woman and purity. Trying to see if something
comes next. Wondering whether he has stalled.
Maybe, he thinks, it is like the Noh: whenever
the script says *dances,* whatever the actor does next
is a dance. If he stands still, he is dancing.

I love that his poems bury and set off a deep implosive charge in the reader's mind. These poems leave behind a wake reminiscent of Basho's:

The Temple bell stops—
but the sound keeps coming
out of the flowers.[2]

When we talk about what is, we talk about what is not. When we talk about Mastery, we must talk about Not Knowing. As the Soto Zen Master, Dogen, said, "A Zen Master's life is one continuous mistake," meaning we find our way through both life and art by trial and error, much as water finds its way downhill, rerouted by each obstacle it hits. Without character and spirit, we're left with knowledge, skill, technique, and excellence. These are, of course, worthy goals, but if we make them ends in themselves, we are not talking about an art, we are talking about a craft. Hazrat Inayat Khan, the founder of the Sufi Order in the West, explained that mastery is "not only a means of accomplishing the things of the world, but it is that by which a person fulfills the purpose of his life."[3]

Daedalus, inventor of the Labyrinth, figured out how to thread nautilus shells onto a necklace by tying an ant to a string. Imprisoned within his own Labyrinth, he escaped not through the maze but through flight: not by focusing on the difficulty of his trap but by thinking about freedom. I have learned, likewise, how to untie certain knots.

Which brings me to my last poetic influence: Jelaluddin Rumi, founder of the mystic Sufi sect of Whirling Dervishes, Persian statesman, politician, chief judge, and one of the world's all-time great poets. Rumi, like King Solomon, saw sensual pleasure, beauty, art, holiness, ecstatic bliss, and surrender to the natural as being natural. His work—which sports the spontaneity of Frank O'Hara, the sudden striking power of *satori* enlightenment, and the ageless wisdom of the Greek sage Heraclitus—taught me to write outside of the box, to leave the self for the Self, to learn *not knowing*. Here's an example from Rumi of what I mean:

JELALUDDIN RUMI
Say Yes Quickly
Translated from the Farsi by Coleman Barks and John Moyne

Forget your life. Say *God is Great*. Get up.
You think you know what time it is. It's time to pray.
You've carved so many little figurines, too many.
Don't knock on any random door like a beggar.
Reach your long hand out to another door, beyond where
you go on the street, the street
where everyone says, "How are you?"
and no one says *How aren't you?*

Tomorrow you'll see what you've broken and torn tonight,
thrashing in the dark. Inside you
there's an artist you don't know about.
He's not interested in how things look different in moonlight.

If you are here unfaithfully with us,
you're causing terrible damage.
If you've opened your loving to God's love,
you're helping people you don't know
and have never seen.

Is what I say true? Say *yes* quickly,
if you know, if you've known it
from before the beginning of the universe.

Under Rumi's spell I wrote a little poem that tries not to stay within the lines:

The Optimist, The Pessimist, and The Other

The optimist believes the cup of desire
is studded with jewels
that turn out to be holes
he pours his desires through.

The pessimist, who has been through all this,
desires to pour forth his story
again and again, as if somewhere
there were a hole in it.

And the other, who seems quite ordinary,
sees the cup of desire is not out there, but within.
He says, so what if it has holes in it!

In seeking answers about the effect of influence on mastery, about the moment of becoming a master, and even about the nature of mastery, one place to look to is your impulse to write in the first place, if you can "re-member" it. I would guess it has more to do with who you were, who you wanted to be, and your sense of your purpose rather than an ambition to produce the poetical equivalent of tourist figurines.

In the Middle East, they say: "Don't show me the grave, show me the body." I don't know if I've written a poem that exhibits trace elements of the development my work and I have been through (a literary correlative to biology's "Ontology recapitulates phylogeny"), but here's a recent little poem I wrote that at least shows the influences of Gilbert and Rumi.

The Flicker

This is in honor of the flicker
that sings its heart out on my roof every day
though no other flicker comes.

If I can't be sure what the language of joy is,
can I at least know what is?

There is a flicker flapping its wings and playing
with the name of whatever it's doing.

The tiny bit of him that weighs something
is holding down the house

while the larger part of him that weighs nothing
lifts it up.

You wouldn't know it, but Dylan Thomas, Anne Sexton, and a host of others are back there playing cards in the Green Room while Rumi, Gilbert, and I are chatting Po' Biz, well aware we're all standing on one another's shoulders just so you can see us.

DONALD REVELL

Donald Revell was born in the Bronx, New York, in 1954. He received his Ph.D. in English literature from the State University of New York at Buffalo in 1980. He has since published six books of poetry: *From the Abandoned Cities* (Harper & Row, 1983), *The Gaza of Winter* (University of Georgia Press, 1988), and *New Dark Ages* (1990), *Erasures* (1992), *Beautiful Shirt* (1994), and *There are Three* (1998), all published by Wesleyan University Press. Revell, who teaches at the University of Utah, lives in Salt Lake City and Las Vegas. He is married to poet Claudia Keelan. They have one son, Benjamin Brecht Revell.

Arcady Siskiyou

Was circus once once Lily
Kisses once imagined are jazz bands

A black great musical man
In the heat of town
On the July fairground
Spread the flowers of his hands
We all for hours were imaginary babies

Lily the sound of water next morning
Lily the light across the sound
Sun a lily circus continuing
Faced the quarter moon down

So July
Like the skittering of dragonflies
Was kisses really

JOHN SKELTON
Uppon a Deedmans Hed

Skelton Laureat, uppon a deedmans hed,
That was sent to hym from an honorable Jentyllwoman for
A token, Devysyd this gostly medytacyon in Englysh:
Convenable in sentence, Commendable, Lamentable, Lacrymable,
Profytable for the soule.

Youre ugly tokyn
My mynd hath brokyn
From worldly lust;
For I have dyscust
We ar but dust,
And dy we must.
    It is generall
To be mortall:
I have well espyde
No man may hym hyde
From deth holow-eyed,
With synnews wyderyd,
With bonys shyderyd,
With hys worme-etyn maw
And hys gastly jaw
Gaspyng asyde,
Nakyd of hyde,
Neyther flesh nor fell.
    Then by my councell,
Loke that ye spell
Well thys gospell:
For wherso we dwell,
Deth wyll us quell
And with us mell.

For all oure pamperde paunchys,
There may no fraunchys
Nor worldly blys
Redeme us from this:
Oure days be datyd
To be chekmatyd,
With drawttys of deth
Stoppyng oure breth;
Oure eyen synkyng,
Oure bodys stynkyng,
Oure gummys grynnyng,
Oure soulys brynnyng!
To whom then shall we sew
For to have rescew,
But to swete Jesu
On us then for to rew?
　　O goodly chyld
Of Mary mylde,
Then be oure shylde!
That we be not exylyd
To the dyne dale
Of boteles bale,
Nor to the lake
Of fendys blake.
　　But graunt us grace
To se thy face,
And to purchace
Thyne hevenly place
And thy palace,
Full of solace,
Above the sky,
That is so hy,
Eternally
To beholde and se
The Trynyte!
　　Amen.

Myrres vous y

Excerpt from **Phyllyp Sparowe**

Pla ce bo,
> Who is there, who?
Di le xi,
> Dame Margery,
Fa, re, my, my.
> Wherefore and why, why?
> For the sowle of Philip Sparowe,
That was late slayn at Carowe,
Among the Nones Blake.
For that swete soules sake,
And for all sparowes soules
Set in our bede rolles,
Pater noster qui,
With an *Ave Mari,*
And with the corner of a Crede,
The more shal be your mede.

> Whan I remembre agayn
How mi Philyp was slayn,
Never halfe the payne
Was betwene you twayne,
Pyramus and Thesbe,
As than befell to me:
I wept and I wayled,
The tearys downe hayled;
But nothynge it avayled
To call Phylyp agayne,
Whom Gyb our cat hath slayne.
> Gyb, I saye, our cat,
Worrowyd her on that
Which I loved best.
It can not be exprest
My sorowfull hevynesse,
But all without redresse;
For within that stounde,
Halfe slumbrynge, in a sounde
I fell downe to the grounde.
> Unneth I kest myne eyes
Towarde the cloudy skyes;
But whan I dyd beholde
My sparow dead and colde,
No creature but that wolde

Have rewed upon me,
To behold and se
What hevynesse dyd me pange:
Wherewith my handes I wrange
That my senaws cracked
As though I had ben racked,
So payned and so strayned
That no lyfe well nye remayned.
    I syghed and I sobbed,
For that I was robbed
Of my sparowes lyfe.
O mayden, wydow, and wyfe,
Of what estate ye be,
Of hye and lowe degre,
Great sorowe than ye myght se,
And lerne to wepe at me!
Such paynes dyd me frete
That myne hert dyd bete,
My vysage pale and dead,
Wanne, and blewe as lead:
The panges of hatefull death
Well nye had stopped my breath.

ROBERT CREELEY
Flowers

> No knowledge rightly understood
> can deprive us of the mirth of flowers.
> —*Edward Dahlberg*

No thing less than one thing
or more—

no sun
but sun—

or water
but wetness found—

What truth is it
that makes men so miserable?

Days we die
are particular—

This life cannot be lived
apart from what it must forgive.

Proper Rites

In poetry, evidence of mastery is first a sound and then a resonance; mastery is a consequence of the simple immediacy of words that bring forth truth. One of the gentlest men I ever knew, Elias Schwartz, a great teacher of prosody, introduced me to the sound and verity of John Skelton when he read this couplet aloud:

> It is generall
> To be mortall.

These remain my favorite lines of poetry. To me, they define mastery as a sound immediately and then continually true; they conduct a conviction to my mind and, I hope, to my behavior as a poet and man. The immediacy of imagination is in the movement of these lines. The physical qualities of the words somehow repair the mediating gaps in language between the material words and their meanings. This reparation ministers through sound, and the sound ministers through time. The whole of *Uppon a Deedmans Hed* moves by way of fleetingly close rhymes; but the sheer force of their velocity protracts these transitory propositions toward a future reader. The doctrine of only a moment—these lines go so quickly—instructs eternity. Mortality endures; the poem is a priest to its readers. It was William Carlos Williams who proposed that a "poet thinks with his poem."[1] Skelton, thinking instantly aloud, thinks *to* me. *"Myrres vous y"* ("See yourself here"), he tells me, and so I do, and so he is my master. In the general mortality of his meaning, Skelton requires my own right and tender conduct.

In *Phyllyp Sparowe*, Skelton requires the syllable itself to be right and tender. Lamenting the death of a sparrow, Skelton looses syllables of the Vespers for the Dead— *"Pla ce bo"* and *"Di le xi"*—into pure sound and pitch— *"Fa, re, my, my"*—recalling the common sound of a sparrow's song. Onomatopoeia is the proper rite in this elegy over the soul of a sparrow. The proper poem evinces a passing sound. The sparrow is my master's master. He sings and dies. The lesson keens forward in every elegy, as every poem elegizes sound. *"Myrres vous y"* while breath remains.

In Robert Creeley's *Flowers,* the simple presence of flowers can move our words into immediacy and a timely conviction. Delight and instruction happen to be one. There is no abstraction, no enduring misery or law, that can prevail over the particular immanence of flowers. The particular flower is a profusion of singularities, as Creeley so beautifully avows, apportioning his lines to one pure fact apiece. Each object is a whole thing unto itself; presence ends refraction. And the lesson of forgiveness shows itself in flowers, in the freedom of passing beauty.

Indeed, it has always been Creeley's *way* to discover comprehension and its techniques dissolving into the better air (or fragrance) of a Virtue or a Love. So in *Flowers,* the taut, particular lines of the poetry ease into atonement. Craft disappears in peace. This *way,* this masterful trajectory, is wonderfully explained by a letter Creeley wrote to Charles Olson in 1951. He begins:

A statement: there is no better poet than Hart Crane/August 15, 1951[2]

The plain bold proposal is the matter of its moment. Timeliness proceeds from faith. The letter goes on to enact a brilliantly detailed appreciation of seven of Hart Crane's lyric poems, emphasizing the sounds of vowels and consonantal shadings. Creeley thereby brings the poems into the present tense, into the proper rite of Presences.

you are going to hear, if you can but listen, can but,
in any sense, hear, sounds as incredible, as finely knit,
caught, as any man ever wrote them[3]

Creeley's point is to present and not to prove the sounds. And so he concludes his understanding with one exclamation:

Dammit/ isn't that gentle![4]

As in *Flowers,* Creeley uses mastery to get beyond mastery, exemplifying craft as conduct. Forgiveness and gentleness design poetic motives. The lesson shows momentous virtue, and then it's done.

My poem *Arcady Siskiyou* was done early in the morning after an evening of jazz on a small town's fairground. The evening had been wonderful, with children and dancing and summer sounds mixing with the music. Driving home afterwards, we played the radio, and a ballad about a girl named Lily came on. Somehow, the several repetitions of "Lily" made onomatopoeic magic, bearing the earlier concert forward into night, into sleep, and into my very first words upon waking. "Lily" had captured the virtue and duration of a sweet memory, and I wanted to make a poem saying so. I wanted my new-found faith in the sound "Lily" to resound with conviction. I thought of Skelton: of the moral force of his rhymes and of his sparrow's soulful song. Immediately I thought, too, of Creeley's couplet at the end of *Flowers*. I'd felt an ecstatic gentleness in the music of the night before, and my two master poets, each in his own way and also as an ensemble, directed me towards entire faith in "Lily." "Lily" was the word to bring dear imagery and moments forward into the present and into immediate, perhaps eternal, keeping. I gave the poem over to "Lily," and, for me, it accomplished a sunrise to face the sinking moon of memory. The awkwardness of my "Lily"'s insistent repetition felt eventually like grace. And grace is candor and the pleasure to say, really, my wife's kisses had been the deepest pleasures of the previous evening. *Arcady Siskiyou* ends there. This is the lesson, then, of mastery to me: candor and the awkward confidence of what is truth to tell.

LEN ROBERTS

Len Roberts was born in Cohoes, New York, in 1947. He attended Siena College; the University of Dayton for his M.A.; and Lehigh University, where he received his Ph.D. in Literature. He has written numerous books of poetry: *Cohoes Theater* (Momentum Press, 1980); *From the Dark* (State University of New York Press, 1984); *Sweet Ones* (Milkweed Editions, 1988); *Black Wings* (Persea Books, 1989); *Learning about the Heart* (Silverfish Review, 1992); *Dangerous Angels* (Copper Beech Press, 1993); *Counting the Black Angels* (University of Illinois Press, 1994); and *The Trouble-Making Finch* (University of Illinois Press, 1998). His most recent book of poems is *The Silent Singer: New and Selected Poems* (University of Illinois Press, 2001). Roberts has translated two books from Hungarian into English, *Call to Me in My Mother Tongue* (Mid-American Review Translation Chapbook, 1989) and *The Selected Poems of Sándor Csoóri* (Copper Canyon Press, 1992). He is currently translating another book of Csoóri's poems. He lives in Hellertown, Pennsylvania. He is married and has three children, Tamara, Bradford, and Joshua.

At the Table

My mother sits across the table,
    reading *Oneida* aloud
from the knife she holds
to the sun filtering through
    her window,

just four feet away yet so distant
I know I can't reach her no matter
    what I say,
all of the names gone into buttered
toast and blue cups of coffee,
all of the screams at that other table
    in that other kitchen
silent here where my mother fingers
the buttons on her bathrobe,
tells me she really ought to go home,
her too-red lips in that perpetual pout
    even now at seventy-eight,
both breasts gone, most of her uterus,
    even the night she high-heeled
off our front porch without one look back,
my mother twelve again, rising for work
    in Cohoes Textile,
scattering the muskrats that crawled
from the canal into those cold rooms
where she knelt on linoleum
with a quick sign of the cross,
making it here, now, in Troy, New York,
before reciting the list of venial sins
she's committed during the week,
asking me, her confessor, her father,
    to forgive the bad thought,
the silence when her uncle kissed her cheek,
my mother down on her arthritic knees
on the fourth floor of this Home for the Elderly
    where I have come for my annual visit
to sulk and remind her I am the last of three
    sons,
flashing pictures of my house and wife and own
    children
before her pudgy face to whisper *See, See what
    I've done,*
let her know our Thanksgiving dinner table was

crammed with relatives and friends

while she sat at the far end of the blue dining
    room

no longer waiting for anyone to come, lifting
    the one glass of milk

she still limits herself to each day because
    she can't break the habit,

sucking the meat from the bones, cleaning
    her plate

with a slice of bread till it gleams back
    like it does today,

my mother staring at the crust in mine,
    the leftover egg,

not sure to tell whoever I am that it's
    not right to waste,

her eyes looking for words I hope she
    never finds.

JOHN KEATS
Ode on a Grecian Urn

I

Thou still unravished bride of quietness,
    Thou foster-child of silence and slow time,
Sylvan historian, who canst thus express
    A flowery tale more sweetly than our rhyme:
What leaf-fringed legend haunts about thy shape
    Of deities or mortals, or of both,
        In Tempe or the dales of Arcady?
    What men or gods are these? What maidens loth?
What mad pursuit? What struggle to escape?
    What pipes and timbrels? What wild ecstasy?

II

Heard melodies are sweet, but those unheard
    Are sweeter; therefore, ye soft pipes, play on;
Not to the sensual ear, but, more endeared,
    Pipe to the spirit ditties of no tone:
Fair youth, beneath the trees, thou canst not leave
    Thy song, nor ever can those trees be bare;

Bold Lover, never, never canst thou kiss,
Though winning near the goal—yet, do not grieve;
She cannot fade, though thou hast not thy bliss,
For ever wilt thou love, and she be fair!

III

Ah, happy, happy boughs! that cannot shed
Your leaves, nor ever bid the Spring adieu;
And, happy melodist, unwearièd
For ever piping songs for ever new;
More happy love! more happy, happy love!
For ever warm and still to be enjoyed,
For ever panting, and for ever young;
All breathing human passion far above,
That leaves a heart high-sorrowful and cloyed,
A burning forehead, and a parching tongue.

IV

Who are these coming to the sacrifice?
To what green altar, O mysterious priest,
Lead'st thou that heifer lowing at the skies,
And all her silken flanks with garlands dressed?
What little town by river or sea shore,
Or mountain-built with peaceful citadel,
Is emptied of this folk, this pious morn?
And, little town, thy streets for evermore
Will silent be; and not a soul to tell
Why thou art desolate, can e'er return.

V

O Attic shape! Fair attitude! with brede
Of marble men and maidens overwrought,
With forest branches and the trodden weed;
Thou, silent form, dost tease us out of thought
As doth eternity: Cold Pastoral!
When old age shall this generation waste,
Thou shalt remain, in midst of other woe
Than ours, a friend to man, to whom thou say'st,
'Beauty is truth, truth beauty,—that is all
Ye know on earth, and all ye need to know.'

RANDALL JARRELL
90 North

At home, in my flannel gown, like a bear to its floe,
I clambered to bed; up the globe's impossible sides
I sailed all night—till at last, with my black beard,
My furs and my dogs, I stood at the northern pole.

There in the childish night my companions lay frozen,
The stiff furs knocked at my starveling throat,
And I gave my great sigh: the flakes came huddling,
Were they really my end? In the darkness I turned to my rest.

—Here, the flag snaps in the glare and silence
Of the unbroken ice. I stand here,
The dogs bark, my beard is black, and I stare
At the North Pole . . .
                    And now what? Why, go back.

Turn as I please, my step is to the south.
The world—my world spins on this final point
Of cold and wretchedness: all lines, all winds
End in this whirlpool I at last discover.

And it is meaningless. In the child's bed
After the night's voyage, in that warm world
Where people work and suffer for the end
That crowns the pain—in that Cloud-Cuckoo-Land

I reached my North and it had meaning.
Here at the actual pole of my existence,
Where all that I have done is meaningless,
Where I die or live by accident alone—

Where, living or dying, I am still alone;
Here where North, the night, the berg of death
Crowd me out of the ignorant darkness,
I see at last that all the knowledge

I wrung from the darkness—that the darkness flung me—
Is worthless as ignorance: nothing comes from nothing,
The darkness from the darkness. Pain comes from the darkness
And we call it wisdom. It is pain.

WALT WHITMAN
Excerpt from *Out of the Cradle Endlessly Rocking*

Out of the cradle endlessly rocking,
Out of the mocking-bird's throat, the musical shuttle,
Out of the Ninth-month midnight,
Over the sterile sands and the fields beyond, where the child leaving
    his bed wander'd alone, bareheaded, barefoot,
Down from the shower'd halo,
Up from the mystic play of shadows twining and twisting as if they
    were alive,
Out from the patches of briers and blackberries
From the memories of the bird that chanted to me,
From your memories sad brother, from the fitful risings and fallings
    I heard,
From under that yellow half-moon late-risen and swollen as if with
    tears,
From those beginning notes of yearning and love there in the mist,
From the thousand responses of my heart never to cease,
From the myriad thence-arous'd words,
From the word stronger and more delicious than any,
From such as now they start the scene revisiting,
As a flock, twittering, rising, or overhead passing,
Borne hither, ere all eludes me, hurriedly,
A man, yet by these tears a little boy again,
Throwing myself on the sand, confronting the waves,
I, chanter of pains and joys, uniter of here and hereafter,
Taking all hints to use them, but swiftly leaping beyond them,
A reminiscence sing.

ROBERT LOWELL
Home After Three Months Away

Gone now the baby's nurse,
a lioness who ruled the roost
and made the Mother cry.
She used to tie
gobbets of porkrind in bowknots of gauze—
three months they hung like soggy toast
on our eight foot magnolia tree,
and helped the English sparrows
weather a Boston winter.

Three months, three months!
Is Richard now himself again?
Dimpled with exaltation,
my daughter holds her levee in the tub.
Our noses rub,
each of us pats a stringy lock of hair—
they tell me nothing's gone.
Though I am forty-one,
not forty now, the time I put away
was child's-play. After thirteen weeks
my child still dabs her cheeks
to start me shaving. When
we dress her in her sky-blue corduroy,
she changes to a boy,
and floats my shaving brush
and washcloth in the flush. . . .
Dearest, I cannot loiter here
in lather like a polar bear.

Recuperating, I neither spin nor toil.
Three stories down below,
a choreman tends our coffin's length of soil,
and seven horizontal tulips blow.
Just twelve months ago,
these flowers were pedigreed
imported Dutchmen; now no one need
distinguish them from weed.
Bushed by the late spring snow,
they cannot meet
another year's snowballing enervation.

I keep no rank nor station.
Cured, I am frizzled, stale and small.

Drinking at the Well: John Keats, Randall Jarrell, Walt Whitman, and Robert Lowell

Whenever I read, there's a part of me that's on the lookout—usually un-
consciously—for something I can use in my own writing, something I
can beg, borrow, or steal. So, in thinking about this essay, I first came up
with a list of about fifty poems that I return to again and again for what-
ever sustenance they provide. I then cut the list down to twenty and then

finally to four poems that appealed most to me during my first ten years
or so of writing: poems that contain the seeds, I can see after the fact, of
attitudes and techniques I have developed in my own poems.

I need to emphasize that "after the fact" phrase, for I was not conscious
of being "influenced" by these poems at the time. All I knew was that
they embodied some quality of poetry I loved, a quality that kept drawing
me back to them. These poems contained themes that were roiling within
me, themes I was often only partially aware of. My process has been to
absorb the techniques of these poems and, while writing, to let them flow
as they will, trusting that the Muse knows a great deal more about writing
than I do.

A quality I love in poems and which I strive to get into my own is
what Federico García Lorca calls duende, that dance with death, so to
speak, that propels the poem's form and content with an urgency felt by
both reader and writer. That sense of vulnerability, impermanence, tran-
sience adds a touch of primitive frenzy to the poetic utterance. As Lorca
says of "The Girl with the Combs," she had to "deny her faculties and her
security . . . turn out her Muse and keep vulnerable, so that her *Duende*
might come and vouchsafe the hand-to-hand struggle. And then how she
sang!"[1] My need for this quality in my poems stems, I think, from the fact
that I experienced the deaths of loved ones in my formative years and I
knew, at some level, that I wanted to express those losses. All of the influence
poems I've selected contain this quality of duende, this agreement to remain
vulnerable, although they present it and come to terms with it in quite
different ways.

I did not know it for years, but that's what kept drawing me back to
John Keats's *Ode on a Grecian Urn:* that moment frozen in time which pre-
vails even against death:

> Bold Lover, never, never canst thou kiss,
> Though winning near the goal—yet, do not grieve;
> She cannot fade, though thou hast not thy bliss,
> For ever wilt thou love, and she be fair!

Forever! Probably due to my father's and brother's early deaths, I've often
felt that hand of the Reaper at my neck. This poem attracted me from
early on with its vision of permanence. But the problem I found, when I

started to write, was how to get this permanence into my poetry. My solution, although I was not fully aware of it at the beginning, has been the image or, as Pound said, that "intellectual and emotional complex in an instant of time."[2] Or, as Robert Hass says in his essay, "Images," there is "some feeling in the arrest of the image that what perishes and what lasts forever have been brought into conjunction."[3] The picture frozen in time suspends time just as the images on the urn do, especially if the image is brought from the past, with meaning, into the present.

I'm aware this is not a new concept, although when I first began writing I did not have that theoretical knowledge, just the need to suspend certain moments of my past. And, because I've always had the need to use the past to inform the present (and to use the present to redeem, when possible, the past), I started writing poems with two suspended, imagistic moments, so that they might energize and inform each other.

My poem *At the Table* uses that image named in the title to present two such moments and to erase the forty or so years between my present visit to my mother and the recollection of her at that "other table/ in that other kitchen." The image bridges the time span, makes the years in between fade and, poetically, the two tables become one: a place where my mother and I confront each other once again. The moment from the past, with her screaming, is frozen into the present at the new table with her babbling, and so the past lives in the present; temporal distinctions cease to exist in the poem's context. The reader's perception of this timelessness joins the two tables and is meant to create that sense of epiphany, a lyrically intense moment risen from the narrative. (This sense of timelessness is also exaggerated by my mother's Alzheimer's; she becomes the child and I the parent.) As the adult in the present, I am able to relive, without the old fears, the anger and terror that I encountered as a child at the old table. I can go back through the poem and imaginatively remake my history. The suspended image makes this possible.

This technique of suspending the moment appears in several other poems I love. William Butler Yeats's *Lapis Lazuli,* for instance, has those stunning last two stanzas in which he describes the three Chinamen, "carved in lapis lazuli," as they climb the stone mountain where they stare on the "tragic scene" as "accomplished fingers begin to play."[4] Isn't this the immortality of art, of the moment suspended? Such images appear, more recently, in the poems of James Dickey, whom I consider to be the contemporary

American master of this poetic move. Dickey presents a timeless moment in his poem *In the Lupanar at Pompeii,* "Where on the dark walls of their home . . . ancient prostitutes hold their eternal postures,/ Doing badly drawn, exacting,/ Too-willing, wide-eyed things/ With dry-eyed art . . ." and, again, in *Chenille,* "Beasts that cannot be thought of/ By the wholly sane/ Rise up in the rough, blurred/ Flowers of fuzzy cloth/ In only their timeless outlines/ Like the beasts of Heaven."[5]

In his poem *90 North,* Randall Jarrell's use of the North Pole and its associated images in scenes from both the speaker's past and present fascinates me for the reasons mentioned above. I am also attracted to its use of dramatic action to create what T. S. Eliot calls in his essay on *Hamlet* the "objective correlative": "a set of objects, a situation, a chain of events which shall be the formula of that particular emotion."[6] In my writing, I sensed from the very beginning that I needed to master this imagistic portrayal of an emotion in order to express what was raging within me: isolation, betrayal, mourning. I knew I had to couch those emotions in physical, sensual terms rather than abstraction, probably because so much of what I had to say, I'd like to stress, was embedded in physical images from my past. The "themes" I needed to deal with came to me in emotionally laden image clusters, so the use of the "objective correlative" was just what I needed to say what I had to say.

Jarrell begins his poem with the speaker as a child imagining his ascent to the North Pole, with all of its attendant adventure and joy. The climb itself, as in Yeats's *Lapis Lazuli,* is an act that creates an air of expectation, of fulfillment. But when the boy is at the top, we see that the promised joy will not be attained, for his "companions lay frozen" and "[t]he stiff furs knocked at [his] starveling throat." This is Lorca's duende at work, and that sense of danger and isolation, of man's vulnerability, is dramatically realized in the adult's second imaginative ascent to the North Pole—in the poem itself—where all is meaningless, where the speaker lives or dies "by accident alone." The dramatic contrast between the two states, for me, is enhanced because they both refer to the same image/situation of the journey to the North Pole.

Jarrell's poem has held me in its sway all these years because it mirrors a seemingly simple way of re-creating an emotion in the reader through the use of image and dramatic action. What better natural image than the North Pole could be found to portray the sense of coldness and isolation he wishes to express? What better way to begin the poem than with the expectant quest of a young man's journey? Again, I did not notice most of this until years after my first reading, but I absorbed the principles enough to attempt my own creations.

At the Table has several dramatic actions which embody (and hopefully re-create in the reader) an emotion, and they all occur "at the table," that central image which is meant to reverberate with meaning. The poem opens, for instance, with my mother repeatedly reading *Oneida* aloud from a knife she holds while sitting at the table, an action meant to embody her incoherence, the arbitrariness of her speech. This inability to speak purposefully, in turn, mirrors her past and present isolation from her family, her community, and possibly even herself:

> just four feet away yet so distant
> I know I can't reach her no matter
>   what I say,
> all of the names gone into buttered
> toast and blue cups of coffee.

This isolation is embodied through a dramatic situation later in the poem, too, where the mother is seen sitting "at the far end of the blue dining room/ no longer waiting for anyone to come." The poem ends with an emphasis on her inability to communicate or to make human contact, and with the speaker hoping "she/ never finds" the words she's looking for, because that wish embodies his anger and desire for her to remain isolated.

Jarrell's poem has fascinated me, I imagine, because he uses poetry to portray his past in its relation to his present. From my first day of writing, I have continuously felt the need to make sense of my past, to let the past inform and perhaps even make sense of my present. That past comes to me in vivid memories of images and dramatic actions, not in abstractions, and so I've naturally tended to render it in those terms. The arrested image has a two-fold effect: we know its moment has perished, and, simultaneously, we know it is made permanent in the poem. This concept, when coupled with the strong belief that the right image and dramatic action can produce an emotion in the reader, accounts for the concentration of sensual detail in all of my work. I also believe I return to certain images from my past, such as the table, because, as Stanley Kunitz once said in an interview about his own work, certain "root" images belong to that part of his life he keeps trying to turn into legend, "converting dross into gold."[7]

This brings me to the vehicle for these imagistic moments: the line, the breath, that articulation of my own body rhythm in words that spin out and pull back in long, convoluted sentences tumbling down the page. Several poets have been important influences on my use of this long breath, including Milton in *Paradise Lost;* Allen Ginsberg in *Howl* and *Kaddish* especially; Theodore Roethke in some of his earlier poems such as *Frau Bauman, Frau Schmidt and Frau Schwartze* and in later poems from the *North American Sequence* of *The Far Field;* and finally C. K. Williams in *Tar* and *With Ignorance.* However, the earliest and most influential poet-breather I'd have to claim is Walt Whitman, especially in *Out of the Cradle Endlessly Rocking.* From looking at Whitman's poem, especially the first, one-sentence stanza that crescendos down the page, I associate the long breath with, again, Lorca's sense of duende. As the speaker confronts his vulnerability, his mortality, his breath keeps him, us, and the poem alive. In *Out of the Cradle Endlessly Rocking,* that urgency finds itself not only in the subject matter but also in the unwinding of line after line, as though the poet must not stop but must hurry to speak, "ere all eludes me, hurriedly." When I sit down to write, I feel just such an urgent need to get my words out: as though I can't get them down fast enough, and if I hesitate, I'll be lost. As long as I keep breathing, I keep living, and I believe my poems don't stop for that very reason. The poem's life-flow is vulnerable, and to stop might kill it.

But no poet merely wants to repeat what's been done: using anaphora, piling up clauses in parallel phrases. So I've tried to alter the line to fit my own worldview to my breath in a stuttering, staggering line that often breaks in unexpected places only to continue in a dropped line. This, I've come to realize, is how my sense of existence finds its breath: jagged, sometimes confusing, trying to balance itself but usually failing to do so as it winds speedily down the page. The clausal line which completes itself in sentences not only slows the poem down—countering my need for urgency—it also gives the delusion of stability, a delusion which does not sit well with most of my topics. A few lines from *At the Table* show this erratic pacing:

> let her know our Thanksgiving dinner table was
>   crammed with relatives and friends

> while she sat at the far end of the blue dining
>   room
> no longer waiting for anyone to come, lifting
>   the one glass of milk
> she still limits herself to each day because
>   she can't break the habit.

I've broken these lines for some musical considerations, but the primary principle is that I don't want the lines to make sense of themselves, I want them to represent the mind's discordant, sometimes disruptive, attention as it tries to find the words. So I enjamb, I drop, I try to create an unsettling pace, but I do not stop. (Some of my recent poems which better demonstrate this principle are *Acupuncture and Cleansing at Forty-Eight, 518, And where were you,* and *Knots,* to name a few.) *At the Table* is one sentence because, as I've said above, I felt such a strong sense of urgency as I was writing it that to stop would mean the death of the poem, of its rhythmic life. I feel this way about many of my poems, and so they unwind in what I hope is some form of what Robert Lowell calls the muscle of syntax, a muscle I hear/feel and respond to strongly in the poets named above and others.

Lowell's work has probably had the greatest and most varied influence on my poetry. When I first read Lowell's poems, I knew he spoke of certain subjects in ways I needed and wanted to speak, and I've never lost my fascination with and admiration for his mastery. *Home After Three Months Away* risks sentiment, has a strong emotional core, that "taste of the self," as Hopkins calls it, but it does not go over the edge into sentimentality. It's presented in clear, accessible language, or, as Lowell has said, in ordinary speech, a quality which makes it a poem of the people, not of the academy. The images also establish a bond between writer and reader: they present so-called ordinary life in common sensual experiences that, as the poem transforms them, are shown to be extraordinary. Finally, the poem rings with vowel and consonant echoes: with word-music. These observations may seem commonplace, since Lowell has influenced so many contemporary American poets, but I would be derelict if I did not at least mention how his poetry showed me ways to find the words (and perhaps even the subjects) of so many of my poems.

Home After Three Months Away is "about" a potentially very sentimental topic: a father who has been institutionalized for three months returns home and is taking a bath with his young daughter. This is the kind of topic I'm drawn to and have often written about: a drunken father singing his favorite songs on the way to work with his young son; a mother who betrayed her husband and sons to live with another man; a husband who fears his wife is having an affair.

One influential technique that Lowell uses, here and in other poems, is what I call a "hard image." Hard images balance the potential sentimentality of the subject, and that's why lines like "gobbets of porkrind in bowknots of gauze" are so significant to me. The hard, arbitrary image sets a tone in the poem right from the start. The "eight foot magnolia tree" and the "English sparrows" that weather the "Boston winter"—all images from stanza one—are also neutral and unemotional. Sure, these images relate to the overall theme of the poem, as we find out later, but they are exact, unsentimental, and objective to the extent that they balance the emotional tone of the entire poem and especially of stanza two. Other examples occur in the third stanza, after the emotional charge of stanza two has registered: "Three stories down below,/ a choreman tends our coffin's length of soil,/ and seven horizontal tulips blow." "*[E]ight foot* magnolia tree," "*[t]hree* stories down," and "*seven* horizontal tulips blow" (emphasis mine) cannot be a coincidence but rather a poetic use of precise images that help create the world as objective fact. This, in turn, distances the reader, or hardens the reader's emotional reaction, to the strong sentiment of stanza two with its core scene of a father washing his daughter in the tub and its accompanying "soft images" such as "[d]impled with exaltation," "[o]ur noses rub," "my child still dabs her cheeks," and so on.

The core situation of my poem, *At the Table*—a son visiting his mother at a home for the elderly—is also potentially sentimental. I therefore try to "harden" some of the images to balance that sentiment, as in my mother "reading *Oneida* aloud." Just the mention of the place name, for me, creates some objectivity. Or when her lost names are "gone into buttered/ toast and blue cups of coffee" or when she lifts "the one glass of milk" or sucks "the meat from the bones," and so on. These objective images and dramatic acts bring the reader back to the arbitrary world of facts and helps to counter the emotional charge of the poem.

Lowell's diction counteracts the sentimentality of his content, and at the same time, Lowell's use of ordinary speech, that frankness to which he often referred, creates a bond with the reader. Right from the start, he uses familiar phrases such as the lioness "who ruled the roost" and made the "[m]other cry," and, at the end of the first stanza, the sparrows who "weather a Boston winter." This sets the easy, familiar, and confidential tone which is carried to the next two stanzas with such phrasing as "nothing's gone," "the time I put away," "child's-play," "to start me," "neither spin nor toil," "[b]ushed by." Such language creates a bond with the reader and in a sense assures us that this is "ordinary" language about an ordinary situation, whereas, of course, it is anything but ordinary! A father has come home, "frizzled, stale and small," as we're told at the end, and all of the seemingly easy language that has come before now reverberates with other meanings; for example, "the time I put away/ was child's-play" becomes dramatically ironic because of the aesthetic distance between the meaning and the colloquial words chosen to convey that meaning.

I love this twisting of everyday language: this use of colloquialisms, even clichés, first to create the usual expectations and then to show other meanings, in context, which hopefully startle the reader into recognizing the extraordinary in the ordinary. In *At the Table,* for instance, when my mother says that "she really ought to go home," the phrase has the ring of any familiar expression, but in the context of this poem, the recognition hits that she's never had a healthy, happy home. Or, at the end of the poem, when she's thinking about telling me "it's/ not right to waste," the familiar chord is struck, but then the insight that she's wasted her life illuminates the phrase. This has been one of Lowell's major influences on my work, and one I greatly enjoy developing.

I did not, at the beginning, study Lowell's use of such familiar language and the twist he gives it; I have written my poems using such language because that's what comes to me when I write, familiar phrases from a lower-class childhood. But as I read more and more of Lowell—especially in *Life Studies* and *For the Union Dead*—I grew to understand how he was using those phrases, which, in turn, helped me to use them more effectively in my first and subsequent drafts.

The last two "influences" Lowell has had on me are fairly common ones and therefore demand little attention, but I need to mention them because they have had a major impact on my work: the use of the so-called "ordinary" events of our lives to illuminate the extraordinary, and the use of word-music, for which he is so well known. The ordinary situation of a father taking a bath with his young daughter is shadowed by the fact that he has just been released from a sanitarium after recuperating from a mental breakdown. The sense of duende, then, of our vulnerability, enters the domestic scene and reminds readers that such "extraordinary" conditions are indeed part of our ordinary existence.

Similarly, my "annual visit" to my mother in her home for the elderly is an ordinary situation, but her Alzheimer's and the subsequent memories it calls up in her and the son infuse the poem with a reminder of our emotional and physical frailty. The familiar setting of eating at a table magnifies this sense of ordinariness and at the same time dramatically contrasts with what's being said (or not said) over that table. I especially like this technique because most of our lives are filled with such so-called ordinary situations that are in fact extraordinary, whether it be a young man making out with his first love at a drive-in or an old man working on a blacktop crew. The trick is, as Lowell shows, to infuse the common scene with the unexpected, to let the lightning strike the tree on the front lawn.

Lastly and perhaps most importantly—for I believe a poem creates itself from its given rhythm and word-music—is the influence of Lowell's tremendous gift of vowel and consonant echoes. He has always been a poet I could rely on to refresh my ear through hearing the clip and swoosh of his language; Seamus Heaney is another such poet, and Keats and Wordsworth, Roethke and Stevens, and some of Whitman. But what I especially find influential in Lowell's word-music is his ability to have riffs of full rhymes countered by near-full and half rhymes, as though it would have been too easy for him to just fully rhyme the poem. (I'm aware that he wrote many rhyming poems he then turned into "free" verse.)

In *Home After Three Months Away,* for instance, he creates all of those wonderful near half rhymes with "nurse" and "roost" and "gauze" and "toast" —matching in tone, I think, with the "harder" images of that stanza— only to go on to stanza two's riff of full rhyme with "tub" and "rub," "gone" and "one," "corduroy" and "boy," and so on, which seem to match the tone and flow of the "softer images" of that stanza. The word-music does not exist just in the end words, either, for there are many echoes within the lines, such as "away" with "play" and "here" and "lather."

Again, I know this is nothing new, but, new or not, his masterful use of such word-music has been a great influence on my work, some instances of which may be seen in *At the Table,* which has "aloud," "holds," and "window" as three of the first five end words, all near half rhymes which are meant to get the poem off to a musical start. Or the internal full rhyme in the next line of "away" with "say," or "buttered" and "other" in the next two lines, or, as the poem progresses, the end words of "back" and "work," or "cross" and "York," "cheek" and "knees," and so on.

As I mentioned earlier, this may be the greatest influence on me because it is to Lowell and poets who make such word-music that I turn when I am unable to write. He helps me to hear the rhythm and music, which in turn helps me to find the words.

These, then, have been the major poetical influences on my work, but there have been so many others, too: William Wordsworth, Seamus Heaney, Sharon Olds, Thomas Hardy, Gerald Stern, Pablo Neruda, George Herbert, Robert Frost, Kenneth Rexroth, Rafael Alberti, Stephen Berg, D. H. Lawrence, Hayden Carruth, William Butler Yeats, Gary Snyder, Robert Hayden, James Wright, Philip Levine, to name just some. The list is long, and one I hesitate even to start making because I know I am not including several important poets. But there is a commonality: whenever I lose my way from words, I return to the well of these poets' words and rhythms to be refreshed, to write again.

MICHAEL RYAN

Michael Ryan was born in St. Louis, Missouri, in 1946. He attended college at Notre Dame and went on to receive an M.A. from Claremont Graduate School as well as an M.F.A. and a Ph.D. from the University of Iowa. His first book of poetry, *Threats Instead of Trees* (Yale University Press, 1974), won the Yale Younger Poets Award and was a nominee for a National Book Award. His next book, *In Winter* (Holt, Rinehart, and Winston, 1981), was a National Poetry Series Selection. His third book, *God Hunger* (Viking Penguin, 1989), won the Lenore Marshall Poetry Prize. He has also won prizes from the *Virginia Quarterly,* the *American Poetry Review,* and the Poetry Society of America, and fellowships from the National Endowment for the Arts and the Guggenheim Foundation, among others. His autobiography, *Secret Life* (Pantheon, 1995), has been translated into German and Spanish and was also imprinted in Britain and Australia. He has just published a new collection of essays on poetry, *A Difficult Grace* (University of Georgia Press, 2000), and is currently at work on a fourth book of poetry. Ryan is Professor of English and Creative Writing at the University of California at Irvine; he also teaches in the M.F.A. Writing Program at Warren Wilson College. He is married to the poet Doreen Gildroy and lives in Irvine.

Reminder

Torment by appetite
is itself an appetite
dulled by inarticulate,
dogged, daily

loving-others-to-death—
as Chekhov put it, "compassion
down to your fingertips"—,
looking on them as into the sun

not in the least for their sake
but slowly for your own
because it causes
the blinded soul to bloom

like deliciousness in dirt,
like beauty from hurt,
their light—*their* light—
pulls so surely. Let it.

EMILY DICKINSON
756

One Blessing had I than the rest
So larger to my Eyes
That I stopped gauging—satisfied—
For this enchanted size—

It was the limit of my Dream—
The focus of my Prayer—
A perfect—paralyzing Bliss—
Contented as Despair—

I knew no more of Want—or Cold—
Phantasms both become
For this new Value in the Soul—
Supremest Earthly Sum—

The Heaven below the Heaven above—
Obscured with ruddier Blue—
Life's Latitudes leant over—full—
The Judgement perished—too—

Why Bliss so scantily disburse—
Why Paradise defer—
Why Floods be served to Us—in Bowls—
I speculate no more—

599

There is a pain—so utter—
It swallows substance up—
Then covers the Abyss with Trance—
So Memory can step
Around—across—upon it—
As one within a Swoon—
Goes safely—where an open eye—
Would drop Him—Bone by Bone.

1304

Not with a Club, the Heart is broken
Nor with a Stone—
A Whip so small you could not see it
I've known

To lash the Magic Creature
Till it fell,
Yet that Whip's Name
Too noble then to tell.

Magnanimous as Bird
By Boy descried—
Singing unto the Stone
Of which it died—

Shame need not crouch
In such an Earth as Ours—
Shame—stand erect—
The Universe is yours.

Influence and Mastery

Reminder was sparked by a conversation with my friend, Jim McMichael, about Emmanuel Levinas's notion of the "alterity of the Other" that is both "the alterity of the human Other and of the Most-High." For Levinas, "the intelligibility of transcendence lies outside ontological structures" and "bears an ethical sense or direction." His argument is that "the structure of transcendence is exemplified not by religious experience" in solitude, but by "the ethical," behavior toward other people. Although Levinas was a Lithuanian Jew, his idea seems to me a radical, illuminating re-vision of the traditional Christian notion that faith without good works is dead: for Levinas, it is possible to experience God only in action toward others. Simone Weil said almost the same thing when she wrote that if you give a crust to a beggar in the right spirit, it will save *your* soul (emphasis hers). Levinas, a Holocaust survivor, added, "and you must take the bread from your own mouth."

Emily Dickinson practiced her own version of this "compassion down to your fingertips" and often wrote about it:

779
The Service without Hope—
Is tenderest, I think—
Because 'tis unsustained
By stint—Rewarded Work—

Has impetus of Gain—
And impetus of Goal—
There is no Diligence like that
That knows not an Until—

When I wrote *Reminder*, I was about four years into a still-unfinished sequence of sixteen-line poems in quatrains and an immersion in Dickinson's work that also continues. She has certainly "influenced" me, a word whose Latin root means the flowing of an ethereal fluid or power from the stars, thought by Roman astrologers to affect a person's character and actions. Dickinson knew herself to be a person who could be this powerfully influenced by writing, and indeed was this powerfully influenced, by the Bible and Shakespeare and lesser constellations. That she knew she could be even more powerfully influenced by people is evident from her first letters and poems, and is part of the reason behind her famous withdrawal from society at large into a society of intimates, a cloister that has been disfiguringly popularized as neurotic isolation and even agoraphobia.

Reminder, as I hope is clear, is addressed to myself. The last sentence of the poem ("Let it.") is meant to occur in a continuous present, the moment in the poem merged with the moment of reading it. As Dickinson said, "Forever is composed of nows." This intense focus she had I constantly forget. I need many reminders, and this poem is one of them. All of my sixteen-line poems in quatrains, including this one, have been influenced (and inspired) by Dickinson's remarkably various and rich adaptations of the hymn stanza. Some of this range can be seen in the three poems of hers I have selected (numbers *756, 599, 1304*). She uses the stanza as a structural grid with slant rhymes at the joists, a recurring melody against the rhythmical and grammatical counterpoint of her sentences, which themselves are often counterpointed against conventional grammar through the agency of the dashes. It is a technically brilliant and inimitable poetic style. My ambition in *Reminder* and the other poems in my sequence is much more modest: simply to use the form differently each time and make sure each particular usage is grounded in the particular poem's structure and subject. She accomplished this over and over again in her 1,789 poems and thirty years of writing. For her to have done so, it must have been part of her intention, yet how she learned such intentions, much less such mastery in realizing them, is a mystery.

Another aspect of her mysterious mastery is somewhat more traceable. Despite their variety, these three poems have in common what Jay Leyda, in his introduction to *The Years and Hours of Emily Dickinson,* mistakenly called the "omitted center": "The riddle, the circumstance too well known to be repeated to the initiate, the deliberate skirting of the obvious—this was the means she used to increase the privacy of her communication." On the contrary, it is by omitting anecdote and incident that she arrives at the "center" in these poems, the place of public communication where the poem is about the reader not the writer, where language articulates not merely the writer's temporary feelings but permanent human feeling and thereby transfigures her private feelings, contextualizes them, and illuminates them. This, as Dickinson well knew, is a religious experience, analogous to using the New Testament's story of Christ to transfigure, contextualize, and illuminate similar moments in any person's life. But she accomplishes it through rhetoric, not narrative; by writing a poem, not preaching the Gospel; by the authority of human words, not God's. All three poems are arguments. She doesn't tell us what occasioned her blessing *(756)* or pain *(599)* or shame *(1304),* but deals in their effects. There is no information in the poem that separates her from us. The poem is made to be an experience instead of referring to one, which is precisely how she says she knows poetry in her famous remark to Higginson: "If I read a book [and] it makes my whole body so cold no fire ever can warm me I know *that* is poetry. If I feel physically as if the top of my head were taken off, I know *that* is poetry. These are the only way I know it. Is there any other way."

I am trying to learn how she learned to write like this. Rhetoric was one of her main subjects during her year at Mount Holyoke Seminary. Her text there was Samuel P. Newman's *A Practical System of Rhetoric.* It is still an interesting and sophisticated book, astonishingly so for high school students (impossibly so for today's high school students). Newman writes, "The first and leading object of attention in every composition of an argumentative kind, is to determine the precise point of inquiry—the proposition which is to be laid down and supported." All three poems have such a proposition, but the way they are "laid down and supported" differ wildly and wonderfully, and constitute a short lesson in the depth of her skill. *756* ("One Blessing had I than the rest") is the simplest: proposition (stanza 1), evidence (stanzas 2–4), conclusion (stanza 5). Its conventional argumentative structure, dull in the hands of Dickinson's Victorian contemporaries, here ground a subject, a mind, and a linguistic inventiveness that are alive in every line. This solidity of structure, and its coincidence with the stanza form, allow for point-to-point variation and improvisation. *599* ("There is a pain—so utter") works differently. The proposition stated in the first two lines is then integrated into a personified drama that is also a description of human response to utter pain—neither a particular human nor a particular pain, much less her or hers, whatever utter pain may have sparked her writing it. The argument is implicit and enacted, and a second drama ("[a]s one within a Swoon") is generated from the first by the pivotal simile, which always implies the mind of the speaker. Her mind is active throughout. We experience her reinterpreting her own words when "swallows" changes from metaphor to dramatic action at the moment the utter pain "*covers* the Abyss with Trance" (emphasis mine). The compounding of the initial action makes us focus on what such utter pain *does,* and what it does, in the last six lines of the poem, is surprisingly palliative, as if such pain contains its own act of grace that allows the sufferer to survive. And what a sentence the poem is—as complex and clear as a sentence can be, laid across eight lines, counterpointed by the famous dashes that in her manuscripts are more often more like dots or like diagonals slashed up or down.

That's how they are in the manuscript of *1304;* those handwritten dashes are impossible to reproduce typographically, and the lineation is different as well. In the manuscript the line breaks appear as follows:

Not with a   *sonnet ?*
Club, the Heart
is broken
Nor with a
Stone
A Whip so
small you
could not see it
I've known

To lash the
Magic Creature
till it fell,
Yet that Whip's
Name
too noble then
to tell.

Magnanimous
as Bird
By Boy descried—
Singing unto the
Stone
of which it died—

Shame need not
    crouch
In such an Earth

as Our's.
Shame—Stand Erect.
The Universe is your's.

This manuscript, unlike the two earlier ones from the fascicles, looks strikingly private—the stanzas are on the page but the lines are only in her ear. The argument, too, is more unruly than those of either earlier poem. The proposition takes two stanzas to state in its entirety and is composed of three smaller propositions: 1) the Heart (conventional symbol for the seat of feeling) is not broken by weapons that break the body; 2) the Heart (characterized as "the Magic Creature") is broken by something invisible (characterized as "A Whip"); 3) the name of that whip (or the person wielding it) may not be revealed because it is "too noble" to the person testifying or at least to this person giving this testimony or perhaps to society at large. The three smaller propositions go from public (even commonplace) to invisible to secret. Nor is that secret revealed by the rest of the poem. If the argument moves forward, it does so obliquely. The third stanza is an unattached sentence fragment, a comparison made by the speaker about the speaker or about anyone in the speaker's position—less evidence than testimony dramatized through figures. (Dickinson often uses birds to stand for herself.) The first sentence of the last stanza is a conclusion: "Shame need not crouch/ in such an Earth as Ours"—shame (personified) need not be invisible or secret. But the conclusion begins another argument, in the surprising form of a command directly addressed to Shame. This same sort of oblique movement occurs in the break between stanza two and three, but here it is contained within a stanza. The reason Shame need not be invisible is that it owns the universe. The speaker's anguish and fury in this moment of the poem are amplified by the direct address, which enacts dramatically the speaker's attempt to distinguish Shame from herself while paradoxically asserting its universal dominance.

Dickinson's mastery here is manifold, and the insight behind it is based on a profound acquaintance with how Shame pervades identity and destroys it, which brings us back from cosmos to microcosm, the Heart's being lashed "[t]ill it fell." The argument as a whole is at best circular, but as Higginson wrote in *Atlantic Essays* (which Dickinson read, both as the individual essays appeared in the *Atlantic Monthly* and as a book when it was published in 1871), "In what is called poetry, *belles-lettres,* or pure literature, the osseous structure is of course hidden; and the symmetry suggested is always that of taste rather than of logic, though logic must always be implied, or at least never violated." "Taste" was one of the main critical terms of the day and does indeed suggest the symmetry of *1304*. According to Newman, "As the result of past experiences of emotions, certain principles seem fixed in the mind, and when taste is called into exercise, it is the immediate application of these principles to particular instances." Poems may have arguments, but they also have many other generative tools and triggers, from large musical patterns to syntactical and sonic rhythms to "past experiences of emotions."

When such compelling poems as this one walk the edge of unintelligibility, it is natural to try to make them more accessible by looking for hints in the person behind the act of speech (or writing) that characterizes her. We want to know exactly what her "past experiences of emotions" were. This is probably why Dickinson has been the subject of rampant biographical speculation ever since the first edition of her poems (which so many readers immediately found "strange" and "powerful") appeared in 1890, four years after her death. The surviving biographical evidence around *1304* is tantalizing, as usual. Dickinson made a copy of the poem on a sheet which Ralph Franklin describes as "wove, cream, and blue-ruled; the stationery is embossed CONGRESS above a capitol." Franklin dates it "about 1873–74" and 1874 in the *Variorum Edition;* Johnson in *The Complete Poems* dated it "c. 1874." Dickinson's father died in 1874. A former United States Congressman, he was serving in the state legislature in Boston, gave a speech on the house floor, felt weak afterwards, walked back to his rented room to which a physician was summoned who apparently gave him opium he was allergic to, and he died. Why would Emily Dickinson copy a poem about shame on her father's official stationery? Maybe for no reason at all, since she seemed to have used any and all available scraps of paper. On the same set of two sheets is *1279,* "The way to know the Bobolink," which is one of her many poems about how to see the natural world à la Emerson and Blake through the eye, not with it. But it also contains these "lines":

> He compliments
> Existence
> Until allured

Away

By Seasons
 or his Children
Adult and
urgent grown-

Between the two poems is an "x" and the word "possibly" above a two-inch horizontal line that may be the markings of her first editor, Millicent Todd Bingham. Below the line is the first stanza of "Not with a club." Did she write these two poems after her father died? When did she copy them onto his stationery? What do they have to do with him?

The other tantalizing bit surrounding a poem about the absolute power of shame is the article that Emily Dickinson certainly read in the *Springfield Republican* on September 24, 1874. It was written by Judge Otis Phillip Lord, and it was about the greatest scandal of the day: the revelation of the long-time extramarital affair between Elizabeth Tilton and Henry Ward Beecher, the famous minister and abolitionist. The Beechers were longtime family friends of the Dickinsons, and Emily Dickinson was in love with Judge Lord, who was her father's age. Whether or not she was in love with him in 1874, while his wife was still alive, is unknown, but she (later?) owned a ring with his middle name engraved inside the band, and her sister Vinnie's last gesture over her coffin was to put two heliotropes by her hand "to take to Judge Lord," who had died two years before. His article in the *Springfield Republican* concluded that Beecher was guilty of adultery.

However "Not with a Club" came to be written, whatever personal shame Emily Dickinson suffered or observed, the poem is ours now. It was also ours when she wrote it, because of the way she wrote. Her mastery derives from a dedication to truth and a belief in her lexicon: the power of language-in-poetry to present truth. This, I think, is what she meant by "my business is circumference" (a term she must have first encountered in reading Emerson): the circle of human articulation is widened, the terra incognita within the circle becomes known. It is mapped by the poem in the writing, forever there for us to discover in reading it—provided that we learn how to read it, which continues to be the challenge of Dickinson's poems, since they continue to be almost as unconventional as they were when she wrote them. Her mastery of grammar and rhetoric were so complete that her failed experiments with them constitute a failure of English to do what she asks of it, although it answered her more often than it didn't. At her best, she put the greatest pressure on it, with faith in its ability to bear it—a direct analogy to her relationship to God. Her love of other people was generous, complex, and (as it is for the rest of us) specific in character to the person she loved; sometimes it was so intense as to constitute what she called "idolatry." "I do not respect 'doctrines,'" she said (quoting the word to emphasize her disdain)—"doctrines" of orthodox grammar no less than of orthodox religion, but in both cases she seems to have absorbed everything in them that was useful to her. Her humility is in her understanding that language, like God, was here before she was, but she used all of her intelligence, wit, courage, and talent to leave them both changed. In my opinion, she did.

IRA SADOFF

Ira Sadoff was born in Brooklyn, New York, in 1945. Before receiving his M.F.A. in fiction writing at the University of Oregon, he studied labor law in the ILR School at Cornell University. He has published one novel, *Uncoupling* (Houghton Mifflin, 1982); five books of poetry, *Settling Down* (Houghton Mifflin, 1975), *Palm Reading in Winter* (Houghton Mifflin, 1978), *A Northern Calendar* (Godine, 1982), *Emotional Traffic* (Godine, 1991), and *Grazing* (University of Illinois Press, 1998); and a collection of his poems, stories, and essays, *An Ira Sadoff Reader* (Middlebury College Press, 1992). Sadoff lives in Hallowell, Maine. He is married to Linda Sadoff and has two stepchildren, Casey and Julie.

Did You Ever Get a Phone Call

Did you ever get a phone call from the past, pleading with you
to come back? Pain pulls up its dress, inviting you to look.
If it's not a husband and wife it's a Serbian hit squad,
the front of the bombed-out building so mangled and open, some
    widow's
cooking in her apartment while next door the bastard's undressing,
we can't see who it is, lying on the quilt in the bed you made together.

You know the voice, the exact pitch and inflection, the flap of it
from the window calling out. Is it yours? It says, I'm tired

of clever metaphors. Can you stare at them like that, at all those
who've been vanquished, without recourse, the doggedly sad
who dream of satin instead of broadcloth? I mean of someone to love
    them
without inventing some self–portrait that looks like a war criminal
as he stands over the bodies with his hands behind his back.

Right now I'm sending this postcard from a resort town on the Isle of
    Wight.
Right now I've got my new wife going down to breakfast, humming.
Right now you can see why I turn away from the sink and its rusty drain.

But the news is like a warning in reverse, a collapsed barn
you remember with the cows still inside, incessantly mooing.
Little Sigmund Freud trying to climb back into the womb because he's
    sick,
there's no other explanation for that origin climbing,
for going back and repainting and replastering as if she were still in bed
begging you to bring her a magazine. I prefer the ruins
of another country: how quaint they are, where the Romans
once built a temple or two. I have friends who say, I can't forgive the
    winter.
Their whole lives, waiting to be asked back.
Dear Gods, I bet they say, you wouldn't pilfer a shadow, would you?

WALT WHITMAN
Excerpts from *The Sleepers*

4
I turn but do not extricate myself,
Confused, a past-reading, another, but with darkness yet.

The beach is cut by the razory ice-wind, the wreck-guns sound,
The tempest lulls, the moon comes floundering through the drifts.

I look where the ship helplessly heads end on, I hear the burst as she
    strikes, I hear the howls of dismay, they grow fainter and fainter.

I cannot aid with my wringing fingers,
I can but rush to the surf and let it drench me and freeze upon me.

I search with the crowd, not one of the company is wash'd to us alive,
In the morning I help pick up the dead and lay them in rows in a barn.

5
Now of the older war-days, the defeat at Brooklyn,
Washington stands inside the lines, he stands on the intrench'd hills
    amid a crowd of officers,
His face is cold and damp, he cannot repress the weeping drops,
He lifts the glass perpetually to his eyes, the color is blanch'd from
    his cheeks,
He sees the slaughter of the southern braves confided to him by their
    parents.

The same at last and at last when peace is declared,
He stands in the room of the old tavern, the well-belov'd soldiers all
    pass through,
The officers speechless and slow draw near in their turns,
The chief encircles their necks with his arm and kisses them on the
    cheek,
He kisses lightly the wet cheeks one after another, he shakes hands and
    bids good-by to the army.

6
Now what my mother told me one day as we sat at dinner together,
Of when she was a nearly grown girl living home with her parents on
    the old homestead.

A red squaw came one breakfast-time to the old homestead,
On her back she carried a bundle of rushes for rush-bottoming chairs,
Her hair, straight, shiny, coarse, black, profuse, half-envelop'd her face,
Her step was free and elastic, and her voice sounded exquisitely as she
    spoke.

My mother look'd in delight and amazement at the stranger,
She look'd at the freshness of her tall-borne face and full and pliant
    limbs,
The more she look'd upon her she loved her,
Never before had she seen such wonderful beauty and purity,
She made her sit on a bench by the jamb of the fireplace, she cook'd
    food for her,

She had no work to give her, but she gave her remembrance and
    fondness.

The red squaw staid all the forenoon, and toward the middle of the
    afternoon she went away,
O my mother was loth to have her go away,
All the week she thought of her, she watch'd for her many a month,
She remember'd her many a winter and many a summer,
But the red squaw never came nor was heard of there again.

C. K. WILLIAMS
Neglect

An old hill town in northern Pennsylvania, a missed connection for a
    bus, an hour to kill.
For all intents and purposes, the place was uninhabited; the mines had
    closed years before—
anthracite too dear to dig, the companies went west to strip, the miners
    to the cities—
and now, although the four-lane truck route still went through—
    eighteen-wheelers pounding past—
that was almost all: a shuttered Buick dealer, a grocery, not even a
    McDonald's,
just the combination ticket office, luncheonette and five-and-dime
    where the buses turned around.
A low gray frame building, it was gloomy and rundown, but
    charmingly old-fashioned:
ancient wooden floors, open shelves, the smell of unwrapped candy,
    cigarettes and band-aid glue.
The only people there, the only people I think that I remember from
    the town at all,
were the silent woman at the register and a youngish teen-aged boy
    standing reading.
The woman smoked and smoked, stared out the streaky window,
    handed me my coffee with indifference.
It was hard to tell how old she was: her hair was dyed and teased, iced
    into a beehive.
The boy was frail, sidelong somehow, afflicted with a devastating
    Nessus-shirt of acne
boiling down his face and neck—pits and pores, scarlet streaks and
    scars; saddening.
We stood together at the magazine rack for a while before I realized
    what he was looking at.

Pornography: two naked men, one grimaces, the other, with a fist
    inside the first one, grins.
I must have flinched: the boy sidled down, blanked his face more and
    I left to take a walk.
It was cold, but not enough to catch or clear your breath: uncertain
    clouds, unemphatic light.
Everything seemed dimmed and colorless, the sense of surfaces
    dissolving, like the Parthenon.
Farther down the main street were a dentist and a chiropractor, both
    with hand-carved signs,
then the Elks' decaying clapboard mansion with a parking space
    "Reserved for the Exalted Ruler,"
and a Russian church, gilt onion domes, a four-horned air-raid siren on
    a pole between them.
Two blocks in, the old slate sidewalks shatter and uplift—gnawed
    lawns, aluminum butane tanks—
then the roads begin to peter out and rise: half-fenced yards with scabs
    of weeks-old snow,
thin, inky, oily leaks of melt insinuating down the gulleys and the
    cindered cuts
that rose again into the footings of the filthy, disused slagheaps ringing
    the horizon.
There was nowhere else. At the depot now, the woman and the boy
    were both behind the counter.
He was on a stool, his eyes closed, she stood just in back of him,
    massaging him,
hauling at his shoulders, kneading at the muscles like a boxer's trainer
    between rounds.
I picked up the county paper: it was anti-crime and welfare bums, for
    Reaganomics and defense.
The wire-photo was an actress in her swimming suit, that famously
    expensive bosom, cream.
My bus arrived at last, its heavy, healthy white exhaust pouring in the
    afternoon.
Glancing back, I felt a qualm, concern, an ill heart, almost parental, but
    before I'd hit the step,
the boy'd begun to blur, to look like someone else, the woman had
    already faded absolutely.
All that held now was that violated, looted country, the fraying fringes
    of the town,
those gutted hills, hills by rote, hills by permission, great, naked wastes
    of wrack and spill,
vivid and disconsolate, like genitalia shaved and disinfected for an
    operation.

EMILY DICKINSON
508

I'm ceded—I've stopped being Theirs—
The name They dropped upon my face
With water, in the country church
Is finished using, now,
And They can put it with my Dolls,
My childhood, and the string of spools,
I've finished threading—too—

Baptized, before, without the choice,
But this time, consciously, of Grace—
Unto supremest name—
Called to my Full—The Crescent dropped—
Existence's whole Arc, filled up,
With one small Diadem.

My second Rank—too small the first—
Crowned—Crowing—on my Father's breast—
A half unconscious Queen—
But this time—Adequate—Erect,
With Will to choose, or to reject,
And I choose, just a Crown—

Multiplicity of Voices

Sometime ago, I got a phone call from my mother, who wanted to patch up some long-term difficulties in our relationship. Her voice was not exactly stiff; it was rather the slow, laborious voice of someone learning a language, enunciating her words slowly, or, even more, it was a voice filled with everything buried inside her for the past four decades: rage, hurt, shame, a tremor of powerlessness, a willed softness, a terrifying self-consciousness. She wanted to project an affectionate image with steadiness and calm, but she couldn't control competing textures of feeling. I am still haunted by all those voices within a single voice, not only in my mother, but in all of us. I think of experience as multiple and simultaneous, and although there's nothing we poets like to do more than "give form" to experience in that Modernist way of moving toward illumination, even if it is an ambiguous or paradoxical closure (mastery), my experience actually suggests something more fragmented and less finite. Until a few years ago, I lacked sufficient vision, confidence, and skill as an artist to express all those textures in an authentic and volatile way within a single poem. I had to give up on both representation and mastery to let all those voices into a poem. I read a lot more of avant-garde poets like John Ashbery, Lyn Hejinian, and Marjorie Welish. Oddly enough, the poet who helped me find that multiplicity of voices was Whitman. I've taught a course on Whitman and Dickinson three times now, and although my love for Dickinson always exceeded my love for Whitman (in part because of his willful and dramatically questionable resolution of the justified cosmos), Whitman finally entered me through the cadences of his lines, not only in their ebb and flow but in his qualifications, his contradictions and differences. In his best poems, like *The Sleepers,* he lets his perceptions breathe and clang against one another without fixing them; he draws both from public and private life, requiring that they bleed onto one another, using his magnifying glass and telescope to express correspondence and difference in unequal measure.

My own poem *Did You Ever Get a Phone Call* didn't begin for me until, watching the news, I found myself mesmerized by the report of a hurricane that had torn the face off a building. You had to look at the devastated insides, the chaos of someone sitting on the couch holding his head in his hands, his possessions having flown far away, perhaps his children buried somewhere under the rubble. In the next apartment was an overturned bed and dresser drawer. So I made the connection between what had been underneath my mother's voice and what was inside the exposed houses. Both experiences felt far away from my own current happiness. That's where I wanted to keep them. But poems wrestle and interrogate, they take a settled truth and toss it away. They reject self-absorbed feelings of pathos and guilt. So I'm in there, too, hovering over that accumulated personal pain, going back to the time when I wasn't merely a spectator to the devastated figures on the bed. For a number of drafts I just trusted that I would probe, inhabit, and flesh out the correspondences, which is one job of the imagination.

This is my most recent poem. I have no way of judging its quality, but it feels authentic and is certainly representative of the way I've been using narrative, imagery, metaphor, and line, with quick cuts and collage, moving from the intensely personal to the public, exploring the gaps and sparks between. It seemed like the right poem with which to talk about process without reducing the poem to "technique" and that limited notion of "craft."

Mastery's a term with many resonances: it has specific meaning for the Modernists, but some poets think of it as learning their trade, and others conceive of it in terms of competitiveness, as in Harold Bloom's *The Anxiety of Influence*. According to Wallace Stevens, "the power of the mind over the possibilities of things" provides the means of self-preservation which enables us to perceive the normal against the abnormal, the opposite of chaos in chaos, the imaginative fiction even if illusory, helps people live their lives and gives life whatever savor it possesses.[1] Although Stevens is one of my "Master" poets, I couldn't agree less with the above passage. It's conservative, cynical, grandiose, even hypocritical, extending faith to the "even if illusory" coherence of an "apposite world." It replicates new criticism's desire to separate the dark, chaotic world from the transcendental and the poetic. I can't write that way. As someone whose intellect has sometimes overpowered feelings, poems, you name it, I've worked hard to relinquish mastery in favor of poems that are more process-oriented, more open-ended. If the world is not quite a text like any other text, it is a shifting field that refuses to be fixed.

The longer I've been writing, the more difficult it is to track literary influences. After thirty years, I suppose I've absorbed less and less from other writers and more from my own poetic diction and syntax. But to deny influence is to deny that you're writing literature and living in the world. I know C. K. Williams's work made an impression on me, especially in *Tar,* for his muscular use of line, his nuanced narratives, and for the way he sought out the complex, ironic relationships between public and private, self and other. I've also intensified the music and broadened the syntactical strategies in my poems, giving the surfaces more density and sensuousness. A number of contemporary poets have helped in this area, but the tautness of line emanating in syntax (coupled with the tension between assonant and consonant music) probably owes a debt to Dickinson and Berryman. Dickinson's poem, "I'm ceded—I've stopped being Theirs," offers the reflexive line an accruing, surprising syntax that I aspire to in my poems. You can also see the poem is at second glance a mess (if, at first glance, you've thematized the poem to "represent" her choosing authentic spirituality over socialized religion). The speaker wants both to serve and to be Jesus, to be feminized and erect (proud and sexual); she desires an autonomous self but chooses to suffer like the son of God. Look at "Called to my Full—The Crescent dropped": what wonderful use of line and syntax to describe not a symmetrical opposition but the askew "full" and "dropped." The richness of this poem lies in Dickinson's inability to decide on her need to acquire self-sufficiency, power, naming and language, desire, vulnerability (she chooses "*just* a crown"). In Bloom's terms, my relationship to this poem would be an Oedipal desire to supercede my poetic ancestors; but rarely have I seen a more solipsistic example of turning a passion into a principle than in the terms of that argument. I'm grateful to these poets, pure and simple: there's infinite room in the world for great poetry. My achievement does not originate in trying to better poets who've made me feel intensely.

I would also claim two non-literary influences. First, having been a passionate fan of jazz for the last thirty years, I finally found a way to use it in my poems, integrating the associative nature of improvisation, taking an idea or an image and transforming it within its own syntax rather than tracking it into a linear trajectory. The saxophone playing of David Murray and James Carter helped me admit more dissonance into my work. And personally, contrary to the cliché that poems require personal tragedy, having found much more pleasure in the world, in love, in my wife-to-be and children, my eyes have been opened more to human possibility, and to the tragedy—cultural, economic, metaphysical—of being deprived of that pleasure and meaning. There's no essence to alienation: that Modernist concept is as culturally bound as Mastery.

Although I wouldn't legislate the relationship between character and work, in my case the connections seem clear. In the last half decade, my poems have acquired more erotic energy, have become more volatile and expansive, have risked making connections between the personal and the social in non-intellectual ways that seemed impossible before. With confidence has come patience: patience for suspending form and connections. I've become more willing to be more open and receptive to the poems' textures and surprises. I've felt the authority to display a wider range of emotions: I've been more willing to be playful with the music in my poem, allowing more virtuosity than I did in earlier poems. In *Sexual Water*, Neruda says his eyes are "held hideously open," which is what, it seems to me, is required to write well and to be human.[2]

HUGH SEIDMAN

Hugh Seidman was born in Brooklyn, New York, in 1940. He received his B.S. in mathematics from the Polytechnic Institute of Brooklyn and his M.S. in theoretical physics from the University of Minnesota. He also holds an M.F.A. in writing from Columbia University. Seidman's books of poetry include *Collecting Evidence* (Yale University Press, 1970), *Blood Lord* (Doubleday, 1974), *Throne/Falcon/Eye* (Random House, 1982), *People Live, They Have Lives* (Miami University Press, 1992), *Selected Poems: 1965–95* (Miami University Press, 1995), and a limited-edition chapbook of the poem *12 Views of Freetown, 1 View of Bumbuna* (Half Moon Bay Press, 2001). He is currently at work on another book of poems. He is married and lives in New York City.

200 IN HELL

200 in hell
Where our sweat is predictable
The part of ourselves
Still fused to the mortal

Often the devil
Drives his convertible
He looks like a model from *Gentleman's Quarterly*
With the pageboy black hair

And the six-pack abdominals
But sometimes he must say
What the hell
And drop the charade
With the hooves and the horns and the big red erection
And the tail and the smoke
Blowing out of his nose
I think it returns us to reality for a while
And then he's gone
With a blonde
And we wonder if we saw him
"And excuse me," anyone, "just where in the hell are we?"
Until the next time he comes
And we're back where we started
Though it's hard to track tears
And I don't mean to bring you down
But even in hell
Your life is your own
The devil told me so
He's not a bad guy
Once you know him

As after a while
However long a while was
He drove the red Cadillac
Beneath the soot
And the brimstone
With the bumper torpedos
And the chrome and the whitewalls
And the shark fins
With the top down
Though up or down
He didn't mind
And he said:
Love and *death* and *redemption*
And of course *resurrection*
It was crazy I admit

To debate
With Satan
But it's what may befall you
If you want to know why
I landed here
To tell the truth I've forgotten
Though the reason must be clear
And that's the damnation
He explained as we rode
Though perhaps it's an error
As when the devil will drive by
To fly me to blue sky
If that's where heaven is—
So be it
Wherever I am
I don't give a damn
I'm not particular
After all these years
Wherever I've been

So smile at the moon
Though there is none
And wind all the clocks that are broken
200 in hell
200 in hell
"And what's the temperature of paradise?"
He said about 72
Give or take a degree
And the angels have halos
Just like in the movies
And it's always
Sunday each day—
And all is as it is in all of our dreams

So here I wish you well
Though the devil fell
And we live down here with him

CZESLAW MILOSZ
The Garden of Earthly Delights: Hell
Translated from the Polish by the author and Robert Hass

If not for the existence of Earth, would there be a Hell?
The instruments of torture are man-made:
Kitchen knives, choppers, drills, enemas.
And implements to create the hellish noise:
Trombones, drums, a mechanical flute, a harp
With a poor damned man entwined in its strings.
The waters in Hell are set by the cold of eternal winter.
Mass meetings, military parades on ice
Under the blood-red and smoke-dark glow of burning cities.
Fire blazing from windows—not sparks, human figures,
Small and black, fly out and then fall into a chasm.
Dirty taverns with wobbly tables. Women in kerchiefs
Cheap, you can have them for a pound of meat,
And a multitude of busy henchmen,
Deft, well trained in their trade.
Thus it's possible to conjecture that mankind exists
To provision and to populate Hell,
The name of which is duration. As to the rest,
Heavens, abysses, orbiting worlds, they just flicker a moment.
Time in Hell does not want to stop. It's fear and boredom together
(Which, after all, happens). And we, frivolous,
Always in pursuit and always with hope,
Fleeting, just like our dances and dresses,
Let us beg to be spared from entering
A permanent condition.

ZBIGNIEW HERBERT
What Mr. Cogito Thinks About Hell
Translated from the Polish by John Carpenter and Bogdana Carpenter

The lowest circle of hell. Contrary to prevailing opinion it is inhabited neither by despots nor matricides, nor even by those who go after the bodies of others. It is the refuge of artists, full of mirrors, musical instruments, and pictures. At first glance this is the most luxurious infernal department, without tar, fire, or physical tortures.

Throughout the year competitions, festivals, and concerts are held here. There is no climax in the season. The climax is permanent and almost absolute. Every few months new trends come into being and nothing, it appears, is capable of stopping the triumphant march of the avant-garde.

Beelzebub loves art. He boasts that already his choruses, his poets, and his painters are nearly superior to those of heaven. He who has better art has better government—that's clear. Soon they will be able to measure their strength against one another at the Festival of the Two Worlds. And then we will see what remains of Dante, Fra Angelico, and Bach.

Beelzebub supports the arts. He provides his artists with calm, good board, and absolute isolation from hellish life.

CHARLOTTE MEW
Fame

Sometimes in the over-heated house, but not for long,
    Smirking and speaking rather loud,
    I see myself among the crowd,
Where no one fits the singer to his song,
Or sifts the unpainted from the painted faces
Of the people who are always on my stair;
They were not with me when I walked in heavenly places;
    But could I spare
In the blind Earth's great silences and spaces,
    The din, the scuffle, the long stare
    If I went back and it was not there?
Back to the old known things that are the new,
The folded glory of the gorse, the sweet-briar air,
To the larks that cannot praise us, knowing nothing of what we do,
    And the divine, wise trees that do not care.
Yet, to leave Fame, still with such eyes and that bright hair!
God! If I might! And before I go hence
    Take in her stead
    To our tossed bed
One little dream, no matter how small, how wild.
Just now, I think I found it in a field, under a fence—
A frail, dead, new-born lamb, ghostly and pitiful and white,
    A blot upon the night,
The moon's dropped child!

CÉSAR VALLEJO
Sermon on Death
Translated from the Spanish by Clayton Eshleman and José Rubia Barcia

And, finally, going now into the domain of death,
which works in squadron, former bracket,

paragraph and brace, piece brace and dieresis,
for what the Assyrian writing desk? for what the Christian pulpit?
the violent jerk of Vandal furniture
or, even less, this proparoxytonic retreat?

Is it in order to end,
tomorrow, as a prototype of phallic boasting,
as diabetes and a white bedpan,
as a geometric face, as a deadman,
that sermon and almonds become necessary,
that there are literally too many potatoes
and this watery spectre in which gold burns
and in which the price of snow is set on fire?
Is it for this, that we die so much?
Only to die,
must we die every second?
And the paragraph that I write?
And the deistic bracket that I raise on high?
And the squadron in which my skull failed?
And the brace that fits all doors?
And the forensic dieresis, the hand,
my potato and my flesh and my contradiction under the bedsheet?

Out of my mind, out of my wolve, out of
my lamb, sensible, out of my absolute equinity!
Writing desk, yes, my whole life; pulpit,
likewise, my whole death!
Sermon on barbarism: these papers;
proparoxytonic retreat: this skin.

In this way, cognitive, auriferous, thick armed,
I will defend my catch in a couple of moments,
with voice and also with larynx,
and of the physical smell with which I pray
and of the instinct for immobility with which I walk,
I will be proud while I live—it must be said;
my horseflies will engorge on their own pride,
because, in the middle, I am, and to the right,
also, and, to the left, likewise.

The Metric is 1

Corpses, corpses, corpses. Shot, gassed, decaying corpses. They seemed to pop out of the ground when a grave was opened. It was a delirium of blood. It was an inferno, a hell. . . .

—Adolf Eichmann, 1960
(Found at the Center for Research on Nazi Crimes, Ludwigsburg, Germany)

THE METRIC IS 1

The metric is 1—to be sung.
Speech song sings (+permutations)

05.30.69

The red, spiteful devil arises in the dream. Horns, stuck-out tongue, pointed tail curled once, his right hand gripping his erection.

In the early 1960s, in Minneapolis, Jean Beauchamp introduced me to Jung—dreams written out and painted, sometimes with a surprising facility, as Jung had predicted. The specific instance coalesced from the archetypes to mirror the personal. For example, the Greek temple with columns over water, built for the Mother, appearing in a dream of rebirth.

Or the *spiteful* devil locked in my rigid neck cords, as Reich would later teach me.

07.17.99

My wife visits her parents in Illinois. Saturday night in Sheridan Square. My thirty-year pilgrimage. The streets hot and thick with people. Suddenly "200 in hell." And the devil's "convertible." I write a first draft in a couple of hours.

Originally I had planned to use the civil war in Sierra Leone for this essay. Both poems meant to be sung. In a peer workshop, the obvious question: how to sing them? Later, I think: *the metric is one.* As Pound had said, *listen.*

RECAPITULATION: INFLUENCE AND MASTERY

The Garden of Earthly Delights: Hell
A couple of summers ago: *Facing the River.* Read over and over. To assimilate Milosz's verbal and intellectual strategies. Irony and emotion at the end of Europe. The opening out at 80. Hell as the absolute zero of the state. The nightmare of this world enacted as the politics of the next. Eternal duration of "boredom and fear," as happens to people.

What Mr. Cogito Thinks About Hell
In the paperback Latin dictionary: *cōgĭtō, -āre vt* to consider, ponder, reflect on; to imagine; (with *inf*) to intend to; *vi* to think, reflect, meditate. I first read Herbert in 1968, in the Penguin *Selected Poems (A Devil, Report from Paradise, The Paradise of the Theologians).* From the very first, the radiance of his uncanny intelligence, not without humor.

This July 4th on a train, I show the poem to my wife, a painter herself, and an energetic foot soldier in the New York art wars. Satan the inquisitor now Satan the bourgeois impresario. In the contemporary world, for the artist, damnation is on earth—the struggle for a one-woman show in a good gallery.

Fame
I originally found Charlotte Mew in *The World Split Open,* a 1974 women's anthology, and later I ordered her thin *Collected Poems* [1953] from England. A probable manic depressive. "Let me go," she said in 1928, after drinking disinfectant.

Over the years she taught me the song—that was in my head. As Louis Zukofsky had said hundreds of times: lower limit = speech, upper limit = song. The sentimental gone over the top in the private catalog. Something so intensely believed it transcends its banal assumptions.

Sermon on Death
I had been reading Vallejo's *The Complete Posthumous Poetry* since it appeared in 1978—amazed by, among so many things to be amazed by, the stupendous metaphorical imagination that was always grounded in the physical world of the poem.

If Milosz broods on hell, and if Herbert subdues hell, shall we say with a straight face that Vallejo is hell? (Heaven too!) Few other poets can stand such an appraisal. He takes off, as they say, the top of your head. So I raise the "deistic bracket" and salute his "horseflies." How shall anyone open themselves up so much?

08.06.99

A color Xerox of the "Black Crook" cigar label—as the Scots say: *black as the crook*—in the mail from a dealer. A cavalier with bat wings, horns, and red pantaloons, bearded and mustachioed, carrying a pitchfork through the fire. He lives somewhere in Europe, sometime in the late nineteenth century.

At another place on the label, he comically sunbathes in a loincloth under an umbrella before a huge red sun as smoke comes out of his mouth.

I remember this line from *Faust: Ich bin der Geist verneinung.*

In another label he writes his name "Herrmann" in the air with a taper and breathes it out of his mouth in fire and smoke.

To be immortal means that everything has happened. Think of us, who have swelled his legions beyond imagining. Vast battalions, as in old Third Reich documentaries. Endless generals and sub-generals, before whom even the angels are astonished.

There is nothing coming through on the airwaves today. Maria Casares as Death in Cocteau's *Orphée* in the back of the black Rolls Royce vainly turns the dials, but her poet is silent. All joking aside, I think they have taken him to a place where one does not hear the screams.

We live in the new age of magic and alchemy and superstition. Satan is very strong. There seems no limit to his power. Bodies tattooed with the signs of an endless zodiac. In the camps it was more abstract: millions of numbers whose sum, like God, is unknowable. We believe in the electron and in the 9-millimeter handgun. In a dream, Flash Gordon flies to the city of the cloud people in his sputtering rocket. Overhead, the satellites turn day and night without rest.

JENNIFER SNYDER

Jennifer Snyder received her M.F.A. from the University of Arizona. Her poems have appeared in the *American Poetry Review,* the *Black Warrior Review,* and the *Iowa Review.* Her first collection of poems, *Train,* is yet to be published. Snyder is currently a seminarian at Emory University in Atlanta, Georgia, where she works in the women's prison system and serves as an advocate for child prostitutes. She is in the process of ordination in the United Methodist Church.

Nurses

Do you want nurses to take your pain away?
They are lovely and milky, a tree of gray moons,
speaking in Spanish, pobre mamacita, pobre mamacita—
so beautiful and white, their smiles before the dark.

They are twilight, bringing us our meals,
giving us pills, kissing our cheeks,
expanding in the forgiving light,
They float through liquid night.
They are never tired.

This one, fat Esmerelda, takes me to bed
and strokes my hair. For years will you long
for her hand on your face? And Helena,
who smells like an auburn wig,
takes my pulse each day and has the little eyes of a bird.

It is a kind of waltz we do, only slower—
breakfast, lunch, dinner. The elegant Cheri,
with her white hair, gives us pills with her pretty hands.
Our hands are not pretty—

they are filled with the memories of tragic violas.
They are the shape of a deformed kiss.
They have cigarette burns and needle marks and warts.
They are not birds. They are how pain looks.

Listen, I would like my hands to be the kisses of sparrows.
I would like my face to be a nurse's face, a wave of roses.
I would like my body to be fat with love.
It is late. Esmerelda puts me to bed.

She will never hold my burned hand in her hand.
I am just a dream of a different life.

PABLO NERUDA
Too Many Names
Translated from the Spanish by Alastair Reid

Mondays are meshed with Tuesdays
and the week with the whole year.
Time cannot be cut
with your weary scissors,
and all the names of the day
are washed out by the waters of night.

No one can claim the name of Pedro,
nobody is Rosa or Maria,
all of us are dust or sand,

all of us are rain under rain.
They have spoken to me of Venezuelas,
of Chiles and of Paraguays;
I have no idea what they are saying.
I know only the skin of the earth
and I know it is without a name.

When I lived amongst the roots
they pleased me more than flowers did,
and when I spoke to a stone
it rang like a bell.

It is so long, the spring
which goes on all winter.
Time lost its shoes.
A year is four centuries.

When I sleep every night,
what am I called or not called?
And when I wake, who am I
if I was not I while I slept?

This means to say that scarcely
have we landed into life
than we come as if new-born;
let us not fill our mouths
with so many faltering names,
with so many sad formalities,
with so many pompous letters,
with so much of yours and mine,
with so much signing of papers.

I have a mind to confuse things,
unite them, bring them to birth,
mix them up, undress them,
until the light of the world
has the oneness of the ocean,
a generous, vast wholeness,
a crepitant fragrance.

ROBERTO JUARROZ
Vertical Poetry, First, 4
Translated from the Spanish by W. S. Merwin

The bottom of things is neither life nor death.
My proof is
the air that goes barefoot in the birds,
a roof of absences that makes room for the silence,
and this look of mine that turns around at the bottom
as everything turns around at the end.

And my further proof is
my childhood that was bread before wheat,
my childhood that knew
that there were smokes that descend,
voices that nobody uses for talking,
roles in which a man does not move.

The bottom of things is neither life nor death.
The bottom is something else
that sometimes comes out on top.

PHILIP LEVINE
They Feed They Lion

Out of burlap sacks, out of bearing butter,
Out of black bean and wet slate bread,
Out of the acids of rage, the candor of tar,
Out of creosote, gasoline, drive shafts, wooden dollies,
They Lion grow.
                    Out of the gray hills
Of industrial barns, out of rain, out of bus ride,
West Virginia to Kiss My Ass, out of buried aunties,
Mothers hardening like pounded stumps, out of stumps,
Out of the bones' need to sharpen and the muscles' to stretch,
They Lion grow.
                    Earth is eating trees, fence posts,
Gutted cars, earth is calling in her little ones,
"Come home, Come home!" From pig balls,
From the ferocity of pig driven to holiness,
From the furred ear and the full jowl come
The repose of the hung belly, from the purpose
They Lion grow.

> From the sweet glues of the trotters
> Come the sweet kinks of the fist, from the full flower
> Of the hams the thorax of caves,
> From "Bow Down" come "Rise Up,"
> Come they Lion from the reeds of shovels,
> The grained arm that pulls the hands,
> They Lion grow.
> From my five arms and all my hands,
> From all my white sins forgiven, they feed,
> From my car passing under the stars,
> They Lion, from my children inherit,
> From the oak turned to a wall, they Lion,
> From they sack and they belly opened
> And all that was hidden burning on the oil-stained earth
> They feed they Lion and he comes.

Second Looking and a Theory of Flamingos

Poems encourage quirky and sudden associations, for they give the mind permission to maneuver away from formulaic interpretations of the world. But these associations are not enough. My mind longs to make sense, and I want poems to interpret in ways that are alternately elegant and clumsy, mysterious and plain, earthy and ethereal. The imagination is flighty, intuitive, obscure, and patterns are a necessary element of restraint. Relationships between the sometimes dizzying quality of the imagination and the prophetic quality of poetic patterns produce a synchronicity that I crave. I notice this synchronicity in every poem I love.

I like Neruda's earthy, intuitive manner of speaking in *Too Many Names*. He effortlessly associates concepts like time with images of the elements —water, sand, roots, skin, flowers. This connecting of impressions with palpable images of the earth lends poems a pretension which is infinitely credible, which permits a poet to say things that are simultaneously ridiculous and true: "Time cannot be cut/ with your weary scissors,/ and all the names of the day/ are washed out by the waters of the night." Many of the poets I love are compelled by contemplative impressions. Poems are roomy. They let us make unlikely generalizations that touch us where we live, where we struggle to find intuitive meaning. But these impressions gather dimensions from the visions that accompany them. Mental landscapes want to be reminded of how connected we are to archetypal images of the earth.

I'm driven to copy Neruda's unexpected association: "Do you want nurses to take your pain away?/ They are lovely and milky, a tree of gray moons." Those areas of the mind that anticipate connections between things imagined and the tangible world appeal to me. Poems gather around these intersections—these points of seeing into images—and embrace the unintended connections the mind makes between the understanding and the visions that represent it. A poem lets us give ideas their proper pictures. Nurses can be "a tree of gray moons," and time can lose its shoes.

Neruda's poem chants and reverberates, mostly in the form of the speaker responding to his own negations: "No one can claim the name of Pedro,/ nobody is Rosa or Maria,/ all of us are dust or sand,/ all of us are rain under rain." I like poems that answer themselves. Reverberations like these move poets to moments of active interpretation and music, and produce a quality of speaking and listening that is circular in shape. In my own poems, I chant through preoccupations. Poems enjoy the musical, trance-inducing properties of obsessions: "Our hands are not pretty—/ they are filled with the memories of tragic violas./ They are the shape of a deformed kiss./ They have cigarette burns and needle marks and warts./ They are not birds. They are how pain looks." Preoccupation gives poems a visionary quality that I adore. Inexplicably, the words become the thing itself.

Roberto Juarroz is the poet I read when I want to be reminded how to temper images with impressions. The poem of his I have included here moves in a linear fashion, with a thesis, an argument, and final deductions. This kind of poem excites me; the appeal is in the crooked logic of its images: "the air that goes barefoot in the birds"; "a roof of absences that makes room for the silence"; "my childhood that was bread before wheat." Here the argument compels the mind to think through association and in pictures. This type of logic instructs me. My imagination is stingy, and I welcome conversations that badger my mind with tangible visions. A kind of magic happens in these associations. Philosophy is transformed into earth and bird and wheat.

Poetry is the art of implication, and just about every time I write, I am lured into metaphors. I want, in my poem, the nurses to be the embodiment of something. Poems hint at a greater geometry—the geometry of the unspoken. That is why I crave metaphor: "They are twilight." Metaphors strike me in ways that are sentient *and* contemplative. I long to interpret the world through images that only make sense in poetry. Poems that speak with images ask for intuitive interpretations and create a nostalgia that I find pleasing. It's as if the images themselves are memories. It's as if I've recalled something from childhood that is important and old.

I enjoy poems that do not ask for proper reasons. The poem is the reason: "And my further proof is/ my childhood that was bread before wheat,/ my childhood that knew/ that there were smokes that descend,/ voices that nobody uses for talking." Poems utter that which is impossible and true, that "[t]he bottom of things is neither life nor death." Paradoxes like these speak elegantly to the mysteries in my life. They demand that I deny absolutes and understand without the logic of understanding. My mind thinks compulsively in paradoxes, not only because they are pleasurable, but also because they give a voice to the messy riddles within and without. Paradoxes are pivotal: "Esmerelda puts me to bed./ She will never hold my burned hand in her hand./ I am just a dream of a different life." My thinking is based on this pivotal motion, for every time I say a thing, I need to say its opposite. So much in a poem depends upon this vicissitude. Negations may be what make me vibrate and hum. Poems nag us with illogical truths. They ask us at once to forget and remember.

I'm also mesmerized by litany in poems. I welcome the canonical severity and the incantational quality of lists in poems like *They Feed They Lion*. Levine's poem is prophetic, speaking its visions in a cumulative manner that resembles biblical vernacular. The stubborn, almost instructive nature of refrains like "They Lion grow" asks me to pay attention to a poem in a certain way. It gives me a nucleus and something to fix my eyes on. Maybe this is what I wish for all along when I read a poem: to recognize lost patterns, to attend to a thing, to remember what's underneath. The real and imagined landscape that Levine scrutinizes reminds me that asylum from difficult images is impossible, that I must visualize the world relentlessly. This poem is a street preacher demanding that I listen against my will.

I love that poems let me be messy. I'm drawn to overgrown gardens, fluorescent bars, dusty houses with broken mason jars, spider webs, and old newspapers. Language is curiously wealthy, and poems ask me to indulge in it. In some ways, I enter a poem when it spoils me. I don't want to squander my time on scrimpy oratory. I want a poem to announce it loves words and sounds and visions. Clumsiness is a lovely thing, and poems that know where to make mistakes excite me. Poetry should animate the quotidian. Cracks in the ordinary are delicious and make me want to sing.

An interesting kind of movement comes from the accumulation of images in a poem. Hillsides, bones, kinetics, boots, fingerprints, musical notes, skin, yellow, fishing nets—these are a poem's nervous system. They walk me through a poem. They stare back at me. What I want to accomplish when I sit down with pen in hand is a certain eloquence in the gathering of images. I am pleasantly covetous about life—I want to be bombarded with sights and sounds and smells, and I want to be told what they mean. That's why I feel satisfied when I write a poem full of lines like "And Helena,/ who smells like an auburn wig,/ takes my pulse each day and has the little eyes of a bird." It's this kind of second look that is imperative to me. I want not only to see the thing itself but also what the thing is speaking to me. Second glances lend the poem a comprehension that is eerily primitive. I think in pictures, and I reverently approach the way language bewitches me with images. Whether poems make me uncomfortable in my bones or offer stillness, they connect me to the sights and sayings of my dreams.

One of my favorite lines of poetry came from an eleven-year-old girl: "I will swim through a book of flamingos." This may be how I finally regard poetry. It swims me through a collection of visions. It mysteriously and painfully and wonderfully teaches me to see past an idea into its form. It is graceful and arduous and wrong. It transforms mind to flamingo.

GERALD STERN

Gerald Stern was born in Pittsburgh, Pennsylvania, in 1925. He taught for many years at the University of Iowa Writers' Workshop. Stern recently published *Last Blue: Poems* (Norton, 2000). *This Time: New and Selected Poems* (Norton, 1998) won a National Book Award. His other books include *Rejoicings* (Fiddlehead Poetry Books, 1973); *Lucky Life* (Houghton Mifflin, 1977), the American Academy of Poets' 1977 Lamont Poetry Selection; *The Red Coal* (Houghton Mifflin, 1981), winner of the Poetry Society of America's Melville Caine Award; *Paradise Poems* (Random House, 1984); *Lovesick* (Perennial Library, 1987); *Two Long Poems* (Carnegie Mellon University Press, 1990); *Leaving Another Kingdom: Selected Poems* (Harper & Row, 1990); *Bread Without Sugar* (Norton, 1992), which was awarded the Paterson Poetry Prize; and *Odd Mercy* (Norton, 1995). Stern has won fellowships and grants from the National Endowment for the Arts, the Guggenheim Foundation, and the Pennsylvania Council on the Arts. He is also the recipient of the *Paris Review*'s Bernard F. Conners Award; the Bess Hokin Award for Poetry; the Ruth Lilly Poetry Prize; the *American Poetry Review*'s Jerome J. Shestack Poetry Prize; and the Pennsylvania Governor's Award for Excellence in the Arts. Stern currently lives in Lambertville, New Jersey.

Larry Levis Visits Easton, PA During a November Freeze

I said "Dear Larry" as I put down his book, *Elegy*,
across the street from the Home Energy Center

and its two embellished secular Christmas trees
and its two red wreathes over red ribbon crosses

enshrining a thirty inch stove in one of its windows
and a fifty gallon water heater in the other,

knowing how wise he would have been with the parking lot
and the tree that refused against all odds and all

sane agreements and codicils to let its dead leaves
for God's sake fall in some kind of trivial decency

and how he would have stopped with me always beside him
to watch a girl in a white fur parka and boots

build the first snowball on Northampton Street she collected
from the hood of a Ford Fairlane underneath that tree

and throw it she thought at a small speed limit sign
although it landed with a fluff just shy of the twin

painted center lines inducing the three of us,
her lover, Larry, and I to make our own snowballs

from the hoods and fenders of our own Fairlanes although
she threw like none of us and to add to it

she was left-handed, so bless her, may she have
a good job and children and always be free of cancer

and may the two of us scrape some roofs before the
rain relieves us, and may we find gloves for our labor.

JOHN BERRYMAN
Dream Songs

149

This world is gradually becoming a place
where I do not care to be any more. Can Delmore die?
I don't suppose
in all them years a day went ever by
without a loving thought for him. Welladay.
In the brightness of his promise,

unstained, I saw him thro' the mist of the actual
blazing with insight, warm with gossip
thro' all our Harvard years
when both of us were just becoming known
I got him out of a police-station once, in Washington, the world is *tref*
and grief too astray for tears.

I imagine you have heard the terrible news,
that Delmore Schwartz is dead, miserably & alone,
in New York: he sang me a song
"I am the Brooklyn poet Delmore Schwartz
Harms & the child I sing, two parents' torts"
when he was young & gift-strong.

157

Ten Songs, one solid block of agony,
I wrote for him, and then I wrote no more.
His sad ghost must aspire
free of my love to its own post, that ghost,
among its fellows, Mozart's, Bach's, Delmore's
free of its careful body

high in the shades which line that avenue
where I will gladly walk, beloved of one,
and listen to the Buddha.
His work downhill, I don't conceal from you,
ran and ran out. The brain shook as if stunned,
I hope he's over that,

flame may his glory in that other place,
for he was fond of fame, devoted to it,
and every first-rate soul
has sacrifices which it puts in play,
I hope he's sitting with his peers: sit, sit,
& recover & be whole.

PAUL GOODMAN
Pagan Rites

Creator Spirit come
by whom
    I'll say what is real
    and so away I'll steal.

When my only son
fell down and died on Percy mountain
    I began
    to practice magic like a pagan.

Around the open grave we ate
the blueberries that he brought
    from the cloud, and then we
    buried his bag with his body.

Upon the covered grave
I laid the hawkweed that I love
    that withered fast
    where the mowers passed.

I brought also a tiny yellow
flower whose name I do not know
    to share my ignorance
    with my son. (But since

then I find in the book
it is a kind of shamrock
    Oxalis corniculata,
    Matty, sorrel of the lady.)

Blue-eyed grass with its gold hexagon
    beautiful as the gold and blue

double in Albireo
that we used to gaze on

when Matty was alive
I laid on Matty's grave
    where two robins were
    hopping here and there;

and gold and bluer than that blue
or the double in Albireo
    bittersweet nightshade
    the deadly alkaloid
        I brought for no other reason
        than because it was poison.

Mostly, though, I brought some weed
beautiful but disesteemed,
    plantain or milkweed,
    because we die by the wayside.

(And if spring comes again
I will bring a dandelion,
    because he was a common weed
    and also he was splendid.)

But when I laid my own forehead
on the withering sod
    to go the journey deep,
    I could not fall asleep.

I cannot dream, I cannot quit
the one scene in the twilight
    that is no longer new yet does
    not pass into what was.

Last night the Pastoral Symphony
of Handel in the key of C
    I played on our piano
    out of tune shrill and slow

because the shepherds were at night
in the field in the starlight
    when music loud and clear
    sang from nowhere.

Will magic and the weeks placate
the soul that in tumbling fright
    fled on August eighth?
    The first flock is flying south

and a black-eyed susan
is livid in the autumn rain
    dripping without haste or strain
    on the oblong larger than a man.

Creator Spirit come
by whom
    I say that which is real
    and softly away I steal.

E. E. CUMMINGS
i sing of Olaf glad and big

i sing of Olaf glad and big
whose warmest heart recoiled at war:
a conscientious object-or
his wellbelovéd colonel(trig
westpointer most succinctly bred)
took erring Olaf soon in hand;
but—though an host of overjoyed
noncoms(first knocking on the head
him)do through icy waters roll
that helplessness which others stroke
with brushes recently employed
anent this muddy toiletbowl,
while kindred intellects evoke
allegiance per blunt instruments—
Olaf(being to all intents
a corpse and wanting any rag
upon what God unto him gave)
responds, without getting annoyed
"I will not kiss your fucking flag"

straightway the silver bird looked grave
(departing hurriedly to shave)

but—though all kinds of officers
(a yearning nation's blueeyed pride)

their passive prey did kick and curse
until for wear their clarion
voices and boots were much the worse,
and egged the firstclassprivates on
his rectum wickedly to tease
by means of skillfully applied
bayonets roasted hot with heat—
Olaf(upon what were once knees)
does almost ceaselessly repeat
"there is some shit I will not eat"

our president,being of which
assertions duly notified
threw the yellowsonofabitch
into a dungeon,where he died

Christ(of His mercy infinite)
i pray to see;and Olaf,too

preponderatingly because
unless statistics lie he was
more brave than me:more blond than you.

Sorrow by Absence

I am writing this to explore what effect some of the grief poems I know
and love the best had on me when I wrote my poem for dear Larry Levis,
who died just before his fiftieth birthday, to the shock and horror of those
who loved him. What comes to me the quickest are the Berryman poems
for Delmore Schwartz, or Dylan Thomas's poem for his father, or Cum-
mings's Olaf poem, or Roethke's *Elegy for Jane.* I turn to those rather than
to Whitman's great lilac poem or Milton's and Shelley's classic elegies. I
am particularly moved by the Berryman poems and find in them the heart-
breaking and almost hysterical emotional tone that dominated our poetic
thinking for so long a time. I find a close connection between Cummings's
extraordinary poem about Olaf, the blond conscientious objector of World
War I, and the Schwartz poems of Berryman. They share heartbreak and
hysteria, though Cummings moves toward anger and back-door redemp-
tion, whereas Berryman ends up in confounded bitterness or just hope-
less—perhaps resigned—sadness. There is no victory or redemption in

those poems. The only other elegy I want to mention is *Pagan Rites,* Paul Goodman's delicate, haunting, gorgeous memorial to his son, killed on Percy Mountain in a climbing accident. This poem, in its form and tone, seems at first out of sync with so many of the recent poems of mourning, but it resembles them, in spite of the rhyme, in its almost unbearable sadness and hopelessness.

Of the four modern poets I mention, three of them were born within a few years of each other and are members, certainly, of a "generation." Roethke's and Thomas's poems are perhaps the best known and the most celebrated, but I am moved more by the rawness, directness, even the incompleteness, of the poems by Berryman and Cummings, as I am moved by the incredible feelings of loss in Goodman's poem. I have selected *149* and *157* from the *Dream Songs,* but Berryman, over a period of several days, wrote poem after poem for "Delmore"—as he says in the beginning of *157*—Schwartz. Among them, these two move me most.

I have indicated already a certain heartbreak and hysteria in the Berryman poems and, as well, a kind of wild desperation, a seeming indifference, if you will, to song, poetic effect obtained through fact, deep-felt raw emotion, literal renderings. Goodman and Cummings, by contrast, are simultaneously concerned with the music, up front, as well as the grief. That is, there is a sense of grief being *accompanied* by song, even rhyme, perhaps especially rhyme. I think *Larry Levis Visits Easton, PA During a November Freeze* is more muted, and more musical (in the sense I am speaking of), than either of the *Dream Songs,* but less "musical" than either *i sing of Olaf glad and big* or *Pagan Rites.* Where it is different from all these poems is in the particular kind of subversion and displacement it shows. One would have to know outside of, or prior to, the poem that Larry Levis died; and that he died suddenly in the midst of a productive, even beautifully exploding, life and career; and that it was a terrible shock to his loving family, his friends, his students, and to the poetry community; and that his last book, put together posthumously, was ironically called *Elegy;* and that he was lonely and whimsical and mostly in exile; and that he was eternally helpful to friends and strangers alike. He appears in this poem as a kind of playful ghost. He is "wise" in the poem: I guess I always looked at him that way and looked to his judgments, though he was much younger than I. I feel certain that the tree that will not lose its leaves is important in the poem and is connected in some basic way with Larry, though I can't explain how. Certainly the tree is erring in its leafy behavior and is in jeopardy: it's in violation of the reasonable rules by which we expect trees to live. Larry would have been "wise" with that tree, though he surely is himself the tree and not too wise in his own leafy behavior. The girl "in a white fur parka and boots"—she is like a creature from the 1970s, as is the Fairlane—is the muse, guide, relief, and center of the poem. We identify with her, "the three of us," and we pray for her. The first line is *my* line, me speaking, which gives the poem a certain literalness, just as the first sentence in *149* is Berryman's own, not Henry's certainly, as are the first two lines in *157*. The last two lines of *Larry Levis Visits Easton, PA During a November Freeze* are an allegory of our two lives, Larry's and mine, and of poets laboring with their fates. The rain relieved Larry, if it hasn't relieved me yet, but I make no judgment about the rain.

I can't get over the beauty and the power of the last two lines of *157* and the first two lines of the third stanza in *149*. Berryman, who wrote that amazing story "The Imaginary Jew," is so much a Jew in his thinking and feeling. It is so Jewish to say, "sit, sit,/ & recover & be whole." He almost says "setz." And remember what "sitting" was to those people. Aren't they old Russian Jews, those immortals with the cube of sugar carefully placed behind their front teeth, sipping hot tea and sighing? I have read *149* a hundred, two hundred times, but always with a chill. "I imagine you have heard the terrible news,/ that Delmore Schwartz is dead, miserably & alone,/ in New York."

Pagan Rites operates with a different voice—and manner, of course. In spite of his agony, Goodman is able to maintain the posture of the poet; indeed what saves him is that royal rhetoric. Yet there is a certain wildness, I want to say a madness, in his line of thought: the distractions, the confessions, the parentheses. If it were Williams or Lowell confessing, instead of a song (a Mozart), we would notice the wildness and the unspeakable agony more. (Look at the fourteenth and fifteenth stanzas.) I think some of the unexpected, or wild, moves in *Larry Levis Visits Easton, PA During a November Freeze* derive from that poem.

i sing of Olaf glad and big has been a tremendous influence on me. I believe it's one of the truly great poems written against sham, bigotry, deceit, caste, bureaucracy, false patriotism, and war itself. I love its bitter irony and its rage against injustice, how it manages, in spite of everything, to create a hero from the most unexpected source; how it turns the false heroism of war on its own head; how it finds a way to name and define goodness, and mercy and humility. There is little of a direct connection between *i sing of Olaf glad and big* and *Larry Levis Visits Easton, PA During a November Freeze.* The theme is different, and the rage has been transformed into something else. Perhaps some more tender elegy has been the influence. But I *feel* the presence of *Olaf* in *Larry Levis,* and I am certain that the connection, even if indirect, is there. Perhaps it is a question of stages, since grief and mourning have different moments. If I don't specifically mention bigotry, deceit, or bureaucracy, I celebrate the opposite: equality, fellowship, love, commonality.

The fact is that at no point does *Larry Levis Visits Easton, PA During a November Freeze* talk about his death, as such. It is a purgatorial moment in which Larry, out of nowhere, appears as if still alive and performs normal human actions, throwing snowballs, enjoying the company. And furthermore, those actions are altogether *conditional.* The only "true" action of the poem is my reading his book, *Elegy,* and putting it down for a moment in reminiscence. It is even the concentration on *something else,* and the careful attention to details, that creates the sorrow. It is sorrow by absence. It is indeed an elegy by absence. It is almost as if the poem that was influenced by Goodman, Berryman, and Cummings existed only by virtue of its own absence. The grief, though, is the same, whatever else is present or absent.

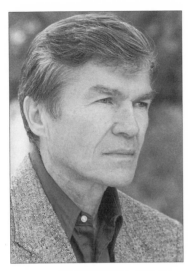

LUCIEN STRYK

Lucien Stryk was born in Kolo, Poland, and came to the United States at the age of four. He was a student of literature and philosophy at Indiana University, the University of Iowa, the University of Maryland, and, finally, the University of Paris. Stryk has authored and edited over thirty books. His recent publications include a collection of poems he translated from the Japanese, together with Takashi Ikemoto, titled *Zen Poetry: Let the Spring Breeze Enter* (Grove Press, 1995); another titled *The Awakened Self: Encounters with Zen* (Kodansha International, 1995); and most recently *And Still Birds Sing: New and Collected Poems* (Swallow Press/Ohio University Press, 1998). He has just published a new edition of translations of Shinkichi Takahashi's poems, titled *Triumph of the Sparrow: Zen Poems of Shinkichi Takahashi* (Grove Press, 2000). He is currently at work on a new poetry manuscript tentatively titled *Blood and Other Poems*. Stryk is a retired Professor of English at Northern Illinois University and lives in DeKalb, Illinois. He is married and has two children.

Remembrance Day

Fingers dance in air, strike
notes on brittle sheets,
as mind pokes in an empty

dustbin, spouts volcanic ash.
Cold sun, a bedlam of birdsong,
a chain of bees nosing

in the hedges. Wild fowl
skim willows round the river
below The Star and Garter,

home for odds and ends of war,
men patched with two minutes
silence and a bloodless poppy

once a year. I sandblast words
into a keening that levitates
into a tapering light, chuck

the grand ritual and the mourning
among planets and the stars.
From here, this gob in space.

SHINKICHI TAKAHASHI

Translated from the Japanese by Lucien Stryk and Takashi Ikemoto

Burning Oneself to Death

That was the best moment of the monk's life.
Firm on a pile of firewood
With nothing more to say, hear, see,
Smoke wrapped him, his folded hands blazed.

There was nothing more to do, the end
Of everything. He remembered, as a cool breeze
Streamed through him, that one is always
In the same place, and that there is no time.

Suddenly a whirling mushroom cloud rose
Before his singed eyes, and he was a mass
Of flame. Globes, one after another, rolled out,
The delighted sparrows flew round like fire balls.

The Pipe

While I slept it was all over,
Everything. My eyes, squashed white,
Flowed off toward dawn.

There was a noise,
Which, like all else, spread and disappeared:
There's nothing worth seeing, listening for.

When I woke, everything seemed cut off.
I was a pipe, still smoking,
Which daylight would knock empty once again.

Thistles

Thistles bloomed in the vast moonlit
Cup of the Mexican sands.

Thistles bloomed on the round hillock
Of a woman's heart.

The stained sea was choked with thistles,
Sky stowed away in thistle stalks.

Thistles, resembling a male corpse, bloomed
Like murex from a woman's side.

At the thorny root of a yellow cactus plant
A plucked pigeon crouched,

And off in the distance a dog whimpered,
As if swallowing hot air.

The Peach

A little girl under a peach tree,
Whose blossoms fall into the entrails
Of the earth.

There you stand, but a mountain may be there
Instead; it is not unlikely that the earth
May be yourself.

You step against a plate of iron and half
Your face is turned to iron. I will smash
Flesh and bone

And suck the cracked peach. She went up the mountain
To hide her breasts in the snowy ravine.
Women's legs

Are more or less alike. The leaves of the peach tree
stretch across the sea to the end of
The continent.

The sea was at the little girl's beck and call.
I will cross the sea like a hairy
Caterpillar

And catch the odor of your body.

What Is Moving

When I turned to look back
Over the waters
The sky was birdless.

Men *were, are* born.
Do I still live? I ask myself,
Munching a sweet potato.

Don't smell of death,
Don't cast its shadow.
Any woman when I glance her way,
Looks down,
Unable to stand it.
Men, as if dead,
Turn up the whites of their eyes.

Get rid of those trashy ideas—
The same thing
Runs through both of us.

My thought moves the world:
I move, it moves.
I crook my arm, the world's crooked.

What's It All About, Then?

The neighbor's tabby squats in tall grass near the birdfeeder. I watch a sparrow land. Cat moves. I shout. Cat bolts. Sparrow whips up onto a mulberry branch, nonchalantly preens, then swooshes down to feast. In an instant Shinkichi Takahashi's sparrows fly through me. So it has always been. Don't ask me why. Poetry, poets are always with me, huddled in doorways, on a bus, up the street, in bed. *Yes,* even on the toilet—poets barge in. Here, I will tell of one. Takahashi's Buddhist disposition enables him to sense the homogeneity of all phenomena and lifts me, as if through a fissure, into the reality of limitless space. Why he or other excelling poets affect me is a mystery that I would never attempt to solve. I just lean back and let their wonder become part of me. How, or if, it shows up in my work I do not know and could never be so bold to claim.

Shinkichi Takahashi, who died in 1987, was totally unique, an enlightened Zenist who wrote from deep within. I never tire of his poetry, as I never tire of great paintings. Each time I look and listen, I hear new music, a freshness of language and imagery that never stales. And there is also his engagement with the world's fullness, its heights and depths. Small wonder that he has become my life companion.

I have chosen five of his poems that suggest the spectrum of his life and art. *Burning Oneself to Death,* the poet told me as we sipped tea, cross-legged under his *inka* (his master's formal testimony to his enlightenment), came after seeing on television Buddhist monks immolating themselves in protest against the savage war in Vietnam. He focused on one of them to show that even sparrows understood his sacrifice. *The Pipe* shows that an enlightened mind can be affected by the creeping dullness of the daily grind and that the pipe—the spirit—must be refilled daily. There is always in his poems the feeling that he is grappling with a *koan,* a puzzling problem set by his Zen master to be pondered in meditation in order to break the monotonous cycle and let in a new-found freedom. *Thistles* is surely such a poem, and all that might have happened was that his master asked him for a vision of the plant. *The Peach* may be the poet's attempt to image the oneness of all that makes up the world: "There you stand, but a mountain may be there/ Instead; it is not unlikely that the earth/ May be yourself." And when the girl climbs the mountain to "hide her breasts in the snowy ravine," we are suddenly aware of the transience of all matter: breasts, snow, everything. *What Is Moving* discovers once and for all the necessity of that oneness with others. He finds just the right remarkable conclusion to this, his most passionate belief. Such ideas and insights make poetry for me. When I read, I wait expectantly for that moment when risks are taken, when visions that startle and enrich are offered, when the poet leaves a legacy in one bold imaginative leap.

Thus I feel uneasy at this point to speak of "influence" and "mastery," as I hold out a poem from a master in the hope that it has somehow crept into some corner to inspire me. But since you've asked it of me, I give you *Remembrance Day*. It is my protest against wars that gnaw through generations and bite into millennia, teaching nothing. It is my hope that this poem has something of the thrust and velocity I admire so deeply in the work of my old friend. Last summer, drifting down the Thames in Richmond; spray splashing our noses, cheeks, eyelids; grand old willows teasing at the ripples, making secret spots for nesting ducks and geese— we passed the remains of Alexander Pope's place and, under a draft of gull wings, caught sight of a heron like a prowhead on an old boat, and the eternal games of squirrels on banks of primroses and nettles. I was at peace, painting this moment in my memory. Suddenly my wife pointed out a building on a hill above the river: the Star and Garter, a home for damaged soldiers. If, while overcome with the wild notes in Takahashi's lines, his voice seeped in at that moment, well, isn't that what this is all about?

KAREN VOLKMAN

Karen Volkman was born in Miami, Florida, in 1967. She studied literature and creative writing at New College and at Syracuse University. A past recipient of an NEA Fellowship, Volkman has recently been a resident at the Camargo Foundation in Cassis, France, and the Akademie Schloss Solitude in Stuttgart, Germany. She has taught at the New School, the 92nd Street Y, the University of Alabama, and the University of Pittsburgh. Her first book of poems is titled *Crash's Law* (Norton, 1996). She has recently completed a second book of poems, titled *Spar*.

Untitled

I have a friend. My friend is a sky. There are dark, starved places that do nothing but blur and spend, and the quick sharp blue-black lightning streaks called *punish*. If you wish to do what is known only as "to rest," "to sleep," "to live," you and my friend will have *nothing* to speak of.

He says, Girls fall through holes, occasionally on purpose. He says, Many shapes of web make the rope that will stay you. He says, A bitter metal forms the bit that slits your tongue.

When they ask, What is your friend, that you ash and azure for him? I sing boxless wind in a blanched meadow, scree and scrawl. It is *not* because doors keep the light out, or doom is mortal. It is *not* because dawn calls weather, wander, weigh. If words are wire and can whip him, *this is* the scar.

THOMAS TRAHERNE
Excerpt from *The First Century*

1

An empty book is like an infant's soul, in which anything may be written. It is capable of all things, but containeth nothing. I have a mind to fill this with profitable wonders. And since Love made you put it into my hands, I will fill it with those truths you love without knowing them; and with those things which, if it be possible, shall show my love: to you, in communicating most enriching truths; to Truth, in exalting her beauties in such a soul.

2

Do not wonder that I promise to fill it with those truths you love, but know not: for tho it be a maxim in the schools, that there is no love of a thing unknown; yet I have found, that things unknown have a secret influence on the soul: and like the centre of the earth unseen, violently attract it. We love we know not what: and therefore everything allures us. As iron at a distance is drawn by the lodestone, there being some invisible communications between them: so is there in us a world of love to somewhat, tho we know not what in the world that should be. There are invisible ways of conveyance, by which some great thing doth touch our souls, and by which we tend to it. Do you not feel yourself drawn with the expectation and desire of some great thing?

3

I will open my mouth in parables: I will utter things that have been kept secret from the foundations of the world. Things strange, yet common; incredible, yet known; most high, yet plain; infinitely profitable, but not esteemed. Is it not a great thing, that you should be heir of the world? Is it not a very enriching verity? In which the fellowship of the mystery, which from the beginning of the world hath been hid in God, lies concealed! The thing hath been from the creation of the world, but hath not so been explained as that the interior beauty should be understood. It is my design therefore in such a plain manner to unfold it that my friendship may appear, in making you possessor of the whole world.

GEORGE HERBERT
The Collar

> I struck the board, and cry'd, No more.
> > I will abroad.
> What? shall I ever sigh and pine?
> My lines and life are free; free as the rode,
> > Loose as the winde, as large as store.
> > > Shall I be still in suit?
> > Have I no harvest but a thorn
> > To let me bloud, and not restore
> What I have lost with cordiall fruit?
> > > Sure there was wine
> > Before my sighs did drie it: there was corn
> > > Before my tears did drown it.
> > Is the yeare onely lost to me?
> > > Have I no bayes to crown it?
> No flowers, no garlands gay? all blasted?
> > > All wasted?
> > Not so, my heart: but there is fruit,
> > > And thou hast hands.
> > Recover all thy sigh-blown age
> On double pleasures: leave thy cold dispute
> Of what is fit, and not forsake thy cage,
> > > Thy rope of sands,
> Which pettie thoughts have made, and made to thee
> > Good cable, to enforce and draw,
> > > And be thy law,
> > While thou didst wink and wouldst not see.
> > > Away; take heed:
> > > I will abroad.
> Call in thy deaths head there: tie up thy fears.
> > > He that forbears
> > To suit and serve his need,
> > > Deserves his load.
> But as I rav'd and grew more fierce and wilde
> > > At every word,
> Me thoughts I heard one calling, *Child:*
> > And I reply'd, *My Lord.*

EMILY DICKINSON
690

Victory comes late—
And is held low to freezing lips—
Too rapt with frost
To take it—
How sweet it would have tasted—
Just a Drop—
Was God so economical?
His Table's spread too high for Us—
Unless We dine on tiptoe—
Crumbs—fit such little mouths—
Cherries—suit Robins—
The Eagle's Golden Breakfast strangles—Them—
God keep His Oath to Sparrows—
Who of little Love—know how to starve—

RAINER MARIA RILKE
Excerpt from ***Sonnets to Orpheus***
Translated from the German by M. D. Herter Norton

II 5

Flower-muscle, that opens the anemone's
meadow-morning bit by bit,
until into her lap the polyphonic
light of the loud skies pours down,

muscle of infinite reception
tensed in the still star of the blossom,
sometimes *so* overmanned with abundance
that the sunset's beckoning to rest

is scarcely able to give back to you
the wide-sprung petal-edges:
you, resolve and strength of *how many* worlds!

We, with our violence, are longer-lasting.
But *when*, in which one of all lives,
are we at last open and receivers?

PAUL CELAN
Your hand full of hours
Translated from the German by Michael Hamburger

> Your hand full of hours, you came to me—and I said:
> Your hair is not brown.
> So you lifted it lightly on to the scales of grief; it weighed more
>   than I . . .
>
> On ships they come to you and make it their cargo, then put it on
>   sale in the markets of lust—
> You smile at me from the depth, I weep at you from the scale
>   that stays light.
> I weep: Your hair is not brown, they offer brine from the sea and
>   you give them curls . . .
> You whisper: They're filling the world with me now, in your
>   heart I'm a hollow way still!
> You say: Lay the leafage of years beside you—it's time you came
>   closer and kissed me!
>
> The leafage of years is brown, your hair is not brown.

Receptivity and Resistance

I wrote the untitled prose poem printed above in February 1998, when I was living for a few months in the south of France. From my window, I could see the cobalt Mediterranean and an endless, relentlessly brilliant sky. The view was opulent, extravagant, unsettling. Coming from New York City, with its street grids and rows of buildings that control sight, I suddenly felt unnervingly exposed. Equally disarming was the extremity of the landscape, full of shifts and contrasts: that lush expanse of water, but just above it, beyond the red-tiled roofs of the town, chalk-dust cliffs, desert scrub, blue and yellow pinflowers punctuating a jagged stretch of scree.

I was reading poets I often read—Dickinson, Rilke, Celan, Traherne, Herbert, Plath—poets I turn to for their strangeness, intensity, beauty, the sense that each is grappling with a large unknowable *thou*. There is an intimacy invested in their work at every level, regardless of whether the poems take on the stance of direct address. I realized once that I most admire writers who have a very personal relationship to the void, and all of these poets have that, whether this void takes the form of (to borrow the distinction Tomas Tranströmer makes in his poem *Vermeer*) the *empty* or the *open*.

What is the nature of their influence? Traherne's strange tenderness in the *Centuries of Meditation*—each century divided into 100 passages that seem nearly prose poems in their rhythm and compactness—seems to distill devotion. His sense of the book as an innocent ground on which to inscribe "profitable wonders"; the extraordinary gesture of receiving this still-nascent text from the hands of the beloved (in this case, a close friend and soul mate); and the longing to reveal, articulate, extol are all expressed with a sweet poise in these writings. His fascination with the expansiveness of infinite space, both inner and outer, is balanced and focused by its initial moment of grasping containment: the offering of the very book being written, "since Love made you put it into my hands," and since Love calls forth its revelations. These hands and what they embody—the receiving, encompassing other—are a lingering presence in the books, in which restless, ranging centuries are bound and compressed in words and space.

The quality of the childlike innocent in Traherne's text is similar to the spare and humble speaker of many celebrated Herbert poems. In this instance, though, it was not the Herbert of renunciation and simplicity who compelled me but, rather, the ravaged, defiant seeker, furiously evading the narrow enclosures of redemption. Where *The First Century* opens with the bliss of its tremulous potential, *The Collar* begins in violence: with a blow and a cry, in the modern cadence of "No more," and the declaration of flight. While Donne is in many ways the more important of the Metaphysicals to me, there may be no single passage in his works that affects me as strongly as this sudden moment of rupture. The fitful, staccato self-questionings and the harried, exhausted harangue summon a beleaguered intelligence shoring up against insoluble crisis. In their hectic topple, the speaker's declarations take the place of actual motion; at no time does he appear to act, even mentally, on the announcement he will abroad. Speech exhausts itself in a circular self-dissection that leads not outward, but further *in* to its more wild rave.

And it can lead nowhere but to the abrupt gesture of its ending. The voice saying "Child" at the end is, of course, the deity, its intervention is benevolent, Christian. But being Jewish, I read it in terms of the deity I know, the one who draws unbreachable boundaries between human and divine proportion: whose definition, in fact, resides in this very difference. To my ear, the lone word seems not a motion of consolation but one that enforces separation and reaffirms the hierarchy of father and child, ending the argument by silencing the speaker. God's word takes the place of the human, the argument (disguised as monologue) is done, and undone. But it is a curious question, this guise of monologue. God's voice at the end is no unexpected occurrence. Though the poem never addresses or alludes to it, the pressure of God's absence is felt constantly in the poem. The speaker's stance seems to me a kind of deflected address, a gaze averted from the object of greatest interest, an object whose importance is measured precisely by the intensity with which it is avoided.

Dickinson's poem, like Herbert's, is one that talks constantly around its intended address. In her interrogation of divine economies, she turns her ire outward. More conversational than many of her poems, and written in a highly uncharacteristic free verse, this poem addresses its harshest inquiry—"Was God so economical?"—not directly to the frugal deity but to the myriad and diminutive disenfranchised—"His Table's spread too high for Us." This deflection emphasizes both distance and the difference of scale between the poem's central antagonistic presences. For Dickinson, the dynamics of sustenance and starvation are highly complex, involving inversions of size, feasts of crumbs, and "Easing my famine/ At my Lexicon—" *(728)*. Her habitual alliance with the small scavenger species serves as a guise, a ruse, and a protection. In the end, the sparrows, and the speaker, "know how to starve," a knowing that distinguishes them from a God whose guilt here lies in not knowing, or overlooking. Size and stupidity are aligned; the great and sated simply do not possess the clear-eyed and astute intelligence of those foraging for daily survival, whether by real crumbs or those of a spiritual "Victory." Both Dickinson and Herbert adamantly resist the posture of supplicant, but this posture, as possibility, lurks at the margin of their poems, as well as in mine.

The question of skewed scale can also be read in terms of receptivity and resistance, a stance of acquiescence or defiance to some radically other, overarching presence. Rilke's poem, the fifth from the second section of the *Sonnets to Orpheus,* approaches this problem in his address directed, not to a flower itself, but to the "flower-muscle," the mysterious, all-responsive force that governs the intricate machinery of an anemone's daily cycle of opening and closing. One of many sonnets addressed to an intimate "du," the poem spans the unnerving distance between the minute, nearly un-representable "muscle" and the encompassing "light of the loud skies," tracing the tremor of response from a hushed but rigorously attentive inner source to the widest expanses of space; though, interestingly, the muscle nearly betrays its own calling, so overwhelmed with saturate light that it nearly ignores—resists—the sunset that should close it. Rilke's shift in the final stanza to "we," humanity with its host of violent intermediaries and defenses (the subject, in part, of the *Duino Elegies*), laments the resistances placed on an absolute receptivity while implicitly defending them. The infinitely receptive flower dies in days. The resistant human achieves open-ness through long difficulty, through solitary struggle, and, ultimately, through death, the one "of all lives" that comes closest to the rapt respon-siveness of the anemone.

Celan's poem places the conflict on a very different ground. Throughout his work, the impossibility of reconciling lyric and lament with an unrepre-sentable extremity of experience forms the central struggle, with language itself as the resisting medium. In this early poem, hair, the dead matter every person carries (here recalling unavoidably the mountainous heaps of the death camps), and leafage, with its eerie evocation of rot and renewal, become the incantatory images of this circular standoff between the irrepar-ably injured speaker and the remote beloved with her sirenlike appeals. The "du" is present in nearly every line, whispering news of her own omniscience: "They're filling the world with me now, in your/ heart I'm a hollow way still!" The speaker's static response is not a defiance but an inability to mend the broken space of distance. The poem ends without motion but with a return to its twin images of fallowness and exhausted growth (in the German original, the final word is the negating "nicht").

My own poem makes its first gesture of receptivity (or resistance) by being in prose. Deprived of the fundamental ordering principle of the line, it signals at the outset an occasion governed by a lack of measure. The identity of the "friend"—lover, deity, or blind destructive force—is quickly cast in doubt, and the attempt to describe, locate, and eventually mark this figure is the poem's central impulse—an impulse interrupted by the inter-vention of the "he." The three sentences of injunction addressed to the speaker all suggest circumscription, captivity, limitation, while the figure who issues those injunctions remains himself unrepresentable, "scree and scrawl." Even the speaker's final gesture of aggression and injury is deflected backward: the "friend" is unwoundable; the poem itself is the scar. What it, and many of my poems, owe to the poets included here, I have approached obliquely. As in Dickinson's and Herbert's poems, the avoidance of address heightens the separation of tangent existences, mutually implicated yet meticulously remote, and perilously unequal in power. As in Traherne's *The First Century,* the poem is a devotion of sorts, assaying the "allure" of a dark unknown. As in Rilke's poem, it seeks to map a thwarted receptivity, a responsiveness that is ultimately non-human, conflicting sharply with the violence within persons and with their violent circumscription within the all-exhausting "open." And as in Celan's poem, it ultimately points to the failure of language as consolation or redress. The speaker is inconsolable but not suppliant. The "boxless wind" is empty or open. The poem is spent.

THEODORE WEISS

Theodore Weiss was born in Reading, Pennsylvania, in 1916. He studied English literature at Muhlenberg College and Columbia University. He and his wife, Renée, have been the editors of the *Quarterly Review of Literature* for over fifty years. Weiss has written two books of criticism, *The Man from Porlock* (Princeton University Press, 1982) and *The Breath of Clowns and Kings: Shakespeare's Early Comedies and Histories* (Atheneum, 1971), as well as fourteen books of poetry, from his first book, *The Catch* (Twayne, 1951), to a recent edition of his *Selected Poems* (Northwestern University Press, 1995). He and Renée live in Princeton, New Jersey. They are currently collaborating on a book of poems. Weiss is also at work on a collection of essays.

Mysterious Matters

Influence and mastery should be attractive topics for anyone interested in poetry, especially when, as in my case, they prompt a survey of the now remote past from the vantage point of age. But age, one might object, is hardly likely to be trustworthy. Well, why shouldn't memories, worked on by the stormy sea of time, the alchemy of dreams, the mind's incessant rearrangements, emerge rich and strange? After all, influence, like parentage itself, is a complicated, mysterious matter.

Influences on young poets are usually easy to spot. Falling in love with a great predecessor, such aspirants yearn to get as close to that poet as possible. Like children donning their parents' clothes, more often than not they flourish that poet's mannerisms. Yet imitating, playing the sedulous ape, is often recommended to young poets as a chief method of discovering the resources of the medium and, at the same time, something basic about their own talents.

Pound urged tyros to imitate, but not just one poet, rather as many as they could. And Eliot remarked that we know the real poets by their stealing from others not this or that quirk but high-handedly substantial amounts. Big haul or small, the worth of the swag depends on the use to which it is put. On the other hand, Hopkins, himself imitated for his distinctive style much more than most, urged that we read and admire but then go and do otherwise.

As I see it, the best influence is one so absorbed in the bloodstream that it is nowhere visible. But such assimilation normally requires hard, deep living in and beyond the older poet and marks the younger poet's achievement of mastery. Then, as Eliot and Borges have observed, the one influenced, turning around, influences the precursor—that is, we discover new qualities in the old poet through the shifting light of the new.

We are in the neighborhood here of Bloom's notion of strong poets, of the life-and-death struggle younger poets must, according to the anxiety of influence, undergo with their great predecessors. For Bloom, writing poetry seems to be predominantly adversarial, rarely conversational: the youngling, enamored of his mother the Muse, longs to eradicate his father who has occupied the Muse much too long. (And what of women poets?) Bloom rejects the idea that, in the loneliness of writing, novices may be grateful for the company of major poets, grateful for the inspiration of their example. Is not one of the profounder delights of writing poetry the way in which, like a gigantic network, the lines are all open and one can argue or agree with, regard as an enemy or as an intimate, any poet of any time and place?

As for my company in the writing of poems, Shakespeare and Robert Browning have been leading influences. Shakespeare has spurred me on to a number of poems involving *The Tempest,* from a long monologue spoken by Caliban, abandoned and alone again on his island and trying to understand the recent amazing events that now seem little more than a taunting dream, to a monologue uttered by Prospero some time after his return to Milan. Shakespeare and Browning, more than anyone else, have underscored for me, even as they have fed my hunger for, the dramatic in poetry, language in action, language as action.

I value Browning for, above all else, returning people to the center of the stage rather than engaging in endless self-exploration. I also value him for his illuminations in a moment's encounter. One stellar instance of such an epiphany occurs in *Andrea Del Sarto,* when the painter's wife, leaving him for an assignation, in a magnificent flurry of diaphanous garments, smudges one of Andrea's still-wet paintings. Here is the moment in all its casualness.

> . . . you don't know how the others strive
> To paint a little thing like that you smeared
> Carelessly passing with your robes afloat![1]

How much these few verses tell us of her indifference to him and his work and of his obsessive love, admiring her loveliness even in its destructiveness (also perhaps for that destructiveness). At the same time, they tell of his pride in his painterly gifts despite his failure, which he in his weakness blames on her.

Having written several long poems, in 1962 I felt encouraged to attempt a book-length poem, *Gunsight.* My *Prometheus Bound,* it sought to amplify the dramatic monologue into a polyphony of interwoven voices. A badly wounded young soldier is about to undergo surgery. The trauma of this experience releases all the voices of his past that compose him. They must be expressed and listened to before he can live again.

In 1982, I wrote another book-length poem, *Recoveries.* Meeting Browning on one of his own most substantial grounds, the world of art, I sought a fundamental change: I presented not a painter but a fresco figure that, as a conservator is restoring it, speaks up. This angel is wholly Promethean; giving light and warmth to human beings, it is bound by its paint and its purpose in the fresco. Through it the conservator uncovers the layers of the fresco's world and the world it has passed through. I quote the first moment of the angel's remembrance of its birth.

> There my one eye,
> glistening with the paint he plies
> as with my first look's fluency,

a spark that sets all April going,
swifter than a bud to sunlight
opens!

      Watching, breathless I,
eye strains, unlidded, out to see—
my straining helps and like a lamp,
casting light to see itself,
attracts—my other eye, the shape
my body comes to,

             ramifying
from itself, an instant, blazing
tree luxuriant with leaves,
into my lasting pose.[2]

Such is the collaboration that goes on between a maker and his making. Once a poet gets going, not only is the language a fundamental influence, but the poet's practice, what he or she has already done, as it prods the poet on, lights the way.

    Meantime, Hopkins had also been an emphatic presence, especially during my graduate school years. I was happily stunned by his magnificent fervor, at times rapture itself, and his bottomless, ferocious despair. He showed me how a trenchant, critical intelligence could produce massive, fiercely compressed poems, from his *Paradiso* epical sonnet, *The Windhover*, a rarely equalled showcase of modulation and intricate musicality, to his *Inferno* terrible sonnets. I quote *The Windhover*, which, Hopkins told Robert Bridges, is "the best thing I ever wrote."

GERARD MANLEY HOPKINS
The Windhover

To Christ our Lord

I caught this morning morning's minion, king-
    dom of daylight's dauphin, dapple-dawn-drawn Falcon, in his riding
    Of the rolling level underneath him steady air, and striding
High there, how he wrung upon the rein of a wimpling wing
In his ecstasy! then off, off forth on swing,
    As a skate's heel sweeps smooth on a bow-bend: the hurl and
      gliding

Rebuffed the big wind. My heart in hiding
Stirred for a bird,—the achieve of, the mastery of the thing!

Brute beauty and valor and act, oh, air, pride, plume, here
    Buckle! AND the fire that breaks from thee then, a billion
Times told lovelier, more dangerous, O my chevalier!

    No wonder of it: sheer plod makes plough down sillion
Shine, and blue-bleak embers, ah my dear,
    Fall, gall themselves, and gash gold-vermilion.

From the later terrible sonnets, I choose:

I wake and feel the fell of dark, not day.

I wake and feel the fell of dark, not day.
What hours, O what black hours we have spent
This night! what sights, you heart, saw; ways you went!
And more must, in yet longer light's delay.

With witness I say this. But where I say
Hours I mean years, mean life. And my lament
Is cries countless, cries like dead letters sent
To dearest him that lives alas! away.

I am gall, I am heartburn. God's most deep decree
Bitter would have me taste: my taste was me;
Bones built in me, flesh filled, blood brimmed the curse.

Selfyeast of spirit a dull dough sours. I see
The lost are like this, and their scourge to be
As I am mine, their sweating selves; but worse.

Some years separate the writing of these poems. But beyond Hopkins's
unique signature on them, they are as far apart as day and night. In *The
Windhover*, Hopkins catches—so it seems for a moment—morning itself.
It is instead a favorite of morning, a little brown-grey falcon, called the
windhover because it hurls itself headlong into the wind. Its ecstasy describes
itself until in the last lines it falls to earth. There, also, little embers, blue-
bleak like the falcon, fall to gall into gold-vermilion, suggesting the splendor
of a Renaissance painting of the Crucifixion.

On the other hand, the terrible sonnet wakes, not to morning, but to night. Rather than a small bird soaring and taking Hopkins with it, this sonnet is the pelt of some hairy beast and of the fallen ("fell" surely proposes that pun) that threatens to smother Hopkins. Whatever tremendous attempt he had made to curb his sensuous and sensual appetite—so his resorting to the rigors of the Jesuit order—boomeranged in all its strength against him through the very asceticism he hoped would save him.

I now think my chance reading of his favorite Oxford professor, Walter Pater, and especially Pater's famous Conclusion to *The Renaissance,* helped to prepare me for Hopkins. One can see how close Pater and Hopkins were in their aesthetics, by juxtaposing this passage from Pater—

> To burn always with this hard, gemlike flame, to maintain this ecstasy, is success in life. . . . Not to discriminate every moment some passionate attitude in those about us, and in the very brilliancy of their gifts some tragic dividing of forces on their way, is, on this short day of frost and sun, to sleep before evening.[3]

—with Hopkins's formulation and advocacy of "inscape" or the seeking out of the essential and unique as it flowers in every moment, in every thing.

Pater, as the English examplar of the French Symbolists, led me to them. An aesthete like them, he maintained that the arts, turning their back on the modern, vulgar world at large, should strive to attain the condition of music. During my days at Columbia University, the Symbolists themselves, most of all Mallarmé, were among my constant companions (rather than the writers I was supposed to be studying). Mallarmé, however impoverished my French (paradoxically an advantage in some respects, since having an additional veil in his dance of a thousand veils only helped to increase the suggestiveness he aimed at), especially charmed me with all he said by not saying. So I yearned to achieve some of his prodigious, not to say lush, economy.

And then, beyond the above worthies, how to calculate the influence of those powerful, contemporary presences, Yeats and that brightest constellation of American poets, Pound, and Eliot (who helped me to discover the pleasure and usefulness of saltation, of leaping from fragment to fragment over vast stretches of time and space), Moore, Williams, and Stevens? Presences made all the more vivid through my editing of the *Quarterly Review of Literature [QRL]*. I can still recall the immense pleasure of receiving brand-new poems from them and the excitement of our correspondence, which soon became personal.

Add to these major poets' work the countless poetry manuscripts I've read for *QRL*, and it shouldn't be hard to see why at times I have been astonished by my persistent need to write. Apparently, rather than depressing me into silence, this huge company has stimulated me.

Yet, however related the main American poets may have been, I soon realized that I stood in the middle of their fundamentally opposing points of view. Eliot and Stevens generally inclined to the elusiveness of the Symbolists, whereas Pound and Williams urged objectivity and precision. Admiring Williams and Stevens as much as I did, I longed to blend the floribunda of Stevens (As he put it in a letter: "I almost always dislike anything that I do that doesn't fly in the window." At that, no doubt, a peacock or at least a cockatoo.) with the plainness, the spareness, of Williams. (So Williams told me that he believed in cutting to the bone. And sometimes beyond.) What a quixotic dream!

I quote Stevens's *Extraordinary References* from the *QRL*.

WALLACE STEVENS
Extraordinary References

The mother ties the hair-ribbons of the child
And she has peace. *My Jacomyntje!*
Your great-grandfather was an Indian fighter.

The cool sun of the Tulpehocken refers
To its barbed, barbarous rising and has peace.
These earlier dissipations of the blood

And brain, as the extraordinary references
Of ordinary people, places, things,
Compose us in a kind of eulogy.

My Jacomyntje! This first spring after the war,
In which your father died, still breathes for him
And breathes again for us a fragile breath.

In the inherited garden, a second-hand
Vertumnus creates an equilibrium.
The child's three ribbons are in her plaited hair.

Next I quote Williams's *To a Lovely Old Bitch*, also out of the *QRL*.

WILLIAM CARLOS WILLIAMS
To a Lovely Old Bitch

Sappho, Sappho, Sappho! initiate,
hand-matron to Astarte,
you praised delicate flowers

and likened them
to virgins of your acquaintance.
Let them grow, thank God!
outside the cemetery barrier—

Burials for cash,
the shares ample security
against—?

The Painted Admiral
or a milk-weed cluster,
untrampled,
keep you company. And pale
blue chickory, frilled
petals—

Butter and eggs,
lady's slipper, close beside
the rust of the dump-heap.

Rust, broken fruit-baskets
and bits of plaster,
painted on one side,
from dismantled bedrooms.

I am amused to point out that, in these poems at least, looked at literally,
Williams, rusty dump and all, is much more floribund than Stevens, armed
only with a second-hand vertumnus. Clearly poets are not—no more than
their critics—to be trusted to behave as they are expected to.

But in all this accumulation, I've failed to talk about my immediate contemporaries. Surely they and their poems must have had a great impact on me? Yes and no. Out of self-protection, I shied away from Lowell's and Berryman's work. Oh, I read them and had to acknowledge their formidable power. But their self-absorption and their filling all the available space served to encourage my reservations.

Recently, I happened on a passage from a letter that Stevens wrote in 1954 when he was seventy-six. (William Logan prints the passage in his volume on contemporary poetry, *All the Rage*.) The passage follows:

> I am not conscious of having been influenced by anybody and have pur-
> posely held off from reading highly mannered people like Eliot and Pound
> so that I should not absorb anything, even unconsciously.[4]

One might ask, "What about your good friend Marianne Moore or William Carlos Williams, whom you even wrote about and with whom you carried on an uneasy friendship?" Stevens's exclusiveness does not, surely, pertain to the past: its poets, even the greatest, whatever his debt to them, were not his rivals. But his saying that he sought to protect himself from absorbing anything, "even unconsciously," makes me question the likelihood of such intactness. Living in the time of Pound and Eliot, as vastly broad-cast as they were, could a poet as sensitive as Stevens have escaped them? And apparently he did see enough of them to recognize that they were highly mannered (so not as different from him as he would like?).

This point brings us to a larger problem: that of originality. From the Romantics on, the stress on the individual, the unique voice, has steadily increased. Originality has become a virtually sacred matter, to be wished for devoutly: a voice, however little it may express. For a poet as realized as Stevens was by 1954, one can understand his irritation at the charge of influence and, at the same time, his resistance to being deflected from his unique course. Yet, if in his later years Stevens read little poetry, he did not hesitate to read philosophy and other kinds of writing. But we might wonder whether fronting one's competitors is not the wiser policy. Shouldn't a poet, secure in his work, rather than worrying about his uniqueness, concern himself with the breadth of what he writes, welcoming new and different attitudes?

One principal local influence from my Columbia days remains to be mentioned. Of course, by far the most important influence, a good deal more basic in my education, was my daily correspondence with Renée, my wife-to-be, as inspired a correspondence course in writing and feeling as one could desire. She also expanded my sense of music and dance through her passion for violin and modern dance. Then there were my classes with Mark Van Doren, as well as my extensive reading of Rilke, whose all-out devotion to art brought me the solace of a sacred text.

The principal local influence, a paramount support for me, was my relationship with David Schubert. David and I met at Columbia and quickly became close friends. Though he was only a few years older, I considered him a full-fledged poet, one thoroughly conversant with the poetry of our time, and I was grateful for his frequent company and his willingness to share his poems with me. He was also the one person with whom I could seriously discuss modern poetry and poets like Lorca and Crane.

His example made me question some of my traits. Until I came to know him, I was very impatient with poems that needed feeding and grooming. Restless youngling that I was, I was always after the next poem and the one after that. (I see now that this conduct grew out of flirtatiousness and a passion for the new. Only later did I come to appreciate the pleasures and surprises that accrue from the long marriage to a long poem.) David convinced me of the folly of my restlessness. Convinced me to a fault. Several times he telephoned to read me a forty- or fifty-line poem that I thought to be altogether realized. Some days later he would call again, having shrunk the poem to twenty lines. A few days after, some six lines. And then, silence. He was worth imitating, but with a bit more self-tolerance!

What I particularly admired and longed to emulate was the mercurial quality of his work, his rare ability to fuse gaiety with the utmost grimness, one very much coloring and intensifying the other. The poignant drama that resulted would be hard to equal. With his powers of amalgamation, he could combine drabbest realism with fairytale magic and elegance. I quote an example of his poetry out of the volume of *QRL* that was devoted to him.

DAVID SCHUBERT
Kind Valentine

She hugs a white rose to her heart—
The petals flare—in her breath blown;

She'll catch the fruit on her death day—
The flower rooted in the bone.
The face at evening comes for love;
Reeds in the river meet below.
She sleeps small child, her face a tear;
The dream comes in with stars to go
Into the window, feigning snow.
This is the book that no one knows.
The paper wall holds mythic oaks,
Behind the oaks a castle grows.
Over the door, and over her
(She dies! she wakes!) the steeds gallop.
The child stirs, hits the dumb air, weeps,
Afraid of night's long loving-cup.

Into yourself, live, Joanne!
And count the buttons—how they run
To doctor, red chief, lady's man!
Most softly pass, on the stairs down,
The stranger in your evening gown.
Hearing white, inside your grief,
An insane laughter up the roof.
O little wind, come in with dawn—
It is your shadow on the lawn.

Break the pot! and let carnations—
Smell them! they're the very first.
Break the sky and let come magic
Rain! Let earth come pseudo-tragic
Roses—blossom, unrehearsed.
Head, break! is broken. Dream, so small,
Come in to her. O little child,
Dance on squills where the winds run wild.

The candles rise in the warm night
Back and forth, the tide is bright.
Slowly, slowly, the waves retreat
Under her wish and under feet.
And over tight breath, tighter eyes,
The mirror ebbs, it ebbs and flows.
And the intern, the driver, speed
To gangrene! But—who knows—suppose
He was beside her! Please, star-bright,
First I see, while in the night

A soft-voiced, like a tear, guitar—
It calls a palm coast from afar.
And oh, so far the stars were there
For him to hang upon her hair
Like the white rose he gave, white hot,
While the low sobbing band—it wept
Violets and forget-me-nots.

At the last I should, I suppose, show the latest fruits of all the above influence. I have taken seriously the importance of other voices, so much so that I have joined with the voice closest to my own, Renée's, and we have just finished a book of poems. Renée is the sharpest critic of my poetry, and since we have judged thousands of poems together in the more than fifty years that we have edited the *QRL,* it seems quite natural, if not inevitable, that we take collaboration the whole distance.

Sharing my long-standing inclination to the dramatic, Renée, even as she has plumped for greater clarity, simplicity, brevity, has spurred us on to composing dialogues. Their speakers are she and he, "R." and "T.," or, as in the medieval *debat,* variations on the body versus the spirit. *The Present,* one such dialogue, is our latest poem.

THEODORE AND RENÉE WEISS
The Present

R: A special present for my birthday?
    How sweet of you. But what are you
    thinking of?

T: Rather than some trinket,
    beaded out of flashy stones, a living
    gift.

R: A living gift! One that grows
    on me?

T: Exactly. A present, out of all
    the past, to keep you constant company.

R: Good! I'll never be lonely. Still
    you haven't said what it's to be.

T: Bee's the word. Or words like
    bees. Plucking words out of the air,
    I'll string them, humming, together.

R: Mmm, a present composed of notes.
    Sounds appealing. But how, beyond
    their buzz, did bees get into this?

T: Even airier than bees, it's words
    I'm after. Also thrumming side by side,
    they'll make a honey-brimming hive.

R: With words mere airiness, how long
    dare I assume they'll cling to me?

T: As long as we depend on breath.

R: That should be time enough.
    But how long before they sting?

T: As long as you are sweet on me.

R: A fragile delicacy!

T: While it lasts,
    this present lasts forever. Roused
    by a breath—

R: Sleeping Beauty waking
    to a kiss?—

T: in turn inspiring the breather,
    such present presents an always present
    present.

R: Riddlesome and knotted
        as it is, I suppose such line is meant
        to bind your words.

T: O more's required:
        being stamped by clover fields these words
        have idled in, by winter bedding down,
        by earthquakes, floods.

R: And most of all
        by men and women storming through?

T: Indeed.
        So flavored, words spread, a preserve,
        over everything.

R: The world become one
        savory dish! Aren't you biting off
        more than we can swallow?

T: I give you what,
        honeycombed by your lips, you give me.

R: A present meant for two, celebrating
        this life that we have lived together
        more than fifty years.

T: A present made
        not only of the said,

R: but the unsaid.

T: As well as the unsayable.

JOE WENDEROTH

Joe Wenderoth is from Baltimore, Maryland. His books of poems include *Disfortune* (Wesleyan University Press, 1995), a chapbook, *The Endearment* (Shortline Editions, 1999), *It Is If I Speak* (Wesleyan University Press, 2000), and *Letters to Wendy's* (Verse Press, 2000). Wenderoth teaches at Southwest State University in Marshall, Minnesota.

SAPPHO
Seizure
Translated from the Greek by Willis Barnstone

To me he seems like a god
as he sits facing you and
hears you near as you speak
softly and laugh

in a sweet echo that jolts
the heart in my ribs. For now
as I look at you my voice
is empty and

can say nothing as my tongue
cracks and slender fire is quick

under my skin. My eyes are dead
to light, my ears

pound, and sweat pours over me.
I convulse, greener than grass,
and feel my mind slip as I
go close to death,

yet, being poor, must suffer
everything.

Withstanding Seizure

It is not easy to *stand with* a world as convulsive as this one. It is difficult. This world, in truth, is a sea—it heaves and bursts and pulls itself apart. And we are not above this world except in pretend. It is not easy to stand here, *as* here—and yet it is perhaps just as difficult *not* to stand here. That is, even if our whole goal is to stand *apart* from the convulsive world, even as we seek with all our might to establish our "selves" upon another firmer ground, the sea comes over us. Of course there are "success" stories— there are those who seem to stand, for a time, upon another firmer ground. While it is true that this other firmer ground is manifest materially (and so is always dependent upon the maintenance of discreet financial and so- cial systems), this other firmer ground is always first and foremost an imagi- nary ground, and for it to be maintained, one must keep in place a specific kind of imaginary practice. This practice might be described as a safe- guarding of the self against knowledge. The development of such a prac- tice seems inevitable and hardly monstrous, so long as it remains humble enough to confess its consistent failure. That is, the instinct to allow for truth, to connect with the world as it truly stands, convulsing, is as in- evitable, or as *pressing*, as the instinct to maintain a firm ground. For me, the struggle to reconcile and accommodate these seemingly contradictory instincts is the fundamental human struggle; it is the struggle to evolve the imagining of a firm ground that is neither rigid nor naïve—a firm ground that is not *set against*, and that can *withstand*, the convulsions that make it live and die, appear and disappear.

Poetic speech is unique in its power to manifest such a ground—a ground which, while it is in some sense firm, nevertheless understands its stability as but a necessary delusion. In poetic speech, the firmness of imaginary ground is a firmness already subtly possessed of the convulsion(s) of the real (the unimaginable); the horizon that poetic speech conjures up nurtures that border—that inherently compromised space wherein it is impossible to see exactly where oblivion begins and order ends and vice-versa. Indeed, if poetic speech is to be reckoned as powerful, it is because of this possession: because it has found a way of capturing (resonating with) the force of the impending unimaginable, such that the imaginary ground —the speaker herself—is implied as a corresponding power, at least to the extent that she is able to *withstand,* even capture, the convulsion that informs and sustains the limits of her ownmost project. The poet is powerful, in short, because she lives in the shadow of that horizon, that border, and knows it will cross over her just as she crosses over it.

Sappho's poem *Seizure* makes us think more carefully about the way in which the poet's experience is convulsive. To "convulse" is to show evidence of inward disruption; it is to be penetrated by something that one cannot abide but at the same time cannot reject. When one convulses, one's unity is shaken and made awkwardly apparent . . . but it is not dissolved; one remains in some sense together, as one body/person, even as that body/person trembles with the secret disruption that has caused it to lose its expectable power, the power to remain upon its way. There is a phrase I have seen in Homer that is generally translated as "loosens his limbs." It is used to describe death in battle; when a warrior is speared, for instance, it is said that he has had his limbs loosed. The phrase speaks to the moment of losing one's power, one's *grasp;* the warrior is still conscious in this moment, but his power, his hold on his fate, has been disrupted. I thought it was curious, then, when I saw the phrase in Sappho, in the first stanza of the poem *To Atthis:*

Love—bittersweet, irrepressible—
loosens my limbs and I tremble.

Here, the convulsion caused by "love" is compared with the moment wherein a warrior is felled by a mortal blow. What are we to make of this comparison? Is this simply a weak analogy, a sentimental exaggeration? Clearly, the blow that love delivers is not the blow that war delivers. What is to stop us from leaping to the conclusion that this is a weak analogy?

For Sappho, the focus is not the blow itself, but the convulsion—the seizure, the trembling—that the blow causes. Love's "weapon" is never specified —the analogy never extends in that direction but instead focuses entirely upon *the resulting state* of the blow. Her "love" has caused her to be filled up with something that she cannot abide yet cannot reject, and here is where the analogy transcends its seeming sentimentality. Rather than being a trite exaggeration of emotional pain, the analogy is a subtly executed glimpse of the physical/mental convulsion that is at once the foundation and the destiny (the end and the beginning) of imagination. This glimpse implies that we continually, "irrepressibly," suffer blows to our grasp of where we are and so continually lose control of our way *through* the world. Just as a felled warrior, in his final moment, looks out across a chasm at the scene he has suddenly been divorced from, so, too, a lover gazes, struck by the voice or the face of the one she loves and cannot possess, reeling in the chasm that holds the two apart.

In every blow, one kind of imagination—the kind that allows the subject to stand securely apart from the convulsions of the real (of our being bodies)—is disabled, and another kind of imagination is forced to arise. We might call the former *imagination asleep and dreaming* and the latter *imagination waking*. Imagination asleep does not cease to be imagination—no, it continues to function, dreaming, creating scenes. It is only different from *imagination waking* in that it creates scenes notwithstanding (not standing with) the world in truth. Imagination, in waking, is faced with the same project: create a scene. And yet, it must do so without the power to overlook the truth, the fundamental instability of its images. This instability may seem, at first, to be a nullifying force—blurring and hollowing out the scene—and yet it becomes, ultimately, the birthing of a new grasp of images, a new scene. This new grasp, because it resonates with the annihilation it has just overcome (and which has promised to return), wrests images into the full strangeness of their ongoing clarity. The subject, in a poem, takes a stand in this chasm—a chasm which is simultaneously void and birthing place; she takes a stand in the yawning of this chasm between the real and the imaginary and, by believing in the real, brings closure to where she has been—thus creating the need for a whole new scene.

I chose to write about Sappho because her poems have impacted upon my own practice of writing in a unique way. Her work, more than any other, has taught me that the poem is always an act of love, or at least it begins there, implying an act of love, or stemming from it, resisting it, or lamenting it. The poet is inevitably a lover, but not a simple lover, not a lover who is able to trust in her love-project. While she loves, she at the same time *knows the limit* of love, the fate of every lover—this is what makes her love poetic. While poetic speech may create a powerful sense of the subject's yearning to possess a specific scene (and within the scene, a specific *other*), it only does so because the poetic subject stands in a uniquely impotent relation to the loved scene. In poetic speech, the subject has always implicitly suffered a blow, and this blow has opened up a chasm between herself and the loved scene; while it in some sense represents a dramatic impotence, this chasm nevertheless births a new power—or, it is perhaps better said, causes a new deployment of the same power. Instead of residing in an ability to make her way *through* the world, the poet's power is shifted toward an ability to stand *in,* to stand *with,* the world, which no longer offers a *through.* Both abilities, of course, are short-lived; they erode one another constantly.

In the poem *Seizure,* I am not as much interested in the specific social contexts of the speaker's desire as much as in what said contexts arrive at —the description of the convulsion itself: "I convulse, greener than grass." To me, this line is perhaps the greatest line of poetry ever written. The metaphor is simple and direct yet resonates with two inextricably bound complexities—the complexity of an *I* (imaginary) and of Nature (real). Underlying the metaphor is this basic equation: *I am grass.* The *I,* like grass, is unshakably passive and utterly vulnerable to the conditions of its existence, which is to say, to being penetrated by what sustains (and ultimately destroys) it. Such passivity is at the heart of the poem's seizure. The love that the speaker is swept up into must be at first assumed as her own definitive potential or inclination, and yet that potential, by going unfulfilled, transforms her—makes *her* the beloved, the penetrated. She is penetrated, moreover, not by *an* other—she is penetrated the way grass is penetrated by sunlight—she is penetrated by the whole of the scene in which she dwells. She becomes the receptive site of everything there is.

This transformation is as joyful as it is painful, and Sappho's metaphor is uniquely able to convey this. The *I,* in its convulsion, is not *as green as grass*—it is *greener* than grass. This means that the *I*'s convulsion, when it is brought into imagery, is more real than the real—for two reasons: a) because the real (the unimaginable) is only ever suspected *as real* in the moment of the poet's being conscious of her inability to bring it into specificity (that is, the ambiguity of the poetic scene is only truly felt via the failure of the specific); and b) because the *I,* which had understood itself as the natural sovereign of the imaginary, is suddenly subservient to unspeakable forces that, in being acknowledged, call into question the imagination's guiding intention.

In poetic space, images attain their greatest radiance, and yet they do so only because that which holds them is neither unified nor eternal. The speaker of poetic speech is a field of grass in bright sunlight; the light is fire, and the grass, if it had not developed a *receptive stance,* would be consumed by this fire. The grass, in the fire, no doubt comes "close to death" and yet is able to survive, even to flourish, in it. Certainly it is possible to argue that Sappho's closing lines depart altogether from the grass metaphor, returning most notably to her social "poverty" as a woman in a man-dominated realm, and yet even this specific poverty must radiate now with the more fundamental poverty, the passivity, of the grass. The "everything" that the speaker "suffers" is the suffering not of any one thing but of a whole condition. Thus, suffering "womanhood" and suffering "existence" blur into the trajectory of one condition, one painful/joyful being in love.

It is important to recognize that "suffering" here can be understood in two ways. First, it is the convulsion itself, the *I*'s moment of being burned, penetrated, and thus, "greener than grass." Secondly, and more profoundly, I think, it is the moment wherein the burning *ceases,* the moment wherein death *withdraws* and the speaker sinks back into a non-convulsive state. In this latter reading (which reminds one of certain Dickinson poems ending with a death that seems co-extensive with a return to the rut of every-dayness), the "everything" that is suffered is history itself, which is to say, this whole process of recognizing and enduring love's inevitable failures. It is interesting that death is not, in this reading, the source of mortal suffering—quite to the contrary, it is the direction in which the *I* moves as it convulses and becomes joyfully receptive to the radiance of where it is. The *I*'s poverty is not its being bound to die, but rather its being bound to love, which is to say, its being incapable of being *timeless* and thereby pursuing the radiance of the world into its full or endless manifestation. The mortal's mortality, that is, consists not of her being toward death but of her being bound *into time,* into *the next love* just as much as into the dimmed radiance of loves lost.

Ex-Lover Somewhere

now to me
you are a flower
living backwards
moving
from bloom to seed
    in just moments
(we have all seen this in school)
retracting beauty, discernible
shape, color—
    slowly,
quickly—
every delicate feature taken back

inside the silent film

My poem *Ex-Lover Somewhere* is founded in one image—that of a flower on a film that is being run backwards. It seems to me that this image conveys several things concerning the practice of love. First, and most obviously, it recognizes a decay, a once-real beloved becoming mere image, image stored on film. And yet, the once-real beloved is acknowledged as being "somewhere," being still real, and so, being in some sense immune to this process of decay. Because of this acknowledgement, the "living backwards" takes on more significance—the image of the beloved is not simply decaying or perhaps not decaying at all—she is not dying but living in a different direction. The lost beloved, "living" in the speaker's mind, has become, or is moving toward being, fully imaginary; as such, she may represent a decaying specificity, but she might just as properly be understood as the birthing of an ambiguity, a "seed."

    This birthing, however, like the film itself, is backwards—the distinct "features" that defined the beloved are not brought out into the light but are instead "taken back/ inside," where they assume a new power, the power of the anonymous, the unspeakable. The film itself can be felt, here, as a devouring chasm, as the silence into which all speech, all distinction, is made to turn. As the poem turns into this silence, an anonymous lover, the poet himself, is felt, and he is an endurance of love; he is that which has not been worn away by love's continual failure. Sappho's poems have taught me many things, but above all they have made me understand that poems must be simultaneously simple and difficult. They are simple insofar as they must at least begin from an act of love, establishing the poetic *I* as a lover of where he has been. They are difficult insofar as they must then proceed to withstand, even joy in, the seizure that, while it opens up a chasm between lover and beloved, nevertheless secures a new birth of love, a new grasp of the "everything" that might be suffered.

NOTES

Introduction

1. Michael Ryan, *A Difficult Grace: On Poets, Poetry, and Writing* (Athens: University of Georgia Press, 2000).

2. Homer, *The Iliad,* Richmond Lattimore, trans. (Chicago: University of Chicago Press, 1951), bk. 11, lines 312–13.

3. Ludwig Wittgenstein, *Zettel,* G.E.M. Anscombe, trans. (Oxford: Blackwell, 1981).

4. Lionel Trilling, *Sincerity and Authenticity* (Cambridge: Harvard University Press, 1972), 131.

5. Robert Frost, "The Figure a Poem Makes," in *Robert Frost: Collected Poems, Prose, and Plays* (New York: Library of America, 1995), 777.

6. Cleanth Brooks and Robert Penn Warren, eds., *Conversations on the Craft of Poetry* (New York: Holt, Rinehart and Winston, 1961), audiotape.

7. Wallace Stevens, *The Necessary Angel* (New York: Random House, 1965), 30.

8. Karen Horney, *Final Lectures* (New York: Norton, 1987), 32.

9. William Wordsworth, *William Wordsworth: Selected Poetry* (London: Penguin, 1992), 179.

10. T. S. Eliot, *Little Gidding,* in *The Complete Poems and Plays* (New York: Harcourt, Brace, 1952), 145.

11. Albert Einstein, *New York Post,* 2 November 1972.

12. William Carlos Williams, *Autobiography* (New York: Random House, 1951), 356.

13. Stevens, *The Necessary Angel.*

14. T. S. Eliot, "The Music of Poetry," in *On Poetry and Poets* (New York: Farrar, Straus & Giroux, 1961).

15. T. S. Eliot, *East Coker,* in *The Complete Poems and Plays,* 128.

16. Robert D. Stevick, ed., *Early Middle English Lyrics* (Indianapolis: Bobbs-Merrill, 1964), 37.

17. Thomas H. Johnson and Theadora Ward, eds., *The Letters of Emily Dickinson* (Cambridge: Belknap Press of Harvard University Press, 1986), 413.

18. T. S. Eliot, "The Music of Poetry," in *On Poetry and Poets.*

19. Frank Sidgwick and E. K. Chambers, eds., *Early English Lyrics* (London: Sidgwick & Jackson, 1966), 150.

Stephanie Brown

1. Nathanael West, *The Day of the Locust* in *Nathanael West: Novels and Other Writings* (New York: Library of America, 1997), 242.

2. Ibid., 380.

3. Ibid., 242.

4. Ibid., 337.

5. Ibid., 286.

6. Mark Singer, "What Are You Afraid Of?", *New Yorker,* 7 September 1998, 62.

7. James M. Cain, *The Postman Always Rings Twice* in *Crime Novels: American Noir of the 1930s and 40s* (New York: Library of America, 1997), 4.

8. Ibid., 9.

9. West, *Miss Lonelyhearts* in *Nathanael West: Novels and Other Writings,* 109.

10. 1 Cor. 13:11.

Gillian Conoley

1. Michel Foucault, *The Order of Things* (New York: Pantheon, 1970), 342.

2. Ibid., 298.

3. Emily Dickinson, *The Complete Poems of Emily Dickinson,* ed. Thomas H. Johnson (New York: Little, Brown, 1960), 129.

4. Stéphane Mallarmé, *An Interrupted Performance, Collected Poems,* trans. Henry Weinfield (Berkeley: University of California Press, 1994), 100–101.

5. Jack Spicer, *Graphemics, The Collected Books of Jack Spicer,* ed. Robin Blaser (Santa Rosa, CA: Black Sparrow Press, 1975), 240.

6. As quoted in ibid., 277–78.

Judith Hall

1. Gertrude Stein, "Why I Like Detective Stories," *Harper's Bazaar,* November 1937.

2. Virginia Woolf to Elizabeth Bowen, 26 September 1935, *The Letters of*

Virginia Woolf, ed. Nigel Nicolson (New York: Harcourt Brace Jovanich, 1975–1980).

3. T. S. Eliot, *Little Gidding,* in *Four Quartets* (New York: Harcourt, Brace, 1943).

4. Ernest J. Gaines, *New York Times* Book Review, 11 June 1978.

Hunt Hawkins

1. Ezra Pound, "A Few Don'ts," *Poetry* vol. 1, no. 6 (March 1913), 201.

2. Frank O'Hara, "Personism: A Manifesto," *Yūgen* 7 (1961).

Jane Hirshfield

1. Jorge Luis Borges, *Selected Poems,* ed. Alexander Coleman (New York: Viking, 1999).

Claudia Keelan

1. Matt. 6:6–7.

2. Martin Luther King, "Nonviolence and the Montgomery Boycott," *Black Protest* (New York: Harper and Row, 1968), 282.

Dana Levin

1. As quoted in Peter Ackroyd, *Blake: A Biography* (New York: Ballantine Books, 1998), 301.

2. As quoted in Ackroyd, 827, 315.

Laurence Lieberman

1. "Interview with Donald Hall," in *A Marianne Moore Reader* (New York: Viking, 1961), 260.

2. Ibid., 261.

3. "Henry James as a Characteristic American," in ibid., 138.

4. *The Complete Poems of Marianne Moore* (New York: Penguin, 1982), 54.

5. "Interview with Donald Hall," in *A Marianne Moore Reader,* 263.

6. Ralph J. Mills, ed., *On the Poet and his Craft: Selected Prose of Theodore Roethke* (Seattle: University of Washington Press, 1965), 61–71.

7. *The Abyss, The Collected Poems of Theodore Roethke* (Garden City, NY: Anchor Press, 1975), 212.

8. *Four for Sir John Davies,* ibid., 101.

9. Kenneth Burke, "The Vegetal Radicalism of Theodore Roethke," *Sewanee Reader,* vol. 58, no. 1 (January–March 1950).

Jane Mead

1. William Hoffer, "A Magic Ratio Occurs Throughout Art and Nature," *Smithsonian Magazine* vol. 6, no. 9 (December 1975), 110–24.

Jack Myers

1. Charles Olson, *Maximus, to Himself, The Maximus Poems* (New York: Jargon/Corinth Books, 1960).

2. Robert Bly, ed., *The Sea and the Honeycomb: A Book of Tiny Poems* (Boston: Beacon Press, 1971).

3. Hazrat Inayat Kahn, *Mastery Through Accomplishment* (New Lebanon, NY: Omega Publications, 1985).

Donald Revell

1. William Carlos Williams, *The Autobiography of William Carlos Williams* (New York: New Directions Publishers, 1967), 390–91.

2. George Butterick, ed., *Charles Olson and Robert Creeley: The Complete Correspondence,* vol. 7 (Santa Rosa, CA: Black Sparrow Press, 1987), 98.

3. Ibid., 99.

4. Ibid., 100.

Len Roberts

1. Federico García Lorca, "The Duende," *The Poet's Work,* ed. Reginald Gibbons (New York: Houghton Mifflin, 1979), 33.

2. Ezra Pound, "A Retrospect," *Literary Essays of Ezra Pound,* ed. T. S. Eliot (Norfolk, CT: New Directions, 1935), 4.

3. Robert Hass, *Twentieth Century Pleasures* (New York: Ecco Press, 1984), 274.

4. William Butler Yeats, *The Collected Poems* (New York: Macmillan, 1933), 294.

5. James Dickey, *Poems, 1957–1967* (Middletown, CT: Wesleyan University Press, 1967), 83, 119.

6. T. S. Eliot, *The Sacred Wood: Essays on Poetry and Criticism* (New York: Methuen, 1920), 100.

7. As quoted in Mary Jane Fortunato, "Stanley Kunitz," *The Craft of Poetry,* ed. William Packard (Garden City, NY: Doubleday, 1974), 27.

Ira Sadoff

1. Wallace Stevens, "Imagination as Value," *The Necessary Angel* (New York: Vintage, 1958), 136.

2. Pablo Neruda, *Agua Sexual,* Residencia en la Tierra I & II, *Poems of Neruda and Vallejo,* ed. Robert Bly (Boston: Beacon Press, 1971), 23.

Theodore Weiss

1. *The Shorter Poems of Robert Browning* (New York: F. S. Crofts & Co., 1934), 150.

2. Theodore Weiss, *Recoveries* (New York: Macmillan, 1982), 19.

3. Walter Pater, *The Renaissance* (New York: Modern Library, 1968), 197.

4. William Logan, *All the Rage* (Ann Arbor: University of Michigan Press, 1988), 3.

ACKNOWLEDGMENTS

Grateful acknowledgment is made for permission to reprint the following previously published works.

A. R. Ammons. "Hymn" from *The Selected Poems, Expanded Edition* by A. R. Ammons. Copyright © 1987, 1977, 1975, 1974, 1972, 1971, 1970, 1966, 1965, 1964, 1955 by A. R. Ammons. Reprinted by permission of W. W. Norton & Company, Inc.

John Ashbery. *"A Wave"* (New York: Viking 1984). Copyright © 1981, 1982, 1983, 1984 by John Ashbery. Reprinted by permission of Georges Borchardt, Inc. for the author.

John Berryman. #149 and #157 from *The Dream Songs* by John Berryman. Copyright © 1969 by John Berryman. Reprinted by permission of Farrar, Straus, and Giroux, LLC.

Elizabeth Bishop. Excerpt from "Crusoe in England" and "The Fish" from *The Complete Poems 1927–1979* by Elizabeth Bishop. Copyright © 1979, 1983 by Alice Helen Methfessel. Reprinted by permission of Farrar, Straus, and Giroux, LLC.

Bertolt Brecht. "The Lovely Fork" from *Bertolt Brecht: Poems 1913–1956* translated by John Willett, published by Methuen. Copyright © 1976. Reprinted by permission of Suhrkamp Verlag.

Stephanie Brown. "No Longer A Girl" from *Allegory of the Supermarket* by Stephanie Brown. Copyright © 1998. Reprinted by permission of University of Georgia Press.

James M. Cain. Excerpt from *The Postman Always Rings Twice*. Copyright © 1934, renewed 1962 by James M. Cain. Reprinted by permission of Alfred A. Knopf, a division of Random House, Inc.

C. P. Cavafy. "Hidden Things" from *Collected Poems* by C. P. Cavafy, translated by Edmund Keeley and Philip Sherrard. Translation copyright © 1992 by Edmund Keely and Philip Sherrard. Reprinted by permission of Princeton University Press.

Paul Celan. "Your hand full of hours" from *Poems of Paul Celan* by Paul Celan, translated by Michael Hamburger. Translation copyright © 1972, 1980, 1988 by Michael Hamburger. Reprinted by permission of Persea Books, Inc.

Hart Crane. "The Air Plant: Grand Cayman" and "Voyages II" from *Complete Poems of Hart Crane* edited by Marc Simon. Copyright © 1933, 1958, 1966 by Liveright Publishing Corporation. Copyright © 1986 by Marc Simon. Reprinted by permission of Liveright Publishing Corporation.

Robert Creeley. "Flowers" from *Collected Poems of Robert Creeley 1945–1975.* Copyright © 1983 by the Regents of the University of California. Reprinted by permission of University of California Press.

E. E. Cummings. "i sing of Olaf glad and big," copyright 1931, © 1959, 1991 by the Trustees for the E. E. Cummings Trust, from *Complete Poems: 1904–1962* by E. E. Cummings, edited by George J. Firmage. Copyright © 1979 by George James Firmage. Reprinted by permission of Liveright Publishing Corporation.

Robert Frost. "Brown's Descent, or The Willy-Nilly Slide" and "The Woodpile" from *The Poetry of Robert Frost* edited by Edward Connery Lathem. Copyright © 1944, 1958 by Robert Frost. Copyright © 1967 by Lesley Frost Ballantine. Copyright 1916, 1930, 1939, © 1969 by Henry Holt and Company, LLC. Reprinted by permission of Henry Holt and Company, LLC.

Amy Gerstler. "Nearby" from *Medicine* by Amy Gerstler. Copyright © 2000 by Amy Gerstler. Used by permission of Penguin, a division of Penguin Putnam Inc.

Jack Gilbert. "To See If Something Comes Next" from *The Great Fires: Poems 1982–1992* by Jack Gilbert. Copyright © 1994 by Jack Gilbert. Reprinted by permission of Alfred A. Knopf, a division of Random House, Inc.

Louise Glück. Excerpt from "The Wild Iris" by Louise Glück. Copyright © 1993 by Louise Glück. Reprinted by permission of HarperCollins Publishers, Inc.

Paul Goodman. "Pagan Rites" from *Collected Poems* by Paul Goodman, edited by Taylor Stoehr, with a memoir by George Dennison, published by Random House, Inc. Copyright © Sally Goodman. Reprinted by permission of Sally Goodman.

Robert Hayden. "The Diver" from *Collected Poems of Robert Hayden,* edited by Frederick Glaysher. Copyright © 1962, 1966 by Robert Hayden. Reprinted by permission of Liveright Publishing Corporation.

Zbigniew Herbert. "What Mr. Cogito Thinks About Hell" from *Mr. Cogito* by Zbigniew Herbert, translated by John and Bogdana Carpenter. Copyright © 1974 by Zbigniew Herbert. Translation copyright © 1993 by John Carpenter and Bogdana Carpenter. Reprinted by permission of HarperCollins Publishers, Inc.

Horace. Odes I, 11 from *The Essential Horace: Odes, Epodes, Satires and Epistles* translated by Burton Raffel. Translation copyright © 1983 by Burton Raffel. Reprinted by permission of North Point Press, a division of Farrar, Straus, and Giroux, LLC.

Randall Jarrell. "90 North" from *The Complete Poems* by Randall Jarrell. Copyright © 1969, renewed 1997 by Mary von S. Jarrell. Reprinted by permission of Farrar, Straus, and Giroux, LLC.

Roberto Juarroz. "First, 4, (the bottom of things)" from *Vertical Poetry* by Roberto Juarroz, translated by W. S. Merwin. Copyright © 1988 by W. S. Merwin. Reprinted with permission.

Bill Knott. "Ignorance 1967," "Poem," and "Widow's Winter" by Bill Knott. Reprinted by permission of the author.

Yusef Komunyakaa. "The Millpond" from *Magic City* by Yusef Komunyakaa, published by Wesleyan University Press. Copyright © 1992 by Yusef Komunyakaa. Reprinted by permission of University Press of New England, Hanover, NH.

D. H. Lawrence. "Butterfly" from *The Complete Works of D. H. Lawrence,* edited by V. de Sola Pinto and F. W. Roberts. Copyright © 1964, 1971 by Angelo Ravagli and C. M. Weekley, Executors of the Estate of Frieda Lawrence Ravagli. Reprinted by permission of Viking Penguin, a division of Penguin Putnam Inc.

Philip Levine. "They Feed They Lion" from *New Selected Poems* by Philip Levine. Copyright © 1991 by Philip Levine. Reprinted by permission of Alfred A. Knopf, a division of Random House, Inc.

Robert Lowell. "Home After Three Months Away" from *Selected Poems* by Robert Lowell. Copyright © 1976 by the Estate of Robert Lowell. Reprinted by permission of Farrar, Straus, and Giroux, LLC.

Robert Lowell. Letter to Stephen Berg beginning "Oh dear, the many paths one might take" by Robert Lowell. Copyright © by the Estate of Robert Lowell. Reprinted by permission of Frank Bidart, Literary Executor of Robert Lowell's estate.

Stéphane Mallarmé. "Saint" and "An Interrupted Performance" from *Collected Poems of Stéphane Mallarmé,* edited and translated by Henry Weinfield. Copyright © 1994 by the Regents of the University of California. Reprinted by permission of University of California Press.

W. S. Merwin, translator. "Berber Song" from *Selected Translations 1948–1968* by W. S. Merwin (New York: Atheneum, 1968). Copyright © 1948, 1949, 1950, 1954, 1956, 1957, 1958, 1959, 1960, 1961, 1962, 1963, 1964, 1965, 1966, 1967, 1968 by W. S. Merwin. Reprinted by permission of Georges Borchardt, Inc. for the author.

W. S. Merwin. "The Child" from *The Lice* by W. S. Merwin. Copyright © 1967 by W. S. Merwin. Reprinted with permission.

Charlotte Mew. "Fame" from *Collected Poems and Prose* by Charlotte Mew, edited and with an introduction by Val Warner. Copyright © 1981 by Carcanet Press, Ltd. Reprinted by permission of Carcanet Press, Ltd.

Czeslaw Milosz. "The Garden of Earthly Delights: Hell" from *Facing the River: New Poems* by Czeslaw Milosz. Copyright © 1995 by Czeslaw Milosz. Reprinted by permission of HarperCollins Publishers, Inc.

Marianne Moore. "The Buffalo" from *The Collected Poems of Marianne Moore.* Copyright © 1935 by Marianne Moore, renewed © 1963 by Marianne Moore and T. S. Eliot. Reprinted by permission of Simon & Schuster.

Jack Myers. "The Optimist, The Pessimist, and The Other" from *OneOnOne* by Jack Myers. Copyright © 1999 by Jack Myers. Reprinted by permission of Autumn House Press.

Pablo Neruda. "Too Many Names" from *Selected Poems* by Pablo Neruda, translated by Alastair Reid, edited by Nathaniel Tarn. Copyright © 1970. Reprinted by permission of Jonathan Cape, Ltd.

Frank O'Hara. "The Day Lady Died" from *Lunch Poems* by Frank O'Hara. Copyright © 1964 by Frank O'Hara. Reprinted by permission of City Lights Books.

Sharon Olds. "Poem to Our Son After a High Fever" from *The Wellspring* by Sharon Olds. Copyright © 1996 by Sharon Olds. Reprinted by permission of Alfred A. Knopf, a division of Random House, Inc.

Ezra Pound. "The Lake Isle" from *Personae* by Ezra Pound. Copyright © 1926 by Ezra Pound. Reprinted by permission of New Directions Publishing Corporation.

Rainer Maria Rilke. Excerpt from *Sonnets to Orpheus* by Rainer Maria Rilke, translated by M. D. Herter Norton. Copyright © 1942 by W. W. Norton & Company, Inc., renewed © 1970 by M. D. Herter Norton. Reprinted by permission of W. W. Norton & Company, Inc.

Theodore Roethke. "The Geranium" from *The Collected Poems of Theodore Roethke.* Copyright © 1963 by Beatrice Roethke, Administratrix of the Estate of Theodore Roethke. Reprinted by permission of Doubleday, a division of Random House, Inc.

Jelaluddin Rumi. "Say Yes Quickly" from *Open Secret* by Jelaluddin Rumi, translated by Coleman Barks and John Moyne. Copyright © 1984 by Threshold Books. Reprinted by permission of Threshold Books.

Sappho. "Seizure" from *Sappho and the Greek Lyric Poets,* translated by Willis Barnstone. Copyright © 1962, 1967, 1988 by Willis Barnstone. Reprinted by permission of Pantheon Books, a division of Random House, Inc.

David Schubert. "Kind Valentine" by David Schubert, published by *Quarterly Review of Literature.* Reprinted by permission of Theodore Weiss.

Sei Shonagon. "Elegant Things," "Rare Things," "Squalid Things" from *The Pillow Book of Sei Shonagon,* translated by Ivan Morris. Copyright © 1967 Columbia University Press. Reprinted by permission of Columbia University Press.

Jack Spicer. "Phonemics" and excerpt from "Graphemics" from *The Collected Books of Jack Spicer.* Copyright © 1975 by the Estate of Jack Spicer. Reprinted by permission of Black Sparrow Press.

Wallace Stevens. "The Snow Man" from *Collected Poems* by Wallace Stevens. Copyright © 1923, renewed 1951 by Wallace Stevens. Reprinted by permission of Alfred A. Knopf, a division of Random House, Inc.

Shinkichi Takahashi. "Burning Oneself To Death," "The Peach," "The Pipe," "Thistles," and "What Is Moving" from *Zen Poetry: Let the Spring Breeze Enter,* edited and translated by Lucien Stryk and Takashi Ikemoto. Copyright © 1995. Reprinted by permission of Grove Press.

César Vallejo. "Sermon on Death" from *Complete Posthumous Poetry* by César Vallejo, translated by Clayton Eshleman and José Rubia Barcia. Copyright © 1979 by The Regents of the University of California. Reprinted by permission of University of California Press.

Theodore Weiss. Excerpt from "Recoveries." Reprinted by permission of the author.

Nathanael West. Excerpt from *The Day of the Locust* by Nathanael West. Copyright © 1939 by the Estate of Nathanael West. Reprinted by permission of New Directions Publishing Corporation.

C. K. Williams. "Neglect" from *Selected Poems* by C. K. Williams. Copyright © 1994 by C. K. Williams. Reprinted by permission of Farrar, Straus, and Giroux, LLC.

William Carlos Williams. "Danse Russe," "Poem," and "To a Lovely Old Bitch" from *Collected Poems: 1909–39, Volume 1* by William Carlos Williams. Copyright © 1938 by New Directions Publishing Corporation. Reprinted by permission of New Directions Publishing Corporation.

James Wright. "The Life" and "The Jewel" from *Above the River.* Copyright © 1990 by Anne Wright. Reprinted by permission of University Press of New England, Hanover, NH.

PHOTO CREDITS

A. R. Ammons/Dede Hatch; L. S. Asekoff/Louise Kalin; Stephanie Brown/Robert Walker; Hayden Carruth/Ted Rosenberg; Gillian Conoley/Domenic Stansberry; Amy Gerstler/Benjamin Weissman; Judith Hall/Steven A. Heller; Hunt Hawkins/Florida State University Photo Lab; Jane Hirshfield/Jerry Bauer; Claudia Keelan/Nolan Rucker; Yusef Komunyakaa/Ted Rosenberg; Dana Levin/P. R. Smith; Lisa Lewis/Linda Leavell; Laurence Lieberman/William Wiegand; Thomas Lux/Barnaby Hall; Jane Mead/Ashley Martin; Jack Myers/Thea Temple; Donald Revell/ Claudia Keelan; Len Roberts/Jim Manis; Michael Ryan/Doreen Gildroy; Ira Sadoff/Linda Sadoff; Hugh Seidman/Jayne Holsinger; Jennifer Snyder/Chip Cooper; Gerald Stern/Ted Rosenberg; Lucien Stryk/Barry Stark; Karen Volkman/Karen Volkman; Ted Weiss/Ted Weiss; Joe Wenderoth/R. A. Norton

INDEX OF POETS